CHEVY VEGA

1971-1977
SHOP MANUAL

By
JIM COMBS

ERIC JORGENSEN
Editor

JEFF ROBINSON
Publisher

CLYMER PUBLICATIONS

*World's largest publisher of books
devoted exclusively to automobiles and motorcycles*

12860 MUSCATINE STREET · P.O. BOX 20 · ARLETA, CALIFORNIA 91331

FIRST EDITION
Published April, 1972

SECOND EDITION
Revised to include 1973-1974 models
Published January, 1975

THIRD EDITION
Revised to include 1975-1976 models
Published December, 1976

FOURTH EDITION
Revised by Mike Bishop to include 1977 models
First Printing June, 1979
Second Printing June, 1980
Third Printing February, 1981
Fourth Printing November, 1981
Fifth Printing October, 1982

Printed in U.S.A.

ISBN: 0-89287-130-X

Photos and illustrations courtesy of
Chevrolet Motor Division, General Motors Corporation

CONTENTS

QUICK REFERENCE DATA

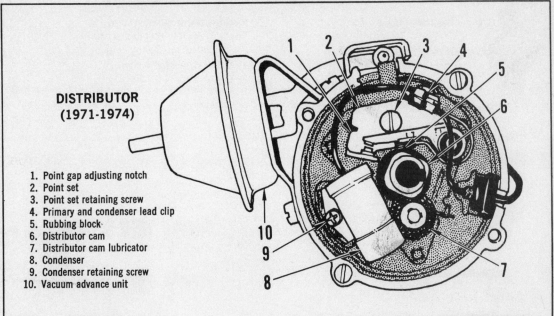

DISTRIBUTOR
(1971-1974)

1. Point gap adjusting notch
2. Point set
3. Point set retaining screw
4. Primary and condenser lead clip
5. Rubbing block
6. Distributor cam
7. Distributor cam lubricator
8. Condenser
9. Condenser retaining screw
10. Vacuum advance unit

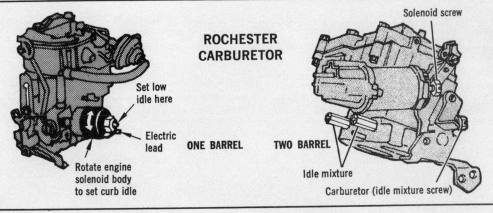

ROCHESTER CARBURETOR

Set low idle here

Electric lead

Rotate engine solenoid body to set curb idle

ONE BARREL

TWO BARREL

Solenoid screw

Idle mixture

Carburetor (idle mixture screw)

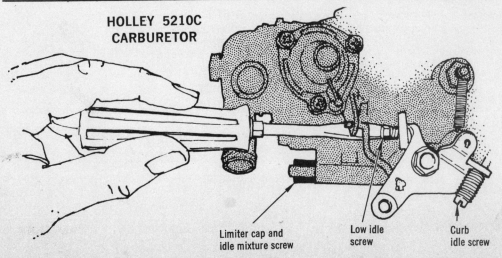

HOLLEY 5210C CARBURETOR

Limiter cap and idle mixture screw

Low idle screw

Curb idle screw

Cylinder head bolt torque   60 ft.-lb. (81 N•m)

Valve clearance (cold)
 Intake   0.014-0.016 in. (0.36-0.40mm)
 Exhaust   0.029-0.031 in. (0.74-0.79mm)

Spark plugs
 Type
  1971-1974   R42TS
  1975   R43TSX
  1976 1 bbl and Calif. 2 bbl. R43TS
  1976 2 bbl 49 states   R43TSX
  1977   R43TS
 Gap (all)   0.035 in.

Point gap
 1971-1974   0.019 in. new; 0.016 in. used

Dwell angle
 1971-1974   31-34°

Timing
 1971
  1 bbl and 2 bbl manual 6° BTDC
  2 bbl automatic   10° BTDC
 1972
  1 bbl   6° BTDC (4° BTDC—Calif.)
  2 bbl manual   8° BTDC
  2 bbl automatic   10° BTDC
 1973
  1 bbl   8° BTDC
  2 bbl manual   10° BTDC
  2 bbl automatic   12° BTDC
 1974
  1 bbl/2 bbl manual   10° BTDC
  1 bbl/2 bbl automatic 12° BTDC
 1975
  1 bbl manual   8° BTDC
  1 bbl automatic/2 bbl manual 10° BTDC
  2 bbl automatic   12° BTDC
 1976
  1 bbl manual   8° BTDC
  1 bbl automatic   10° BTDC
  2 bbl manual—49 states and Calif. 10° BTDC
  2 bbl automatic—49 states and Calif. 12° BTDC
 1977
  Manual—49 states and high altitude 0°
  Manual—Calif.   2° ATDC
  Automatic—49 states and high altitude 2° BTDC
  Automatic—Calif.   0°

Firing order   1-3-4-2

Table 3 BULB SPECIFICATIONS

	Candle Power	Bulb Type
Headlight unit—high beam	60W	6014 (6012)①
—low beam	50W	Sealed beam
Front park and directional signal	32-3	1157③
Front fender side marker light	2	194
Rear side marker light	2	194
Tail, stop, and rear directional signal	32-3	1157
License plate light	4	168 (194)②
Back-up lights	32	1156
Dome light	12	211 or 211-1 (561)②
Instrument panel cluster lights	2	194
Transmission control indicator	2	194
Heater or air conditioner control panel light indirect lighting		(194)①
Indicator lights		
Automatic transmission	2	194
Generator	2	194
High beam headlight	2	194
Oil	2	194
Temperature system	2	194
Brake warning	2	194
Turn signal	2	194
Stop engine	2	194
Radio dial light	3	1816
Rear window defogger	3	168
Seat belt warning light	2	194
Glove compartment	3	1891

① 1976-1977   ② 1975-1977   ③ 1157NA G.T. equipped

ADJUSTMENTS

Drive belt deflection

Distance between pulley centers	Deflection
7-10 in.	¼ in.
10-13 in.	⅜ in.
13-16 in.	½ in.

Clutch pedal free play   1 in.

TORQUE SPECIFICATIONS

Item	Torque	Item	Torque
Battery cable	80 in.-lb.	Generator pulley	50 ft.-lb.
Battery hold down	70 in.-lb.	Starter mount	30 ft.-lb.
Generator brace adjustment	120 in.-lb.	Starter brace	18 ft.-lb.

RECOMMENDED LUBRICANTS

Component	Temperature Range, °F	Recommended Lubricant	Capacity
Engine crankcase	−30 to 20 0 to 60 20 to 110	5W-20, 5W-30[1] 10W, 5W-30, 10W-30, 10W-40[1] 20W, 10W-30, 10W-40, 20W-40[1]	3 quarts (4 with filter) change)
Transmission (std.)	All	SAE 80 or 90 weight	2.4 pints
Transmission (auto.)	All	Dexron® II ATF	1½ pints
Differential	All	SAE 80 or 90 weight	2 pints
Steering gear (std.)	All	GM4673m or equivalent	13 ounces
Steering and parking brake linkage	All	Water-resistant EP chassis lubricant	—
Front wheel bearings	All	High temperature bearing grease[2]	—
Compressor	All	Compressor oil, 525 viscosity	11 ounces

1. Rated "FOR SERVICE MS, SD OR SE"
2. Do not use long fiber or viscous type grease

CAPACITIES

Engine oil	3 quarts (4 quarts with filter change)
Transmission	
Manual	fill to LEVEL plug
Automatic	fill to ½ in. of ADD mark
Differential	fill to LEVEL plug

VALVE ADJUSTMENT SEQUENCE

Rotor position	Valves to be adjusted
Pointing to No. 1 cylinder	Intake No. 1 and 2 Exhaust No. 1 and 3
Pointing to No. 2 cylinder	Intake No. 3 and 4 Exhaust No. 2 and 4

CHEVY VEGA

1971-1977

SHOP MANUAL

CHAPTER ONE

GENERAL INFORMATION

This book covers all Vega models from 1971 through 1977, with the exception of the Cosworth Vega. The Cosworth version uses a different engine with fuel injection and electronic ignition. Although introduced in 1975, only a limited number of these cars have been made. The sophistication of these high-performance engines makes it impractical for any but specially-trained mechanics to work on them.

Vega standard equipment includes the 4-cylinder, 140 cubic-inch-displacement, single-overhead-cam engine with a one-barrel carburetor and a 3-speed manual transmission. In all production years options have included a 4-speed transmission, a 2-barrel carburetor, and an automatic transmission (either Powerglide or Turbo-Hydramatic). In early model years a semi-automatic Torque Drive transmission was offered, and a 1976-1977 option is a 5-speed manual transmission. The lightweight (Opel) 3- and 4-speed transmissions used in 1971-1972 models were replaced in 1973 by the "Saginaw" 3- and 4-speed transmissions used in other General Motors applications since 1969.

Numerous safety, convenience, comfort, and trim options have been offered through the years, and some of these have become standard equipment items.

This chapter contains information on the location of identification numbers, a description of manual organization, some service hints, and general specifications (**Tables 1 and 2**).

IDENTIFICATION NUMBERS

The vehicle serial number plate is located on the top of the instrument panel, left side. It is stamped with the manufacturer's identity number, the division series number, body style number, either the last one or 2 digits of the model, year, a code identifying the assembly plant, and finally, the vehicle identification number (VIN), or serial number. Numbering begins at 100,000 for the first Vega produced. The VIN is also stamped on the engine and on the transmission. The exact location of these and other component serial or unit numbers are shown in **Table 3**.

MANUAL ORGANIZATION

This service/repair handbook has been carefully prepared to provide the latest service information and complete overhaul procedures for the Vega vehicles.

This chapter provides general information and specifications. Chapter Two covers all

Table 1   GENERAL SPECIFICATIONS — 1971-1974

Item	1971-72	1973	1974
Curb weight	2,190 lb.		
Maximum length	169.8 in.	172.2 in.	175.4 in.
Maximum height	51.2 in.	51.9 in.	51.9 in.
Maximum width	65.4 in.	65.4 in.	65.4 in.
Wheelbase	97.0 in.	97.0 in.	97.0 in.
Track, front	54.6 in.	55.2 in.	55.2 in.
Track, rear	54.1 in.	54.1 in.	54.1 in.
Turning diameter	33 ft.	33 ft.	33 ft.
Window area (sedan)	3,635 sq. in.		
Fuel capacity	11 U.S. gal.	11 U.S. gal.	16 U.S. gal.
Air conditioning compressor	Frigidaire	Frigidaire	Frigidaire
Engine model/type	L-4/OHC, 4 cyl.	L-4/OHC, 4 cyl.	L-4/OHC, 4 cyl.
displacement	140 cu. in. (2300cc)	140 cu. in. (2300cc)	140 cu. in. (2300cc)
bore	3.5 in.	3.5 in.	3.5 in.
stroke	3.625 in.	3.625 in.	3.625 in.
compression ratio	8.50 : 1	8.00 : 1	8.00 : 1
horsepower/rpm	90/4,800	72/4,400	75/4,400
	110/4,800	85/4,800	85/4,400
carburetor	Rochester MV single barrel	Rochester MV single barrel	Rochester MV single barrel
	Rochester 2GV double barrel	Holley 5210C double barrel	Holley 5210C double barrel
Transmission	3- or 4-speed standard	3- or 4-speed standard	3- or 4-speed standard
	Torque Drive (semi-automatic)	Turbo Hydramatic (fully automatic)	Turbo Hydramatic (fully automatic)
	Powerglide (fully automatic)	Powerglide (fully automatic)	Powerglide (fully automatic)
Brakes	Disc (front), Drum (rear)	Disc (front), Drum (rear)	Disc (front), Drum (rear)
Tires	6.00 x 13, A70-13 or A78-13	6.00 x 13, A70-13 or A78-13	6.00 x 13, A70-13 or A78-13

periodic lubrication and scheduled maintenance required to keep your car running smoothly. Tune-up information is also included in Chapter Two, eliminating the need to consult several chapters on components requiring periodic replacement or adjustment.

Chapter Three provides numerous methods and suggestions for finding and fixing troubles fast. Troubleshooting procedures discuss typical symptoms and methods to pinpoint the trouble. It also discusses test equipment useful for preventive maintenance and troubleshooting.

Subsequent chapters describe specific systems such as the engine, transmission, or electrical system. Each provides complete disassembly, repair, and reassembly procedures in easy to follow, step-by-step form. If a repair is impractical for the owner/mechanic, this is indicated. Such repairs are usually quickly and more economically done by a Chevrolet dealer or other competent repair shop. Specifications concerning a particular system or component are provided in the applicable chapter.

Some of the procedures in this manual specify special tools. In all cases, the tool is illustrated either in actual use or alone. A well-equipped mechanic may find he can substitute similar tools already on hand or can fabricate his own.

Table 2   GENERAL SPECIFICATIONS — 1975-1977

Item	1975	1976-1977
Maximum length	175.4 in.	175.4 in.
Maximum height	51.8 in	51.8 in.
Maximum width	65.4 in.	65.4 in.
Wheelbase	97.0 in.	97.0 in.
Track, front	55.2 in.	54.8 in.
Track, rear	54.1 in.	53.6 in.
Fuel capacity	16 U.S. gals.	16 U.S. gals.
Air conditioning compressor	Frigidaire	Frigidaire
Engine model/type	L-4/OHC, 4 cyl.	L-4/OHC, 4 cyl.
Displacement	140 cu. in.(2300cc)	140 cu. in. (2300cc)
Bore	3.5 in.	3.5 in.
Stroke	3.625 in.	3.625 in.
Compression ratio	8.00:1	8.00:1
Horsepower/rpm	78/4200	69/4000
	87/4400	87/4400
Carburetor	Rochester MV single barrel	Rochester MV single barrel (1976 only)
	Holley 5210C double barrel	Holley 5210C double barrel
Transmission	3- or 4-speed std.	3-, 4-, or 5-speed std.
	Turbo Hydramatic (fully automatic)	Turbo Hydramatic (fully automatic)
Brakes	Disc (front)	Disc (front)
	Drum (rear)	Drum (rear)
Tires	BR78-13, A78-13	A78-13, BR78-13, A70-13

SERVICE HINTS

Notes, Cautions, and Warnings

The terms NOTE, CAUTION, and WARNING have specific meanings in this book. A NOTE provides additional information to make a step or procedure easier or clearer. Disregarding a NOTE could cause inconvenience, but would not cause damage or personal injury.

A CAUTION emphasizes areas where equipment damage could result. Disregarding a CAUTION could cause permanent mechanical damage; however, personal injury is unlikely.

A WARNING emphasizes areas where personal injury, or even death, could result from negligence. Mechanical damage may also occur. WARNINGS are to be taken seriously. In some cases serious injury or death has occurred when mechanics disregard similar warnings.

General Hints

Observing the following practices will save time, effort, and frustration, as well as prevent possible injury.

1. Throughout this manual keep in mind 2 conventions. "Front" refers to the front of the car. The front of any component such as the engine or transaxle is that end which faces toward the front of the car. The left and right side of the car refer to a person sitting in the car facing forward. For example, the steering wheel is on

Table 3   VEHICLE IDENTIFICATION NUMBERS

Identification	Location				
	1971-72	1973	1974	1975	1976-1977
Vehicle identification plate	①	①	①	①	①
Body number, trim & paint plate	②	②	②	②	②
Engine and transmission identification numbers					
3-speed standard	③	③	③	③	③
4-speed standard	④	④	④	④	④
5-speed standard					⑤
Powerglide and Torque Drive	⑥	⑦			
Turbo Hydramatic		⑧	⑨	⑨	⑨
Rear axle number	⑩	⑩	⑩	⑩	⑩
Alternator	⑪	⑪	⑪	⑪	⑪
Starter	⑫	⑫	⑫	⑫	⑫
Battery	⑬	⑬	⑬	⑬	⑬

① Left front top of instrument panel.
② Upper right side of dash panel.
③ On pad at right side of cylinder block above starter.
④ Centered on lower rear face of case.
⑤ On metal tag bolted to right side of case.
⑥ On left upper flange of converter opening of transmission housing.
⑦ On boss on lower right side of converter housing.
⑧ On boss on left side of manual control lever.
⑨ On right vertical surface of oil pan.
⑩ On right or left axle adjacent to carrier.
⑪ On top, drive end flange.
⑫ Stamped on outer case, toward rear.
⑬ On cell cover segment, top of battery.

the left side. These rules are simple, but even experienced mechanics occasionally become disoriented.

WARNING
When working under a car, never trust a hydraulic or mechanical jack to hold the car up by itself. Always use jackstands.

2. Disconnect battery ground cable before working near electrical connections and before disconnecting wires. Never run the engine with the battery disconnected; the alternator could be seriously damaged.

3. Tag all similar internal parts for location and mark all parts which mate together for position. Record the quantity and thickness of any shims as they are removed. Small parts, such as bolts, can be identified by placing them in plastic sandwich bags. Seal and label the bags with masking tape.

4. Protect finished surfaces from physical damage or corrosion. Keep gasoline and brake fluid off painted surfaces.

5. Frozen or very tight bolts and screws can often be loosened by soaking with penerating oil, then sharply striking the bolt head a few times with a hammer and punch (or screwdriver for screws). Avoid heat unless absolutely necessary, since it may melt, warp, or remove the temper from many parts.

6. Avoid flames or sparks when working near a charging battery or flammable liquids such as brake fluid or gasoline.

7. No parts, except those assembled with a press fit, require unusual force during assembly. If a part is hard to remove or install, find out why before proceeding.

8. Cover all openings after removing parts to keep dirt, small tools, etc., from falling in.

9. When assembling 2 parts, start all fasteners, then tighten evenly.

10. Completely read each procedure while looking at the actual parts *before* beginning. Many procedures are complicated and errors can be disastrous. When you thoroughly understand what is to be done, carefully follow the procedure step-by-step.

PARTS REPLACEMENT

Chevrolet and other GM divisions make frequent changes during a model year; some minor, some relatively major. When you order parts from the dealer or other parts distributor, *always order by manufacturer's identity number*. Write the numbers down and carry them in your wallet. Compare new parts to old before purchasing them. If they are not alike, have the parts manager explain the difference.

CHAPTER TWO

LUBRICATION, MAINTENANCE,
AND TUNE-UP

To ensure good performance, dependability, and safety, regular preventive maintenance is necessary. This chapter outlines periodic checks, lubrication, and maintenance for a car driven by the average owner. One driven more than average may require more frequent attention. But even without use, rust, dirt, and corrosion cause unnecessary damage. Whether performed by the owner or a Chevrolet dealer, regular routine attention helps avoid expensive repairs.

The recommended maintenance in this chapter includes routine checks easily performed at each fuel stop (**Table 1**), periodic checks performed less often, preventive maintenance of items requiring attention at regular intervals, and periodic lubrication. **Table 2** summarizes the periodic maintenance. The last part of this chapter presents tune-up information in a sequence to facilitate this important task.

No sophisticated instruments or tools are required for procedures in this chapter. You will, however, need a vacuum gauge, tachometer, timing light, and a set of feeler gauges. A dwell meter, often included with a tachometer in one package, is not required but permits more accurate ignition points adjustment.

ROUTINE CHECKS

The following checks should be performed at each stop for gas.

1. Check engine oil level. Shut off engine and allow a few moments for the oil to return to the crankcase. Remove dipstick (located at left rear corner of engine compartment), wipe, and replace, making sure it is seated in the tube. Remove it again and inspect; add oil only when the level is *below* the ADD mark. One quart will

Table 1   ROUTINE CHECKS

Interval	Item	Procedure
Fuel stop	Engine oil	Check level
	Coolant	Check level
	Windshield washer fluid	Check level
Monthly	Battery electrolyte	Check level
	Tire pressures	Check (or when tires are visibly low)

Table 2   SCHEDULED MAINTENANCE

Interval	Item	Procedure
6,000 miles or 4 months (7,500 miles or 6 months on 1975-1977 vehicles)	Engine oil	Change
	Distributor cam lubricator	Rotate 180°
	Front suspension	Lubricate
	Steering linkage	Lubricate
	Brake fluid	Check level
	Power steering fluid	Check level
	Transmission fluid	Check level (manual and automatic)
	Differential	Check level
	Transmission linkage and parking brake cable	Lubricate
	Hood latch and door hinges	Lubricate
	Air conditioning condenser	Clean external surfaces
	Accessory drive belt	Check tension
	PCV valve	Check operation
12,000 miles or 12 months (15,000 miles or 12 months on 1975-1977 vehicles)	Spark plugs ②	Replace
	Ignition points ①	Replace
	Condenser ①	Replace
	Ignition timing ②	Set timing, check vacuum advance
	Intake manifold	Check torque
	Fuel filter	Clean or replace
	Carburetor	Adjust
	Oil filter ③	Replace
	Battery terminals	Clean
	Fuel evaporative canister ④	Replace
	Headlight aim	Adjust
	Air conditioning refrigerant	Check charge
24,000 miles (30,000 miles on 1975-1977 vehicles)	Distributor cam lubricator ①	Replace
	Distributor cap and rotor ②	Replace
	Automatic transmission fluid	Replace
	Automatic transmission low band	Adjust
	Front wheel bearings	Repack
	PCV valve	Replace
	Valves (1975 and earlier) ②	Adjust
	Brake lines and linings	Check
24 months (regardless of miles)	Engine coolant	Replace
50,000 miles	Air cleaner assembly	Replace

① Not applicable to 1975-1977 models.
② Every 22,500 miles on 1975-1977 models (valves on 1976-1977 cars require no adjustment).
③ Replace filter at first oil change, then every second oil change.
④ Every 30,000 miles on 1975-1977 models.

raise the level from ADD to FULL. See **Table 3** for recommended grades.

2. Check coolant level. It should be from ¾ inch to 1½ inches below the filler neck. Use caution when removing radiator cap. Later models use a coolant recovery system. Visually check that there is some coolant in the reservoir at normal operating temperatures.

3. Check the level of the windshield washer container. It should be kept full.

4. Check tire pressures once a month or when tires are visibly low. This should be done when the tires are cold. Correct pressures for your tire size are listed on the right-hand door lock pillar. Maximum pressures are also imprinted on the tires.

5. Check the battery electrolyte level about once a month, or more often in hot weather. It should be up to the ring inside each filler hole (**Figure 1**). Fill with ordinary tap water unless local water is hard. Use distilled water in hard water areas.

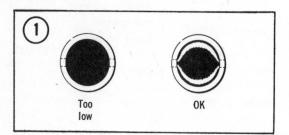

NOTE: *Some late models may be equipped with the sealed "Freedom Battery." Water cannot be added to this battery. Check battery condition as shown in* **Figure 2** *by checking charge indicator on battery.*

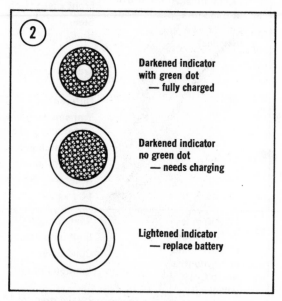

Darkened indicator with green dot — fully charged

Darkened indicator no green dot — needs charging

Lightened indicator — replace battery

PERIODIC CHECKS

Regular inspection and adjustment each time your Vega is lubricated can prevent untimely breakdown and prolong vehicle life. Inspect all rubber hoses (brakes, power steering, radiator, heater, and small lines to carburetor, distributor,

Table 3   RECOMMENDED LUBRICANTS

Component	Temperature Range, °F	Recommended Lubricant	Capacity
Engine crankcase	— 30 to 20 0 to 60 20 to 110	5W-20, 5W-30[1] 10W, 5W-30, 10W-30, 10W-40[1] 20W, 10W-30, 10W-40, 20W-40[1]	3 quarts (4 with filter change)
Transmission (std.)	All	SAE 80 or 90 weight	2.4 pints
Transmission (auto.)	All	Dexron® II A.T.F.	1½ pints
Differential	All	SAE 80 or 90 weight	2 pints
Steering gear (std.)	All	GM4673m or equivalent	13 ounces
Steering and parking brake linkage	All	Water-resistant EP chassis lubricant	——
Front wheel bearings	All	High temperature bearing grease[2]	——
Compressor	All	Compressor oil, 525 viscosity	11 ounces

1. Rated "FOR SERVICE MS, SD OR SE"
2. Do not use long fiber or viscous type grease

etc.) for cracks and wear. Check accessory drive belt for wear. Look for evidence of coolant or fluid leaks on all lines.

Check headlights, taillights, stoplights, and directional signals. Inspect exhaust system for leaks. Examine shock absorber bushings. Make certain that shock absorbers are securely mounted. Check for tire wear and correct pressure. Tire rotation every 6,000 miles will extend mileage. Some authorities note, however, that unless you do it yourself, the cost of tire rotation may exceed any savings gained through longer life.

Drive Belts

Tension on the accressory drive belt can be checked as follows.

1. Depress the belt by placing moderate pressure midway between the pulleys.

2. Measure the amount of deflection and compare to **Table 4**.

Table 4   BELT DEFLECTION

Center-to-center distance between pulleys, inches	Belt deflection, inches
7-10	¼
10-13	⅜
13-16	½

3. Adjust the accessory drive belt tension by inserting a large screwdriver between the alternator body and the mounting bracket for leverage and loosening the ½ in. adjusting nut. The alternator is located on the left side of the engine on cars with standard steering and on the right side for those equipped with power steering. Retighten the nut securely after adjusting tension.

Timing belt tension need not be checked regularly. A special tool (strand tension gauge, Tool J-23600) is required to check this. See *Timing Belt and Water Pump*, Chapter Four, for adjustment.

Steering Gear

The manual steering gear requires no lubricant change. If visual inspection reveals a severe grease leak, the gear should be overhauled.

Power Steering Pump

Every 4 months or 6,000 miles (6 months or 7,500 miles on 1975-1977 cars) remove the filler cap on the power steering pump located at the left front of the engine compartment. At operating temperature, the level should be high on the dipstick; at cooler temperatures, the level will be lower, but should never be allowed to fall below the end of the dipstick. Either power steering fluid or automatic transmission fluid may be added.

Manual Transmission Level

Manual transmission lubricant need not be changed. Check level every 4 months or 6,000 miles (6 months or 7,500 miles on 1975-1977 cars). The filler plug is located on the left side of the transmission case, and can be removed with a 9/16 in. wrench. Using SAE 80 or 90 weight gear lubricant, fill to within ½ in. of the filler hole if unit is cold, or level with the filler hole if the unit is hot.

Automatic Transmission Level

Check transmission fluid level every 4 months or 6,000 miles (6 months or 7,500 miles on 1975-1977 cars). Transmission must be at operating temperature, in NEUTRAL or PARK. The engine should be idling and the parking brake set. The dipstick is located near the distributor. Add Dexron® automatic transmission fluid through the dipstick tube and only enough to bring the level to the FULL mark. One pint will raise the level from ADD to the FULL mark. *Do not overfill.*

Differential

It is not necessary to change the standard differential lubricant. Check level every 4 months or 6,000 miles (6 months or 7,500 miles on 1975-1977 models). If the unit is cold, fill to ½ in. below the filler hole with SAE 80 or SAE 90 weight gear lubricant. At operating temperature, the lubricant level should reach the filler hole.

Positraction rear axles use a special lubricant made for limited-slip differentials. This lubricant should be changed at the end of the first 12,000 miles (15,000 miles on 1975-1977 cars).

Thereafter, check level as indicated for the standard differential.

Clutch Free Play

Periodically check clutch free play. Normal clutch plate wear reduces free play to a point where clutch wear may be accelerated. With a tape measure, measure distance between floorboard and underside of clutch at rest. Depress clutch by hand until resistance is felt. Measure distance again. The difference (clutch free play) should be approximately one inch. If adjustment is necessary, refer to Chapter Eight.

Brakes

At every lubrication, check all brake lines and cylinders for leakage. Check fluid level in both sides of master brake cylinder. Clean cover, then snap off retaining clip. Do not bend clips. The fluid level should be within 1/4 in. of top. Use only Delco Hydraulic Supreme No. 11 or DOT-3 brake fluid.

Inspect front disc pads whenever a front tire is removed or at 7,500-mile intervals. There is an access hole in the front and rear of each caliper. Pads need replacing when there is less than 1/32 in. of pad exposed. At the same time, remove either rear tire and wheel and inspect rear linings. Rear brake linings should be replaced when less than 1/32 in. of available lining remains. If difficulty is encountered when removing rear wheel, release the brake adjuster. Remove the oblong rubber plug covering the access hole or punch out the knock-out plug. Push in on the adjuster rod until it is clear of the shoe. This allows the brake shoes to retract and the wheel can now be removed.

> NOTE: *The punch out will drop inside the wheel. Remove and discard this piece and replace with a rubber plug available from your Chevrolet dealer.*

If a brake pedal appears spongy, there is air in the system and the hydraulic system must be bled. Refer to Chapter Nine.

Headlight Aim Check

For safety and maximum visibility at night, the headlight aim should be checked at 12,000 miles (15,000 miles on 1975-1977 cars) and anytime front end damage has occurred. It is necessary to have the car on a level surface and perpendicular to a vertical wall 25 ft. in front of the car (garage door works well). The gas tank should be approximately 1/2 full and all extra weight (not including spare tire or jack) should be removed from the interior and trunk. Refer to **Figure 3**.

1. Move the car until it is 25 ft. from wall.

2. Measure distance between center of headlight and ground.

3. Mark a horizontal line this height on wall.

4. Run a string forward from one rear tire, alongside the front tire on the same side of the car, to the wall. Mark a spot on line drawn in Step 3.

5. Do Step 4 for other side of car and find center point between these 2 spots.

6. Measure distance between center of headlights and divide distance by 2. Mark dark spots at this distance on each side of center point located in Step 5. This is where the center of the high beam should shine.

7. Turn lights on low beam. Both headlights should project below and to the right of the 2 spots located in Step 6 (Figure 3).

8. If necessary, adjust aim by turning one or both Phillips head adjusting screws at the top and at the outside edge of the headlight. It is not necessary to remove molding around headlight.

Air Conditioning

At 4 months or 6,000 miles (6 months or 7,500 miles on 1975-1977 cars), clean dirt and debris from the condenser located in front of engine radiator. Clean evaporator drain tube. Adjust compressor belt tension, if necessary.

Refrigerant Charge Check

1. Set parking brake and run engine at fast idle with transmission in NEUTRAL.

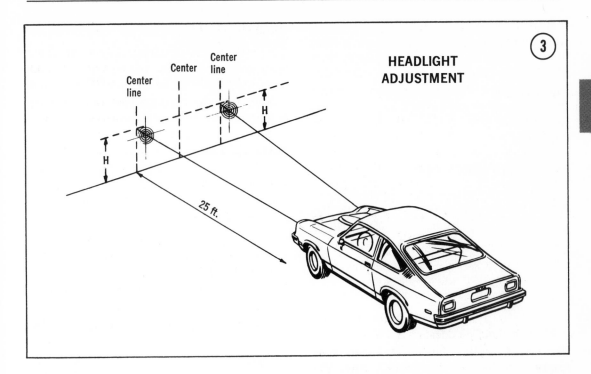

2. Set air conditioning controls for maximum cooling (blower on high).

3. Remove sight glass protective cover.

4. If bubbles are observed, system is low on refrigerant.

5. A clean sight glass indicates a full charge of refrigierant if cold air is being produced. If the system is not producing cold air, and if there is no temperature difference between the 2 hoses at the compressor, then the system is empty.

WARNING

Leave air conditioning system recharge and repairs to your dealer or a qualified refrigeration technician. Without adequate knowledge and special tools, there is danger of personal injury and damage to the system.

PERIODIC MAINTENANCE

The following procedures are for replacement of items that are exposed to dirt and wear. The items may be cleaned and reused until the replacement interval is reached. In cases where your Vega is used under severe conditions or when performance has deteriorated, it may be well to perform this maintenance sooner than called for.

Air Cleaner Replacement

Vegas are equipped with a new 50,000-mile air cleaner which is replaced as a unit. When driving in dusty areas or if gas mileage has been dropping, replace more often. Remove hold-down screws or nuts on top of air cleaner. Pull vent hose out and lift air cleaner straight off carburetor. Save grommet and gasket for reuse. While air cleaner is off, check and clean choke and throttle linkage.

Fuel Filter Replacement

The fuel filter is located in the fuel filter fitting to which the fuel line attaches. Remove the fuel line, then unscrew the fuel filter fitting. There are 2 filter types; one for single-barrel carburetors, the other for the 2-barrel carburetor. Be sure you obtain correct replacement.

Positive Crankcase Ventilation (PCV)

The PCV system draws contaminating vapors from the crankcase during engine operation and routes them through the carburetor into the combustion chambers. The metered PCV valve is located on the camshaft cover beneath the engine oil cap. It should be checked at every engine oil change. Remove it by merely pulling it from the rubber grommet. Start the engine. The valve needs replacement if no air is being drawn through the system. Replacement every 24,000 miles (30,000 miles on 1975-1977 cars) is recommended. Pinch valve retaining clip with pliers and remove valve. Check associated hoses for cracks or plugged hoses. Replace hoses as necessary.

Evaporation Control System

This system consists of a vapor separator located on the fuel tank and an evaporative canister in the left front corner of the engine compartment.

> NOTE: *A pressure-vacuum fuel tank cap is required for this system to function properly. Do not replace with a vented cap.*

Replace the filter located in the bottom of the canister every 12 months or 12,000 miles (every 30,000 miles on 1975-1977 cars). The canister must be disconnected and removed from its mounting to replace the filter. See **Figure 4**. When replacing the canister filter, examine all hose connection openings for obstruction. Apply vacuum to the small hose leading to the cap of the canister purge valve. If it does not hold vacuum, snap off the cap (slowly, as it is under spring tension) and replace necessary parts.

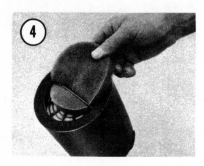

Intake Manifold

Torque intake manifold bolts to 30 ft.-lb. (moderate torque) at each 12,000 miles (15,000 miles on 1975-1977 cars) before beginning tune-up. Slight leaks here can cause rough idle and poor performance. At first 12,000 miles (15,000 miles on 1975-1977 cars) also tighten

carburetor hold-down bolts to compensate for gasket compression.

PERIODIC LUBRICATION

Refer to Table 3 and **Figure 5** for a summary of lubrication points and requirements.

Engine Oil Change

Check for engine oil leaks both *before* and *after* changing oil. Select oil of viscosity suitable for the coldest temperature anticipated before the next oil change. See Table 3.

> WARNING
> *Use safety stands when working under the car. Do not rely solely on hydraulic or mechanical jacks.*

Run the engine until warm. Replace engine crankcase drain plug with a 9/16 in. wrench and drain into pan. Replace and tighten drain plug. Fill with 3 quarts recommended engine oil, or 4 quarts if the filter is changed. Check oil level with dipstick. *Do not overfill.*

Oil Filter

The oil filter should be replaced at every other oil change beginning with the first. The entire unit, located at the front left side of the engine, unscrews and should be replaced with an AC type PF-25 filter or equivalent. Removal can be done without tools, although an inexpensive tool available at auto supply stores may make the job easier.

> CAUTION
> *Do not install a filter with any tool. Tighten by hand only.*

Distributor (1971-1974)

Every other oil change, rotate cam lubricator (**Figure 6**) 180°. Replace every 24,000 miles.

Distributor (1975-1977)

The 1975-1977 Vegas are equipped with the High Energy Ignition (HEI) system which is permanently lubricated at the factory and does not require any further lubrication. At 22,500-mile intervals, however, the distributor cap and

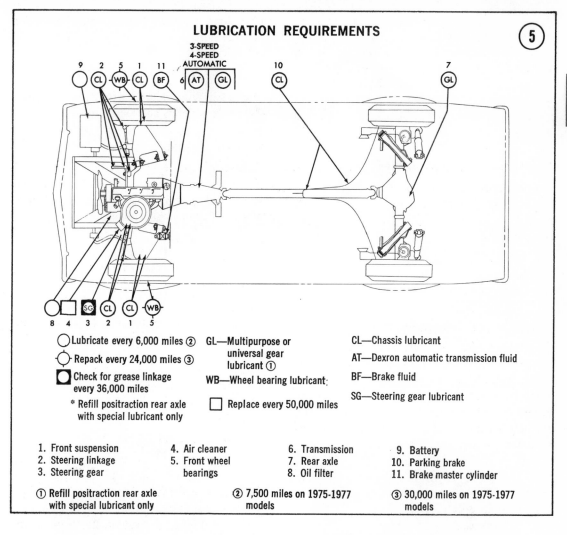

LUBRICATION REQUIREMENTS ⑤

- ◯ Lubricate every 6,000 miles ②
- ◇ Repack every 24,000 miles ③
- ◼ Check for grease linkage every 36,000 miles
- * Refill positraction rear axle with special lubricant only
- ☐ Replace every 50,000 miles

GL—Multipurpose or universal gear lubricant ①

WB—Wheel bearing lubricant:

CL—Chassis lubricant

AT—Dexron automatic transmission fluid

BF—Brake fluid

SG—Steering gear lubricant

1. Front suspension
2. Steering linkage
3. Steering gear
4. Air cleaner
5. Front wheel bearings
6. Transmission
7. Rear axle
8. Oil filter
9. Battery
10. Parking brake
11. Brake master cylinder

① Refill positraction rear axle with special lubricant only

② 7,500 miles on 1975-1977 models

③ 30,000 miles on 1975-1977 models

rotor (**Figure 7**) should be inspected for chips, cracks, corrosion, carbonized paths, and evidence of wear. Replace if in doubtful condition.

Front Suspension and Steering Linkage

Clean each grease fitting with a rag or paper towel. Apply chassis lubricant with a hand-held grease gun to the 7 fittings on the steering linkage. See **Figure 8** for location. Sufficient lubrication is indicated when grease begins to seep from around the rubber seals. Remove excess grease with rag. Apply same grease to the 2 fittings (top and bottom) of the control arm ball-joint next to each front wheel as pointed out in **Figure 9**. These 4 fittings are reached best with the wheels turned to one extreme, then the other.

NOTE: *Ball-joints should not be greased unless temperature is 10°F or higher.*

Front Wheel Bearings

Repack bearings every 24,000 miles (30,000 miles on 1975-1977 cars) with water-resistant, high melting point, front wheel bearing lubricant.

CAUTION
Do not use long fiber or viscous lubricants.

Refer to Chapter Ten for disassembly and assembly of front hubs, including correct wheel bearing adjustment.

1. Clean all old grease from spindle.

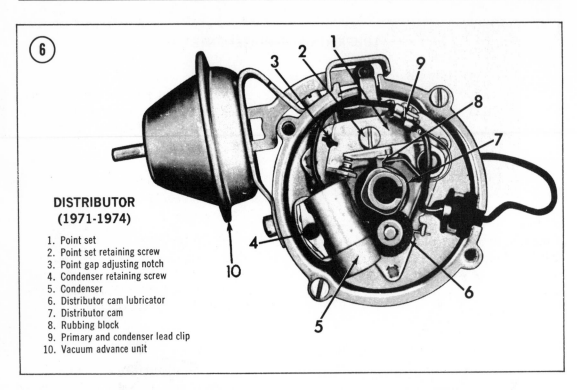

(6)

DISTRIBUTOR
(1971-1974)

1. Point set
2. Point set retaining screw
3. Point gap adjusting notch
4. Condenser retaining screw
5. Condenser
6. Distributor cam lubricator
7. Distributor cam
8. Rubbing block
9. Primary and condenser lead clip
10. Vacuum advance unit

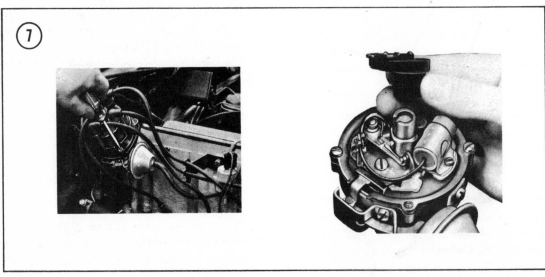

(7)

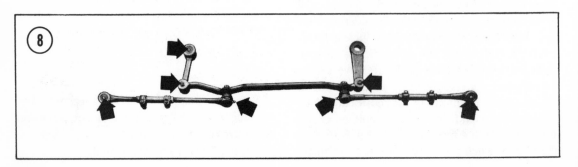

(8)

2. Insert wooden dowel, or small hammer handle, through the front of the hub and tap out dust seal to release inner bearing.

3. Clean inside of hub and bearings with solvent, or kerosene, removing all old grease and foreign matter.

CAUTION

If an air hose is used after cleaning bearings with solvent, do not direct air stream to cause bearings to spin.

4. Repack bearings by forcing lubricant through the bearing—a little at a time—with the palm of your hand. Remove excess grease by wiping with your fingers. *Do not pack grease into hub or dust cap.*

5. Reassemble with new dust seal if needed. Thoroughly clean disc surface before installing caliper brake assembly.

Automatic Transmission

At 24,000-mile (30,000 miles on 1975-1977 cars) intervals, the transmission fluid should be changed. Check for leaks *before* and *after* changing fluid. Clean the area around the transmission drain plug, then remove it with a ⅞ in. wrench and drain into pan. Replace and tighten drain plug. Fill to ¼ in. below the ADD mark to allow for expansion during operation. Start the engine and move selector lever through all positions; recheck the level. *Do not overfill.*

> NOTE: *Adjust low band at first transmission fluid change (Chapter Eight).*

Lubricate transmission linkage and parking brake cable, guides, links, and levers every 4 months or 6,000 miles (6 months or 7,500 miles on 1975-1977 cars).

Body

Every 6 months lubricate all movable body parts with a light spray lubricant such as WD-40. Work the oil in several times and wipe off excess. Some of the points that should not be overlooked are:

    a. Hood latch and hinges

    b. Passenger door latches and hinges

    c. Rear deck lid latch and hinges

    d. Trunk torque rods

If weatherstripping begins to squeak, rub a silicone stick (obtainable at most auto parts stores) over the weatherstrip. This also preserves the rubber and inhibits cracking.

ENGINE TUNE-UP

Periodic tune-ups are necessary to maintain a car in proper running condition. Procedures outlined here should be performed every 12,000 miles on 1971-1974 models and every 22,500 miles on 1975-1977 models.

The specifications used in tune-up work vary from model to model and may even change during a model year. For this reason, always consult the label located on the underside of the hood for the specifications that apply to your particular vehicle. If this label is missing or cannot be read, use the specifications given in **Table 5**. If your vehicle does not run properly after using these specifications, consult your dealer.

Since different systems in an engine interact to affect overall performance, tune-up must be accomplished in the following order:

    1. Valve clearance adjustment (except 1976-1977 cars)

    2. Ignition adjustment and/or timing

    3. Carburetor adjustment

Valve Clearance (1971-1975)

> NOTE: *All 1976-1977 Vega 140 cu. in. engines have hydraulic valve lifters which require no adjustment.*

Table 5 TUNE-UP SPECIFICATIONS

Year	Carburetor	Transmission	Idle Speed (RPM)		Compression (PSI) ①	Distributor		Spark Plugs		Timing (° BTDC)
			Solenoid Disconnected	Solenoid Connected		Point Setting (Inch) ②	Dwell Angle (Degrees)	Type	Gap (Inch)	
1971	1 bbl	M	700	850	140	0.019	31-34	R42TS	0.035	6
	1 bbl	A	550D ③	650 ③	140	0.019	31-34	R42TS	0.035	6
	2 bbl	M	700	1,200	140	0.019	31-34	R42TS	0.035	6
	2 bbl	A	550D ③	700 ③	140	0.019	31-34	R42TS	0.035	10
1972	1 bbl	M	700/800 ④	850 ⑤	140	0.019	31-34	R42TS	0.035	6 ⑤
	1 bbl	A	550D ③	700/800 ④ ③	140	0.019	31-34	R42TS	0.035	6
	2 bbl	M	700/800 ④	1,200	140	0.019	31-34	R42TS	0.035	8
	2 bbl	A	550D ③	700/800 ④ ③	140	0.019	31-34			
1973	1 bbl	M	800/700	1,000	140	0.019	31-34	R42TS	0.035	8
	1 bbl	A	550 ③	800/750/800 ④ ③	140	0.019	31-34	R42TS	0.035	8
	2 bbl	M	800/700/800 ④	1,200	140	0.019	31-34	R42TS	0.035	10
	2 bbl	A	500 ③	1,000	140	0.019	31-34	R42TS	0.035	12
1974	1 bbl	M	800/700	800/750/800 ④ ③	140	0.019	31-34	R42TS	0.035	10
	1 bbl	A	550 ③	800/750 ③	140	0.019	31-34	R42TS	0.035	12
	2 bbl	M	800/700	1,200	140	0.019	31-34	R42TS	0.035	10
	2 bbl	A	500 ③	800/750 ③	140	0.019	31-34	R42TS	0.035	12

① Maximum 20 psi allowable between high and low cylinder.
② 0.016 in. for used points.
③ In DRIVE.
④ Use last number for air conditioned cars.
⑤ 4° BTDC for cars first sold in California.

Table 5   TUNE-UP SPECIFICATIONS (continued)

Year	Carburetor	Transmission, Emission Class	Idle Speed (RPM) Solenoid Disconnected	Idle Speed (RPM) Solenoid Connected	Compression (PSI) ①	Distributor	Spark plugs Type	Spark plugs Gap (Inch)	Timing (° BTDC)
1975	1 bbl	M	700	1,200	140	Equipped with HEI system	R43TSX	0.068	8
	1 bbl	A	550 ②	750 ②	140	Equipped with HEI system	R43TSX	0.060	10
	2 bbl	M	700	1,200	140	Equipped with HEI system	R43TSX	0.060	10
	2 bbl	A	600 ②	750 ②	140	Equipped with HEI system	R43TSX	0.060	12
1976	1 bbl	M	750	1,200	140	Equipped with HEI system	R43TS	0.035	8
	1 bbl	A	550 ②	750 ②	140	Equipped with HEI system	R43TS	0.035	10
	2 bbl	M, 49 states	550	700 ③	140	Equipped with HEI system	R43TSX	0.035	10
	2 bbl	A, 49 states	600 ②	750 ②	140	Equipped with HEI system	R43TSX	0.035	12
	2 bbl	M, Calif.	700	1,000	140	Equipped with HEI system	R43TS	0.035	10
	2 bbl	A, Calif.	600 ②	750 ②	140	Equipped with HEI system	R43TS	0.035	12
1977	2 bbl	M, 49 states	700	1,250	140	Equipped with HEI system	R43TS	0.035	0 @ 700 rpm
	2 bbl	M, Calif.	800	1,250	140	Equipped with HEI system	R43TS	0.035	−2 @ 700 rpm
	2 bbl	M, high-alt.	800	1,250	140	Equipped with HEI system	R43TS	0.035	0 @ 700 rpm
	2 bbl	A, 49 states	650 ②	850 ②	140	Equipped with HEI system	R43TS	0.035	2 @ 650 rpm
	2 bbl	A, Calif.	650 ②	850 ②	140	Equipped with HEI system	R43TS	0.035	0 @ 650 rpm
	2 bbl	A, high-alt.	700 ②	850 ②	140	Equipped with HEI system	R43TS	0.035	2 @ 700 rpm

① Maximum 20 psi allowable between high and low cylinders.
② In DRIVE.
③ With air conditioner override switch disconnected and air conditioner on, adjust solenoid to 1,200 rpm in neutral.

This is a series of simple mechanical adjustments which is performed every 24,000 miles (22,500 miles on 1975 cars) while the engine is hot or cold. Valve clearance for your engine must be carefully determined. If the clearance is too small, the valves may be burned or distorted. Large clearance results in excessive noise. In either case, the engine power is reduced.

1. Remove spark plugs.

2. Remove the air cleaner, cam cover, coil wire, and distributor cap, noting the position of the spark plug wire for cylinder No. 1.

3. With a ¾ in. socket, turn the crankshaft clockwise until the distributor rotor is at the No. 1 firing position (ignition points open). See **Figure 10**.

4. Using a leaf-type feeler gauge and a ⅛ in. Allen wrench, check and adjust the intake valves for cylinders 1 and 2 and the exhaust valves for cylinders 1 and 3 (intake, 0.014-0.016 in.; exhaust, 0.029-0.031 in.). *Turn the screw in 360° increments.* Each complete revolution of the screw changes the clearance 0.0003 in. If you apply a slight downward pressure to the tappet when turning the adjusting screw, you will feel it seat against the valve stem. Turn the adjusting screw until the feeler gauge no longer

can be inserted between the cam lobe and tappet, and back off one revolution on the adjusting screw for correct clearance.

5. Now turn the crankshaft until the distributor rotor is at the No. 4 firing position (ignition points open). Check and adjust the intake valves for cylinders 3 and 4 and the exhaust valves for cylinders 2 and 4.

Ignition Wiring

Inspect all ignition wiring. Replace wiring that has become brittle or oil soaked. Look for broken wire strands at terminal connectors. If ignition wires are oily or dirty, wipe clean with a cloth dampened with solvent.

Distributor (1971-1974)

Servicing the distributor includes rotating or replacing the cam lubricator, replacing and regapping contact points, replacing condenser, inspecting, cleaning, or replacing rotor and cap.

1. Turn distributor rotor clockwise, then release it. If it does not snap back to its original position, the distributor should be removed and disassembled to locate trouble in the centrifugal advance mechanism.

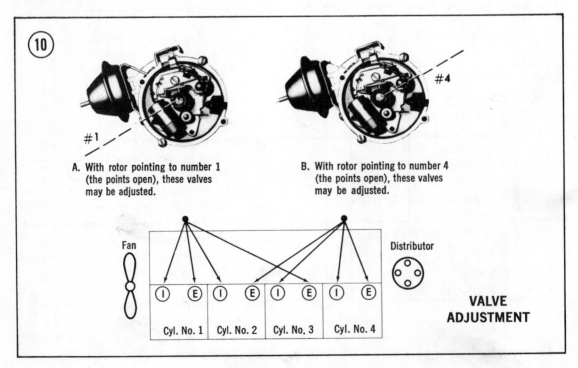

(10)

A. With rotor pointing to number 1 (the points open), these valves may be adjusted.

B. With rotor pointing to number 4 (the points open), these valves may be adjusted.

Fan

Distributor

Cyl. No. 1   Cyl. No. 2   Cyl. No. 3   Cyl. No. 4

VALVE ADJUSTMENT

2. Disconnect the hose from the vacuum advance (Figure 6). Turn the breaker plate counterclockwise and firmly place your finger over the end of the hose fitting on the vacuum diaphragm chamber. Keep your finger in place and release the breaker plate. It will remain in relatively the same position if there are no leaks in the vacuum unit. Now remove your finger. The breaker plate should snap back to its original position.

3. Remove distributor cap by depressing and rotating the 2 retaining screws.

4. Wipe cap with clean, dry cloth and inspect for cracks, chips, carbon paths or corrosion, or wear on the high voltage contacts. If cap is in good condition, it can be reused.

5. Remove rotor by pulling straight up with thumb and forefinger. Check spring on top of rotor. Clean and inspect wear at end of contact. If only slightly rough, file smooth, wipe clean, and reuse. Replacement is necessary anytime the distributor cap is replaced.

6. Visually inspect contact points for wear and alignment before removing. If the points are gray and only slightly roughened (0.020 in. or less) they need not be replaced and often have a greater area of contact than new points. If points need to be replaced, continue with the next procedure. Smooth points with several strokes of a point file and check gap.

Contact Point Replacement (1971-1974)

Remove the 2 leads that fasten to points. Remove the point set retaining screw (Figure 6) carefully so it does not drop down inside the distributor. Lift out the old points and replace with a new set by reversing the procedure. Clean any residue on the surface of the new points with a clean cloth drawn between them.

Contact Point Alignment and Gapping (1971-1974)

Flat surfaces of closed points should be parallel. If misaligned, bend the fixed contact support, *not* the movable breaker lever arm.

Rotate the engine by hand or with starter motor until the points open completely (cam opposite rubbing block). Loosen retaining screw

slightly and manually adjust gap to 0.019 in. for new points or 0.016 in. for used points. Tighten retaining screw and recheck gap.

Distributor Cam Lubricator (1971-1974)

Every 24,000 miles replace distributor cam lubricator. Pull straight off its retaining stud. Slip a new lubricator over the stud. It will return to its original shape in a few minutes. Reassemble distributor in reverse procedure.

Distributor (1975-1977)

The only distributor service required for 1975-1977 Vegas is inspection of the distributor cap and rotor for signs of damage, wear, or other deterioration. Replace damaged or doubtful parts. Lubrication and adjustment are not required.

Spark Plug Replacement

Remove spark plug wire by pulling on the boot over the spark plug insulator.

CAUTION
Do not pull directly on the spark plug wire itself. The carbon center in the resistance wire is subject to separation when the wire is stretched. The separation may be unnoticeable from the outside but may cause intermittent missing. Repair of damaged wires is impossible and replacement is necessary.

Inspect the wiring and replace as a set if any wiring or connectors appear cracked, brittle, or broken. Clean any loose debris and dirt lodged around base of spark plug.

Remove plugs with a ⅝ in. deep standard spark plug wrench keeping them in order so you can identify which cylinders they were associated with. Compare plug appearance with **Figure 11** to identify any abnormal condition associated with one or more cylinders.

Plugs having a normal appearance even if coated with powdery red, brown, yellow, and/or white deposits may be cleaned, regapped, and reused if they have been used less than 12,000 miles (22,500 miles for 1975-1977 cars). Nor-

⑪   **SPARK PLUG CONDITION**

NORMAL

• Identified by light tan or gray deposits on the firing tip.
• Can be cleaned.

GAP BRIDGED

• Identified by deposit buildup closing gap between electrodes.
• Caused by oil or carbon fouling. If deposits are not excessive, the plug can be cleaned.

OIL FOULED

• Identified by wet black deposits on the insulator shell bore electrodes.
• Caused by excessive oil entering combustion chamber through worn rings and pistons, excessive clearance between valve guides and stems, or worn or loose bearings. Can be cleaned. If engine is not repaired, use a hotter plug.

CARBON FOULED

• Identified by black, dry fluffy carbon deposits on insulator tips, exposed shell surfaces and electrodes.
• Caused by too cold a plug, weak ignition, dirty air cleaner, defective fuel pump, too rich a fuel mixture, improperly operating heat riser, or excessive idling. Can be cleaned.

LEAD FOULED

• Identified by dark gray, black, yellow, or tan deposits or a fused glazed coating on the insulator tip.
• Caused by highly leaded gasoline. Can be cleaned.

WORN

• Identified by severely eroded or worn electrodes.
• Caused by normal wear. Should be replaced.

FUSED SPOT DEPOSIT

• Identified by melted or spotty deposits resembling bubbles or blisters.
• Caused by sudden acceleration. Can be cleaned.

OVERHEATING

• Identified by a white or light gray insulator with small black or gray brown spots and with bluish-burnt appearance of electrodes.
• Caused by engine overheating, wrong type of fuel, loose spark plugs, too hot a plug, low fuel pump pressure, or incorrect ignition timing. Replace the plug.

PREIGNITION

• Identified by melted electrodes and possibly blistered insulator. Metallic deposits on insulator indicate engine damage.
• Caused by wrong type of fuel, incorrect ignition timing or advance, too hot a plug, burned valves, or engine overheating. Replace the plug.

mally the plugs will be replaced at every tune-up since the time and effort to remove, clean, adjust, etc., costs more than a new set of 4 plugs. If an abnormal plug condition is noted on one or more cylinders do not merely replace the plug; locate and correct the problem before it becomes more serious.

Adjust the plug gap to 0.035 in. (0.060 in. for 1975 models only) with a round or wire gap gauge. A flat gauge as used for setting distributor point gap can give misleading spark plug gap settings.

If the spark plugs need adjustment gently bend the side electrode to meet specifications. Do not pound on electrode with a heavy tool. Many plug gap gauges have handy notches in the side to conveniently bend electrode.

Insert plugs and tighten by hand until they seat. Tighten plugs firmly (15 ft.-lb. torque). Replace spark plug wires by pushing boot firmly over top of plug.

> NOTE: *The remainder of the engine tune-up procedure consists of ignition timing and carburetor adjustments which are made with the engine running and at operating temperature.*

Ignition Point Dwell Check (1971-1974)

If a dwell meter is available, check ignition point dwell while the engine is warming up. Dwell angle should be 31-34 degrees. Check this between idle and 1,750 rpm. Variation should not exceed 3 degrees. If dwell is steady, but above or below specifications, recheck the point setting. If dwell cannot be brought to within specifications, or dwell variation exceeds specifications, check for a loose breaker plate or a worn distributor shaft and bushing.

Ignition Timing

All tune-up specifications should be strictly adhered to for proper engine and emission control performance. Various model years will have slightly different tune-up specifications which are indicated on the plate located on the underside of the hood.

Warm up the engine and then shut it off. Rub the timing marks, located on the right side of the engine at the crankshaft pulley, with white chalk; also mark the timing notch on the pulley. See **Figure 12**.

1. Connect a timing light to No. 1 spark plug (Figure 10).

2. Disconnect hose from vacuum advance unit and plug with pencil or golf tee.

3. Check that all test equipment leads are clear of fan and belt. Start engine.

> WARNING
> *When working around an idling engine, remember the fan will sometimes appear to be stationary. Do not allow test leads or hands to fall where they may be struck by the fan.*

4. Point the timing light to illuminate the timing index tab on the lower left of crank pulley and read timing. Note that each point on the index tab is 4 degrees; the numbers toward the top of the engine are after top dead center (ATDC) and toward the bottom are before top dead center (BTDC). Remember "before" means "advanced."

5. Timing specifications vary according to year and state in which sold. Consult either Vehicle Emission Control Information sticker or Table 5 for proper setting.

6. To reset timing, loosen distributor locknut and slowly rotate distributor to bring timing into specification.

7. Tighten distributor locknut and recheck timing.

8. When finished, shut off engine. Disconnect timing light. Do not remove plug from vacuum hose until after carburetor idle adjustment discussed later.

Choke and Throttle Linkage Adjustment

Hold the throttle partially open and operate choke linkage up and down. If it sticks, clean with solvent. Do not oil. Oil attracts dirt and will aggravate the problem. Have an assistant slowly floor the accelerator pedal and visually check for twisting or kinking. Observe whether the throttle return spring brings the throttle all the way back against the idle solenoid. If not, bend the spring holding tab to increase the spring tension.

Carburetor Adjustment

Because of anti-pollution regulations the only routine adjustments that should be made by the owner/mechanic without special test equipment (exhaust gas analyzer) is idle speed. Carburetor mixture screws are factory set and covered by limiter caps. These are not adjusted on a routine basis. This section will cover only the 2 idle speed adjustments. Remaining adjustments are found in Chapter Six.

> NOTE: *All carburetor adjustments must be made with engine at operating temperature, choke open, air cleaner on, and air conditioning off.*

Carburetor Idle Adjustment

This adjustment is made with the engine running and manual gearshift in NEUTRAL or automatic transmission in DRIVE. With automatic transmissions, it will be necessary to block up the back wheels so they will not contact the pavement.

1. Set parking brake on hard and block up rear wheels if automatic transmission.

2. Disconnect hose labeled FUEL TANK (second from right) for evaporation emission canister.

3. Disconnect hose to vacuum advance unit and plug it. This may have been done during ignition timing.

4. Observe the proper rpm settings on Vehicle Emission Control Information sticker or Table 5.

5. Refer to **Figures 13 and 14**, set curb idle with electrical lead connected to idle stop solenoid on carburetor. On 2-barrel carburetors, momentarily open throttle to allow plunger to extend before adjusting.

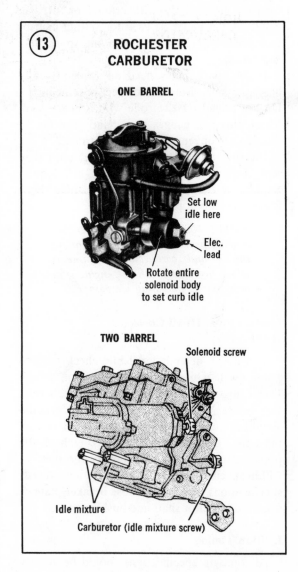

⑬ **ROCHESTER CARBURETOR**

ONE BARREL

Set low idle here

Elec. lead

Rotate entire solenoid body to set curb idle

TWO BARREL

Solenoid screw

Idle mixture

Carburetor (idle mixture screw)

6. Set low idle with solenoid lead disconnected. On single-barrel carburetors use ⅛ in. Allen wrench inserted in the end of solenoid to make adjustment.

7. Reconnect solenoid lead, vacuum advance hose, and emission control hose.

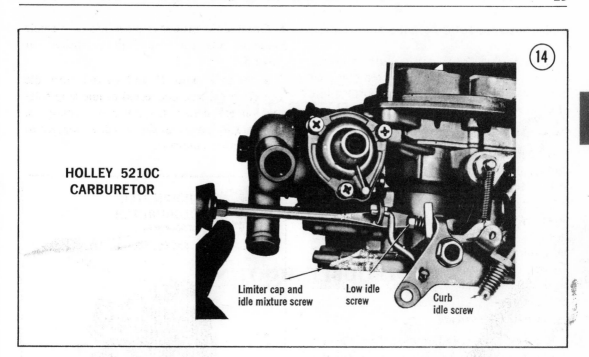

HOLLEY 5210C
CARBURETOR

Limiter cap and
idle mixture screw

Low idle
screw

Curb
idle screw

CHAPTER THREE

TROUBLESHOOTING

Troubleshooting the Vega can be relatively easy if done in a logical, orderly manner. The first step in any troubleshooting procedure must be defining the symptoms as closely as possible. After the symptoms are defined, areas which could cause the problems are tested and analyzed. Guessing at the cause of a problem may provide the solution, but it can easily lead to frustration, wasted time, and a series of expensive, unnecessary parts replacements.

TROUBLESHOOTING INSTRUMENTS

The following equipment is necessary to properly troubleshoot any engine:

a. Voltmeter, ammeter, and ohmmeter
b. Hydrometer
c. Compression tester
d. Vacuum gauge
e. Fuel pressure gauge
f. Dwell meter
g. Tachometer
h. Strobe timing light
i. Exhaust gas analyzer

Items a-f are basic for any car. Items g-i are necessary for exhaust emission control compli-

ance. The following is a brief description of each instrument.

Voltmeter, Ammeter and Ohmmeter

For testing the ignition system and electrical system, a good voltmeter is needed. A voltmeter covering 0-20 volts is satisfactory. It should have an accuracy of about ±½ volt, which excludes the type found in car instrument panels.

An ohmmeter measures electrical resistance. It is useful for checking continuity (open and short circuits) and testing fuses and lights.

The ammeter measures electrical current. Ammeters for automotive use should cover 0-10 amperes and 0-100 amperes. These are useful for checking battery starting and charging current.

Some inexpensive VOM's (volt-ohmmeters) combine all 3 instruments into one. Unfortunately, the ammeter ranges are usually too small for automotive work.

Hydrometer

The hydrometer gives a useful indication of battery condition and charge by measuring the specific gravity of the electrolyte in each cell. Complete details on use and interpretation of readings are given in Chapter Seven.

Compression Tester

The compression tester measures the compression pressure built up in each cylinder. Interpretation of compression test results can indicate general cylinder and valve condition. **Figure 1** shows a compression tester in use.

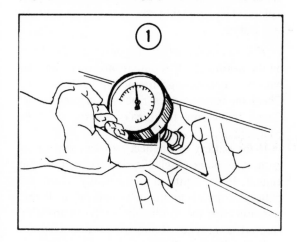

There are 2 types of compression test, "wet" and "dry." These tests are interpreted together to isolate problems in cylinders and valves. The dry compression test is performed first. If the engine fails to pass the compression test, correct the condition before proceeding with the engine tune-up.

1. Warm the engine to normal operating temperature. Remove air cleaner and make sure the choke valve is completely open.

2. Remove spark plugs one at a time, and examine each for evidence of improper combustion. Put them aside for further examination later. Keep them in order so you'll know which cylinder is causing trouble.

CAUTION

To avoid damage to the grounding circuit in the ignition switch, disconnect the distributor primary lead at the coil (negative post) and turn the ignition switch to ON *whenever cranking the engine remotely.*

3. Connect the compression tester to one cylinder following manufacturer's instructions.

4. Have an assistant crank the engine over until there is no further increase in compression. Hold the accelerator to the floor while cranking.

5. Remove the tester and record each reading.

6. Repeat Steps 3-5 for each cylinder.

When interpreting the results, actual readings are not as important as the differences in readings. The lowest reading must be within 75% of the highest. A greater difference indicates worn or broken rings, leaky or sticking valves, or a combination of all.

If the dry compression test indicates a problem (excessive variation in readings), isolate the cause with a wet compression test. This is done in the same way as the dry compression test, except that about 1 tablespoon of oil is poured down the spark plug hole before performing Steps 3-5. If the wet compression readings are much greater than the dry compression readings, the trouble is probably due to worn or broken rings. If there is little difference between wet and dry readings, the trouble is probably due to leaky or sticking valves.

There may also be head gasket leaks if oil or engine coolant is found in a cylinder. The following simple test will confirm and locate coolant leakage into engine cylinders.

1. Remove the radiator cap and bring the coolant level to the lip of the pressure cap valve seat.

2. Reinstall a spark plug in the suspected cylinder.

3. Look into the radiator filler neck and crank the engine several times.

4. If bubbles are observed, leakage is confirmed; head gasket must be replaced, or cracks repaired.

Vacuum Gauge

The vacuum gauge is one of the easiest instruments to use, but one of the most difficult for the inexperienced mechanic to interpret. The results are interpreted with other findings to isolate problems.

To use the vacuum gauge, connect it to the intake manifold at any convenient location, such as the distributor vacuum advance unit. Start the engine and let it warm up thoroughly. Vacuum reading should be steady at 17-21 in.

NOTE: *Subtract 1 in. from reading for every 1,000 ft. of altitude.*

Figure 2 shows numerous typical readings with interpretations. Numbers given are approximate. Results are not conclusive without comparing to other tests, such as compression.

Fuel Pressure Gauge

This instrument is necessary for testing fuel pump performance. Fuel system troubleshooting procedures in this chapter use a fuel pressure gauge. The fuel pressure gauge should read to 10 pounds per square inch (psi).

Dwell Meter

A dwell meter measures how many degrees of cam rotation that the distributor points remain closed when the engine is running. Since this angle is determined by breaker point gap, the dwell angle is an accurate indication of point gap. Dwell angle for all Vega models is 31°-34°.

Many tachometers intended for testing and tuning include a dwell meter. Follow the manufacturer's instructions to measure dwell.

Tachometer

A tachometer is necessary for setting ignition timing and adjusting the carburetors. The best instrument for this purpose is one with a range of 0-2,000 rpm. Tachometers with an extended range (0-6,000 or 0-8,000 rpm) lack accuracy at lower speeds. The tachometer should be capable of detecting changes of 25 rpm.

Strobe Timing Light

This instrument is necessary for tuning and emission control adjustments. It permits very accurate ignition timing. The light flashes precisely at the same instant that No. 1 cylinder fires, so the position of the crankshaft pulley at that instant can be seen. Refer to Chapter Two for location of timing index marks.

Exhaust Analyzer

This instrument is necessary to check emission control adjustments accurately. It samples the exhaust gases from the tailpipe and measures the thermal conductivity of the exhaust. Since different gases conduct heat at varying rates, thermal conductivity of the exhaust is a good indicator of the gases present.

Exhaust analyzers are relatively expensive to buy, but some large rent-all dealers have them available at a modest price.

STARTER

Starter system troubles are relatively easy to isolate. The following are common symptoms and causes.

1. *Engine cranks very slowly or not at all*—Turn on the headlights. If the lights are very dim, the battery or connecting wires are probably at fault. Check the battery as described in Chapter Seven. Check the wiring for breaks, shorts, or dirty connections.

If the battery or connecting wires are not at fault, turn the headlights on and try to crank the engine. If the lights dim drastically, clean the battery terminals and clamps and retest. If this does not clear the trouble the starter is probably shorted to ground. Remove it and test as described in Chapter Seven.

If the lights remain bright or dim only slightly when trying to start the engine, the trouble may be in the starter, relay, or wiring. On automatic transmission models, the neutral start switch may also be at fault. Perform the following steps to isolate the cause.

> **WARNING**
> *Disconnect the coil wire to prevent accidental starting. Keep away from moving parts (fan, alternator, etc.) when working in the engine compartment.*

a. If the starter doesn't respond at all, connect a 12-volt test lamp between the starter terminal and ground. Turn the ignition key to START. If the lamp lights, the starter is probably at fault. Remove it and test as described in Chapter Seven. If the lamp doesn't light, the problem is somewhere in the starting circuit. Perform the next steps.

b. On automatic transmission models, disconnect the wiring connector from the neutral start switch (Chapter Seven). Connect a jumper wire between the terminals on the wiring connector, then turn the ignition key to START. If the starter turns, adjust or replace the neutral start switch.

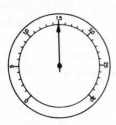

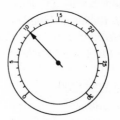

1. NORMAL READING .
Reads 15 in. at idle.

2. LATE IGNITION TIMING
About 2 inches too low at idle.

3. LATE VALVE TIMING
About 4 to 8 inches low at idle.

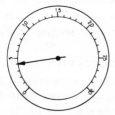
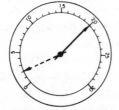

4. INTAKE LEAK
Low steady reading.

5. NORMAL READING
Drops to 2, then rises to 20 when accelerator is rapidly depressed and released.

6. WORN RINGS, DILUTED OIL
Drops to 0, then rises to 18 when accelerator is rapidly depressed and released.

7. STICKING VALVE(S)
Normally steady. Intermittently flicks downward about 4 in.

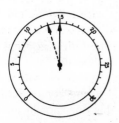
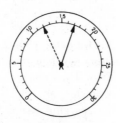
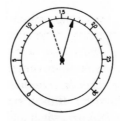
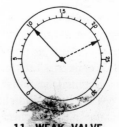

8. LEAKY VALVE
Regular drop about 2 inches.

9. BURNED OR WARPED VALVE
Regular, evenly spaced down-scale flick about 4 in.

10. WORN VALVE GUIDES
Oscillates about 4 in.

11. WEAK VALVE SPRINGS
Violent oscillation (about 10 in.) as rpm increases. Often steady at idle.

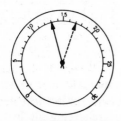
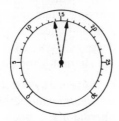
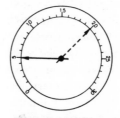

12. IMPROPER IDLE MIXTURE
Floats slowly between 13-17 in.

13. SMALL SPARK GAP or DEFECTIVE POINTS
Slight float between 14-16 in.

14. HEAD GASKET LEAK
Gauge floats between 5-19 in.

15. RESTRICTED EXHAUST SYSTEM
Normal when first started. Drops to 0 as rpm increases. May eventually rise to about 16.

c. Connect a jumper wire between the battery and starter terminals on the starter relay (**Figure 3**). If the starter doesn't respond at all, the relay is probably defective. If the starter cranks normally, perform next step.

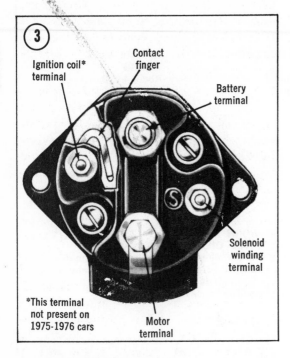

Ignition coil* terminal

Contact finger

Battery terminal

Solenoid winding terminal

*This terminal not present on 1975-1976 cars

Motor terminal

d. Connect a test lamp between the starter terminal on the starter relay and ground. Turn the ignition key to START. If the lamp doesn't light, check the ignition switch and associated wiring. Turn the key to START and work it around in the switch. If the lamp lights erratically, the ignition switch is probably defective.

e. If the problem still has not been isolated, check all wiring in the starting circuit with an ohmmeter or other continuity tester. Starting circuit efficiency can easily be checked by connecting a voltmeter across the following points: positive battery terminal and solenoid battery terminal; negative battery terminal and starter housing; solenoid battery terminal and solenoid motor terminal. Disconnect the coil wire to keep the engine from starting. The voltage drop on any of these circuit checks should not exceed 0.2V with the starter switch closed and the engine cranking.

2. *Starter turns, but does not engage with flywheel ring gear*—This problem may be caused by a defective starter drive mechanism, or broken pinion or ring gear teeth. Remove and inspect the starter as described in Chapter Seven.

3. *Loud grinding noises when starter runs*—This may mean the teeth on pinion or flywheel are not meshing properly, or it may mean the starter drive mechanism is damaged. In the first case, remove the starter and examine the gear teeth. In the latter case, remove the starter and repair the starter drive mechanism.

CHARGING SYSTEM

Charging system troubles may be in the alternator, solid-state regulator, or fan belt. The following symptoms are typical.

1. *Battery dies frequently, even though ammeter shows no discharge*—This can be caused by a fan belt that is just slightly too loose. Grasp the alternator pulley and try to turn it. If the pulley can be turned without moving the fan belt, the fan belt needs to be tightened.

2. *Ammeter shows constant discharge*—First check fan belt tension as described in Chapter Two. Then check battery condition with a hydrometer, and check all wiring connections in the charging system. If this does not locate the trouble, check the alternator and voltage regulator, using test procedures described in Chapter Seven.

3. *Ammeter shows intermittent discharge*—This usually indicates the charging system is working intermittently. Check the fan belt tension and check all electrical connections in the charging system for loose connections. Check the alternator for worn brushes.

4. *Battery requires frequent additions of water, or lights require frequent replacement*—The alternator is probably overcharging the battery. The voltage regulator is probably at fault. Check as described in Chapter Seven.

5. *Excessive noise from alternator*—Check for loose alternator mounting. The problem may also be worn alternator bearings. If the alternator whines, a shorted diode may be indicated.

ENGINE

These procedures are to be used when the starter cranks the engine over normally. If not, refer to starter section in this chapter.

1. *Engine will not start*—This problem could be caused by the ignition system or the fuel system. First find out if there is high voltage to the spark plugs. To do this, disconnect one of the spark plug wires. Hold the wire about ¼ in. to ½ in. from ground (any metal in the engine compartment) with an insulated screwdriver. Crank the engine over. If sparks do not jump to ground, or the sparks are very weak, the problem may be in the ignition system. See the *Ignition System* section of this chapter for further details. If long, blue sparks occur, the trouble may be in the fuel system. See *Fuel System* section of this chapter.

2. *Engine misses steadily*—Remove one spark plug wire at a time and ground the wire. If engine miss increases, *that* cylinder was working properly. Reconnect the wire and check the others. When a wire is disconnected and the miss remains the same, *that* cylinder is not firing. Check spark as described in Step 1. If no spark occurs for one cylinder only, check the distributor cap, wire, and spark plug. If spark occurs on the non-firing cylinder, check compression and intake manifold vacuum to isolate the trouble.

3. *Engine misses erratically at all speeds*—There are several possible causes, which may be difficult to find. The problem could be in the ignition system, exhaust system (exhaust restriction), or fuel system. Trouble can be dirty gas, water in the gas, dirty carburetor jets. A worn distributor shaft or cam lobe, weak coil, or incorrect plug or point gap can cause intermittent ignition trouble. A leaky exhaust gas recirculating valve can also cause this problem.

4. *Engine misses at idle only*—Most often an ignition problem, vacuum (intake manifold) leak, worn valves, low compression, EGR or PCV valve leaky, carburetor idle set too low or mixture incorrectly adjusted.

5. *Engine misses at high speed only*—This is generally an indication of poor fuel delivery. Check fuel pump. Sometimes ignition crossfire can occur. Clean and relocate the ignition coil high tension and the plug wires. Check for clogged fuel filter.

6. *Engine stalls*—Carburetor idle speed or mixture needs adjustment, sticky carburetor fuel inlet valve, dirty or watery gas, incorrect timing, exhaust restricted, overheated engine, vacuum leaks in intake manifold or vacuum lines can cause constant stalling. Sometimes indicates need for tune-up.

7. *Low performance and/or poor fuel economy* —This is to be expected with emission devices of later models. Check all emission control devices for proper operation. Review driving habits. Consider a tune-up. Try different brands of gasoline. Premium may help slightly but generally not enough considering the higher price. Check carburetor float level and jets. Replace air cleaner, check compression for faulty valves, leaking cylinder head gasket. High fuel consumption can also be caused by many factors seemingly unrelated to fuel consumption. Check for clutch slippage (manual transmissions), brake drag, defective wheel bearings, and poor front end alignment, or low tire pressures. Sometimes a capacitor-discharge (CD) ignition kit will improve mileage slightly. It also pays for itself in longer point and plug life.

IGNITION SYSTEM (1971-1974)

These procedures assume the battery is in good enough condition to crank the engine at a normal rate.

1. *No spark to one plug*—The only possible causes are a defective distributor cap or spark plug wire. Examine the distributor cap for moisture, dirt, carbon tracking between the contacts, or other visible defects.

2. *No spark to any plugs*—This could be caused by trouble in the primary or secondary circuits. First remove the coil wire from the center of the distributor cap. Hold the end of the wire about ¼ in. from ground with an insulated screwdriver. Crank the engine. If sparks occur, the trouble is in the rotor, distributor cap, or points. Remove the cap and check for burns, moisture, dirt, carbon tracking, etc. Check the rotor for excessive pitting, burning, wear, or

cracks. Replace if necessary. Check the points for excessive gap (or none at all), burning, pitting, or looseness. Replace or adjust them if necessary.

If the coil does not produce any spark, check the secondary (high voltage) wire for opens. If the wire is good, crank the engine so the breaker points are open. With the points open, check voltage from the negative terminal of the coil to ground with a voltmeter or test lamp. If voltage is present, the coil is probably bad. Have it checked or substitute a coil known to be good. If voltage is not present, check wire connections to the coil and distributor. Temporarily disconnect the wire from the coil negative terminal and measure voltage from the terminal to ground. If voltage is present, the distributor is shorted. Examine breaker points and connecting wires carefully. If voltage is still not present, measure voltage from the coil positive terminal to ground. Voltage on the positive terminal, but not on the negative, indicates a defective coil. No voltage on the positive terminal indicates an open wire between the positive terminal and the battery.

3. *Weak spark*—If the spark is so small it cannot jump ¼-½ in. to ground, check the battery condition as described in Chapter Seven. Other causes are bad breaker points, condenser, incorrect point gap, dirty or loose connections in the primary circuit, or dirty or burned rotor or distributor. Also check for worn distributor cam lobes.

4. *Missing*—This is usually caused by fouled or damaged plugs, plugs of the wrong heat range, or incorrect plug gap. Clean and regap the spark plugs. This trouble can also be caused by weak spark (Step 3) or incorrect ignition timing.

IGNITION SYSTEM
(1975-1977 HEI)

The following procedures are for diagnosis of problems in the High Energy Ignition (HEI) system distributors used on 1975-1977 Vegas.

1. *Engine cranks but will not start* — Turn ignition on and place automatic transmission selector in PARK or manual transmission selector in NEUTRAL. Connect a test light to the BAT lead terminal on the coil. Connect other test light

lead to ground. If light goes on, remove a spark plug wire and hold it ¼ inch from engine block and crank engine. If a healthy spark is present, the problem is not in the HEI system. Check spark plugs, fuel system, and for flooded condition. If test light does not go on, check ignition switch and BAT terminal and wire lead and replace if faulty, then repeat spark test above. If no spark is present, turn off ignition and remove and inspect distributor cap and rotor for cracks, evidence of moisture, dust, or burns, carbonized paths, etc., and replace defective or questionable components. If no defects are noted, disconnect green and white wire leads from electronic module and connect an ohmmeter between either lead and ground. If a reading of less than infinity is obtained (on the X1,000 scale), replace pickup coil.

If engine still does not start, connect an ohmmeter to coil terminals as shown in **Figure 4**. If a reading of above one ohm is obtained (on the X1 scale), replace the ignition coil.

If the reading between the green or white electronic module leads and ground is infinite, connect the ohmmeter between the 2 leads (green and white). If the reading is between 500 and 1,500 ohms, repeat the reading while moving the vacuum advance with a screwdriver. If the reading remains between 500 and 1,500 ohms, check the ignition coil as outlined in the paragraph above.

If a reading of less than 500 or more than 1,500 ohms is obtained, replace the pickup coil. If engine still does not start, check the ignition coil as outlined above.

If the ohmmeter reads less than one ohm (on the X1 scale) when the ignition coil is checked, connect the ohmmeter to the ignition coil as shown in **Figure 5**. If the reading is above 30,000 or less than 6,000 ohms, replace the ignition coil. If the reading is between 30,000 and 6,000 ohms, connect the ohmmeter as shown in **Figure 6**. If reading is less than infinity, replace coil. If infinity, check electronic module.

NOTE: *Checking of the electronic module requires a special tester. This task should be referred to your Chevrolet dealer or a qualified me-*

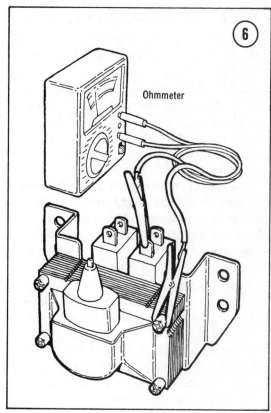

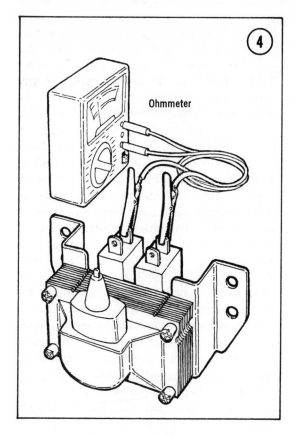

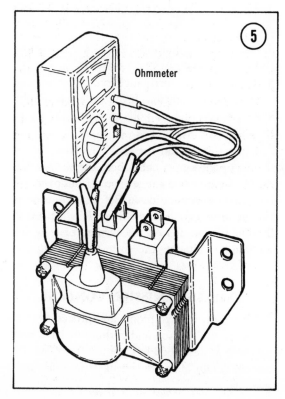

chanic who has the necessary special
equipment.

2. *Engine runs rough or cuts out*—First check
spark plugs and spark plug wires and replace as
required. If engine still runs rough, have the
electronic module checked and replace if indicated. If this is not the problem, remove the
distributor cap and inspect the cap and rotor
for evidence of dust, moisture, cracks, burns,
etc., and repair or replace as necessary. If electronic module is OK, remove green and white
leads from module and connect an ohmmeter
between either lead and ground. If the reading is
less than infinity (on the X1,000 scale), replace
the pickup coil. If the reading is infinity, connect the ohmmeter between the green and white
leads. If the reading is between 500 and 1,500
ohms, retake the reading while moving the vacuum advance with a screwdriver. If the reading
is still within the 500-1,500 ohm limits, check
the ignition coil as outlined below. If the reading is not within the 500-1,500 ohm limits, replace the pickup coil. If engine still does not run

properly, check the ignition coil as outlined below.

To check the ignition coil, connect an ohmmeter as shown in Figure 5. If the reading is more than 30,000 ohms or less than 6,000 ohms, replace the ignition coil. If the reading is between 30,000 and 6,000 ohms, repeat the procedure above until the problem is isolated.

FUEL SYSTEM

Fuel system problems must be isolated at the fuel pump, fuel lines, or carburetors. These procedures assume the ignition system has been checked and properly adjusted, and that gas is in the tank.

1. *Engine will not start*—First make sure fuel is being delivered to the carburetor. Remove the air cleaner, look into the carburetor throat, and depress the accelerator several times. There should be a stream of fuel from the accelerator pump nozzle each time the accelerator is depressed. If not, check the fuel pump delivery (described later), float valves, and float adjustment (Chapter Five).

If fuel is delivered and the engine still won't start, check the automatic choke to make sure it is not stuck, out of adjustment, or damaged. If necessary, rebuild or replace the carburetor. See Chapter Five.

2. *Engine runs at fast idle*—Check the choke setting. Check the idle mixture, idle speed, and decel valve adjustments. See Chapter Five.

3. *Rough idle or engine miss with frequent stalling*—Check idle mixture and idle speed adjustments. See Chapter Five.

4. *Engine "diesels" (keeps on running) when ignition is switched off*—Check idle mixture (probably too rich), ignition timing, and idle speed (probably too fast). Check the throttle solenoid for proper operation (Chapter Five). Check for overheated engine.

5. *Stumbling when accelerating from idle*—Check the idle speed and idle mixture adjustments. Check the carburetor accelerator pump. See Chapter Six.

6. *Engine misses at high speed or lacks power*—This indicates possible fuel starvation. Check

fuel pump pressure and capacity. Check float needle valves. Check for a clogged fuel filter or air cleaner.

7. *Black exhaust smoke*—This indicates a badly overrich mixture. Check idle mixture and idle speed adjustment. Check choke setting. Check for excessive fuel pump pressure, leaky floats, or worn needle valves.

8. *Excessive fuel consumption* — Check for overrich mixture. Make sure choke mechanism works properly. Check idle mixture and idle speed. Check for excessive fuel pump pressure, leaky floats, or worn float needle valves.

Fuel Pump Pressure Testing

An inefficient fuel pump will affect high speed engine operation. The Vega is equipped with an electric fuel pump which can be tested for delivery volume and pressure without the engine running.

1. Unplug the oil pressure safety switch located on left front of the engine block.

2. Insert a jumper wire across the 2 outside terminals in the plug.

3. Disconnect the fuel line at the carburetor and direct it into a one pint container.

4. Turn on the ignition switch. The container should fill within 30 to 45 seconds.

5. Connect a pressure gauge to the fuel line and operate the pump again. If the battery is supplying the required 12.6 volts or more, the gauge should read 3 to 4½ psi.

If there is fuel in the tank, but none is delivered by the pump, check both the electric fuel fuse (20 amp) and gauge fuse (10 amp) in the fuse panel under the dash. Before reconnecting the fuel line, install a new filter. It is located in the fuel filter fitting on the carburetor to which the fuel line attaches.

EXHAUST EMISSION CONTROL

The following symptoms and procedures apply when the ignition and carburetor have been adjusted as described in Chapters Two and Six, and the results have been checked on an accurate gas analyzer.

1. *CO content too low*—Make sure idle speed is not too low. Check idle mixture adjustment. Check engine condition with a compression and vacuum test.

2. *CO content too high*—Check idle mixture adjustment. Check for clogged or dirty air cleaner. Make sure choke is all the way open. Check carburetor condition. Clean or replace as necessary. Check engine condition with a compression and vacuum test.

CLUTCH

All clutch problems, except adjustments or cable replacement, require removal of the transmission to identify the cause and make repairs.

1. *Slippage*—This condition is most noticeable when accelerating in high gear at relatively low speed. To check slippage, drive at a steady speed in second or third gear. Without letting up the accelerator, push in the clutch long enough to let engine speed increase (1 or 2 seconds). Then let the clutch out rapidly. If the clutch is good, engine speed will drop quickly or the car will jump forward. If the clutch is slipping, engine speed will drop slowly and the car will not jump forward.

Slippage results from insufficient clutch pedal free play, oil or grease on the disc, worn pressure plate, or a weak diaphragm spring. Riding the clutch pedal can cause the disc surface to become glazed, resulting in slippage. Also check the withdrawal lever to make sure it isn't binding and preventing full engagement.

2. *Drag or failure to release* — This trouble usually causes difficult shifting and gear clash especially when downshifting. The cause may be excessive clutch pedal free play, warped or bent pressure plate or clutch disc, stretched clutch cable, or broken or loose disc linings. Also check condition of the transmission input shaft splines.

3. *Chatter or grabbing*—There are several possible causes. Check tightness of transmission-to-frame and engine-to-transmission mounting bolts. Check for worn or misaligned pressure plate and clutch disc.

4. *Other noises*—Noise usually indicates a dry or defective release bearing. Check the bearing and replace if necessary. Also check all parts for misalignment or uneven wear.

MANUAL TRANSMISSION

Most transmission problems are evidenced by one or more of the following symptoms:

   a. Difficulty in shifting gears

   b. Gear clash when downshifting

   c. Slipping out of gear

   d. Excessive noise in gear

   e. Oil leaks

Transmission troubles are sometimes difficult to distinguish from clutch trouble. Eliminate the clutch as a source of trouble before suspecting the transmission.

1. *Slips out of high gear*—Could be caused by loose mounting bolts or worn, misaligned or binding shift rods or linkage. A loose or damaged pilot bearing or a broken or loose main drive gear retainer could also cause the problem. Dirt between the transmission case and the clutch housing can also cause this symptom. Another cause could be a stiff shift lever seal.

2. *Noisy in all gears*—This problem can be caused by one or more of the following:

   a. Insufficient lubricant

   b. Worn countergear bearings

   c. Worn or damaged main drive gear and countergear

   d. Damaged main drive gear or main shaft bearings

   e. Worn or damaged countergear anti-lash plate

3. *Noisy in high gear*—Can be caused by damaged main drive gear bearing, main shaft bearing or high speed gear synchronizer.

4. *Noisy in neutral*—Could be caused by damaged main drive gear bearing, damaged or loose main shaft pilot bearing, worn or damaged countergear anti-lash plate, or worn countergear bearings.

5. *Noisy in all reduction gears*—Usually caused by insufficient lubricant or worn or damaged main drive gear or countergear.

6. *Noisy in second gear only*—This could be

caused by damaged or worn second-speed constant mesh gears, worn or damaged countergear rear bearings, or damaged or worn second-speed synchronizer.

7. *Noisy in third gear only* (4-speed)—Usually caused by worn or damaged third-speed constant mesh gears or worn or damaged countergear bearings.

8. *Noisy in reverse only*—Probable causes are worn or damaged reverse idler gear or idler bushing, worn or damaged reverse gear on main shaft, damaged or worn reverse countergear, or damaged shift mechanism.

9. *Excessive backlash in all reduction gears*—Suspect worn countergear bearings or excessive end play in countergear.

10. *Main drive gear bearing retainer burned or scored by input shaft*—Can be caused by loose or damaged main shaft pilot bearing or misalignment of the transmission.

11. *Leaking lubricant*—Can be caused by any of the following.

   a. Too much lubricant in transmission
   b. Loose or broken main drive gear bearing retainer
   c. Main drive gear bearing retainer gasket damaged
   d. Side cover loose or damaged gasket
   e. Rear bearing retainer oil seal leaking
   f. Countershaft loose in case
   g. Shift lever seal leaking

AUTOMATIC TRANSMISSIONS

Most automatic transmission repairs require specialized knowledge and tools. Is is impractical for the home mechanic to invest in tools which cost more than the price of a properly rebuilt transmission. There are some corrective measures that can be taken, however (see Chapter Eight). If these measures do not correct the problem, the home mechanic usually can save on labor charges by removing the defective transmission from the automobile, having it repaired, and then replacing it in the car. Removal and installation procedures are given in Chapter Eight.

Following are lists of symptoms and probable causes. Compare unusual transmission behavior to these symptoms to help isolate problems.

Powerglide Transmission Troubleshooting

1. *No drive in any gear*—Low fluid level; check for defective fluid pump; check pressure as described later; broken gears.

2. *No drive in reverse*—Incorrect manual valve lever adjustment. Defective reverse clutch.

3. *Engine races excessively during upshift*—Improper fluid level. Improper band adjustment. Burnt or worn high clutch friction linings. Improper fluid pressure. Check as described later.

4. *Transmission will not upshift*—Low band not releasing. This could be caused by improperly adjusted manual valve lever, stuck low drive valve, defective governor, stuck or improperly adjusted throttle valve, or defective rear pump.

5. *Harsh upshifts*—Improper low band adjustment. Defective vacuum modulator or modulator line. Defective hydraulic modulator.

6. *Harsh downshifts when throttle is closed*—Improper low band adjustment. High engine idle speed. Defective downshift timing valve. High mainline pressure.

7. *Transmission will not downshift*—Sticking low drive shift valve. High governor pressure.

8. *Incorrect shift points* (see **Table 1**)—Carburetor-to-transmission linkage incorrectly adjusted. Throttle valve incorrectly adjusted. Defective governor. Rear pump priming valve stuck.

9. *Poor acceleration; engine output good*—Normally caused by defective torque converter. Could be low fluid level, slipping bands or clutches, also.

10. *Transmission fluid discolored or smells burnt*—Burnt band or friction lining.

11. *Unusual scraping, grinding or screeching noises* — Defective converter or planetary gear set.

12. *Excessive fluid consumption*—If accompanied by smoking exhaust, vacuum unit is probably leaking and engine is drawing fluid out. Otherwise check for leak around transmission

Table 1   POWERGLIDE SHIFT POINTS

	Shift Points, MPH		
	2.73 axle, A78-13 tire	2.92 axle, A78-13 tire	2.92 axle, A70-13 tire
Closed throttle			
Up	19-23	16.3-19.8	17-23
Down	22-18	19.0-15.4	20-15
Detent touch			
Up	54-67	46.5-57.5	51-64
Down	54-39	46.5-33.5	51-37
Wide open throttle			
Up	63-73	54.0-63.0	60-69
Down	69-59	59.5-51.0	65-55

case and extension, transmission oil pan gasket, and converter cover pan.

13. *Oil forced out of filter tube*—Oil level too high. Water in oil. Leak in pump suction circuits.

14. *Vehicle creeps excessively at idle; transmission in drive*—Idle speed too high.

15. *Vehicle creeps in neutral*—Incorrect manual valve lever adjustment. High clutch or low band not releasing.

Powerglide Basic Pressure Checks

Several basic pressure checks are used to diagnose Powerglide troubles. All checks should be made only after thoroughly warming up the transmission.

1. Warm transmission by idling at 750 rpm for 2 minutes with transmission in DRIVE range with parking brake set tight. As an alternative, drive car for 5 miles making frequent starts and stops. Return engine to proper idle after warm-up.

2. Connect pressure gauge as shown in **Figure 7**. Route connecting hose so gauge can be observed while car is being driven.

3. Verify that a wide open throttle upshift occurs at the pressure indicated in Table 1.

4. Apply parking brake and move shift selector to DRIVE. Compare idle pressure to Table 1.

5. Connect a tachometer. Apply parking brake and move shift selector to low. Adjust engine speed to 1,000 rpm. Compare mainline pressures to **Table 2**.

Turbo-Hydramatic Troubleshooting

1. If car does not drive in DRIVE range, this could be caused by low fluid level, incorrectly adjusted manual linkage, low fluid pressure (see

Table 2   POWERGLIDE MAINLINE PRESSURE CHECK

	Mainline Pressure (PSI)		
	1971-1972	1973 Base	1973*
Wide open throttle upshift	90	91.1	87.2
Idle at 16 in. Hg in DRIVE	50	60.1	80.1
Idle at 10 in. Hg in DRIVE	80	80.9	80.9
1,000 rpm in manual low	90	91.1	91.1
20-25 mph coast in drive (approx. 20 in. Hg)	50	50.8	50.8

* With 2-barrel carburetor and all vehicles first sold in California.

Servo apply pressure

Step 2b below), malfunctioning forward clutch, or defective roller clutch.

2a. If line pressure is high, check for disconnected or leaking vacuum, or leak in other vacuum operated accessories. This symptom also can be caused by the modulator (stuck, damaged, or presence of water), a fault in the detent system (defective detent switch, shorted wiring, defective solenoid, restricted feed orifice, or damaged valve bore plug), or by a defective oil pump.

2b. If line pressure is low, check for low fluid level, or a restricted or blocked filter or screen. Low pressure also can be caused by a defective oil pump, internal circuit leaks, defective regulator valves, and leaky or damaged case assemblies.

3. If transmission shifts from D1 to D2 at full throttle only, the cause could be a sticking (or misadjusted linkage) detent valve, faulty or leaking vacuum line or fittings, a defective control valve assembly, or a porous or leaking case assembly. Suspect a sticking detent switch if symptom occurs only in wet or cold weather.

4. If transmission refuses to shift from D1 to D2, check for a binding detent (downshift) cable. This also may be caused by a sticking or damaged governor assembly, damaged control

valves or gaskets, or a faulty intermediate clutch. Case defects may also cause the problem.

5. If shifting occurs between D1 and D2, but the transmission will not shift from D2 to DRIVE, suspect a defective control valve, detent switch or solenoid, or a damaged or malfunctioning direct clutch.

6. If the transmission skips D1 and starts in D2, suspect a defective intermediate clutch.

7. If drive occurs while the transmission is in NEUTRAL, check the manual linkage for correct adjustment. This symptom also can be caused by damaged internal linkage, defective fluid pump, or a damaged forward clutch.

8. If no motion or slippage occurs in REVERSE, check for low fluid level, misadjusted manual linkage, or low fluid pressure. This can also be caused by defective control valve, defective or sticking servos, and malfunctioning clutches.

9. If slipping occurs in all ranges, or when starting, check for low fluid level, low fluid pressure, or leaking case assembly. This can also be caused by defective direct or forward clutch.

10. If slipping occurs during the D1-D2 shift, check for low fluid level, low fluid pressure, or leaking case. Possible causes also include defective control valves, mispositioned or damaged pump-to-case gasket, or damaged intermediate clutch.

11. If slipping occurs during the D2-D3 shift, again check for low fluid level and/or pressure, or a leaking case. This can also be caused by a defective direct clutch.

12. If rough shifting occurs in the D1-D2 shift, check for high fluid pressure. Other possible causes include defective control valve, damaged intermediate clutch, and damaged case.

13. If roughness occurs in the D2-D3 shift, check for high fluid pressure. This can also be caused by defective servo accumulators, or damaged direct clutch.

14. If engine braking does not occur in L1 or L2, check for low fluid pressure. This can also be caused by defective control valves, clutches, and servos.

15. If downshift does not occur at part throttle, check for high or low fluid pressure. This can

also be caused by defective detent valve and linkage, or damaged control valve.

16. If no detent downshift (wide open throttle) occurs, check for improperly adjusted or disconnected detent downshift cable or retainer. This can also be caused by malfunctioning valve body or solenoid.

17. If low or high shift points occur, check for high or low fluid pressure and for vacuum leaks and/or faulty vacuum connections. This symptom can also be caused by a faulty governor, a stuck detent valve and/or linkage, a sticking control valve assembly, or a leaking case assembly.

18. If the transmission will not hold in PARK, check the adjustment of the manual linkage. This can also be caused by defective internal linkage.

19. If the transmission seems to sound noisy, verify that the noise is not coming from the water pump, alternator, power steering, air conditioner compressor, or other belt-driven accessories. This can be done by removing the belt to each accessory and operating the engine momentarily. If this procedure isolates the noise to the transmission, check for low fluid level or for external transmission or cooler lines grounded against underbody of vehicle, or loose or broken engine mounts. Also check for water in fluid. If these checks fail to uncover the problem, the transmission should be taken to a competent mechanic.

Turbo-Hydramatic
Basic Pressure Check

1. Warm engine by iding at approximately 750 rpm for 2 minutes in DRIVE range with parking brake set and wheels blocked. As an alternative, drive the car for about 5 miles, making frequent starts and stops.

2. Connect oil pressure gauge to line pressure tap (**Figure 8**). Route connecting hose so gauge is visible from driver's position in car.

3. Disconnect vacuum modulator tube and firmly apply parking brake. Operate the engine at 1,200 rpm (connect tachometer if required) and check pressures obtained in the various

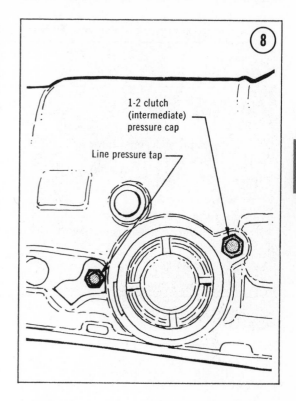

1-2 clutch (intermediate) pressure cap

Line pressure tap

transmission ranges against those given in **Table 3**.

4. Reconnect the vacuum modulator tube and connect a vacuum gauge to the intake manifold.

5. Operate engine at a speed required to maintain an absolute manifold pressure of 16 in. Hg (operate engine at 12 in. Hg for Hydramatic 350). Compare the pressures obtained in the various transmission ranges with those given in Table 3.

BRAKES

1. *Brake pedal goes to floor*—There are numerous causes for this, including excessively worn linings, air in the hydraulic system, leaky brake lines, leaky wheel cylinders and disc brake calipers, or leaky or worn master cylinder. Check for leaks and thin brake linings. Bleed the brakes. If the problem still exists, rebuild the wheel cylinders and calipers and/or the master cylinder.

2. *Spongy pedal*—Normally caused by air in the system; bleed the brakes.

3. *Brakes pull*—Check for wet or greasy brake linings, leaky wheel cylinders and calipers, loose

Table 3   TURBO HYDRAMATIC PRESSURES

	Pressure (PSI)		
	D/N/P	L1/L2	R
Turbo Hydramatic 350			
Idle, vacuum modulator disconnected	165	157	263
Idle, vacuum modulator connected*			
At sea level	49	73	78
At 6,000 ft.	70	88	111
Turbo Hydramatic 250			
Idle, vacuum modulator disconected	153	139	245
Idle, vacuum modulator connected**			
At sea level	55	82	88
At 6,000 ft.	96	106	154

* Engine vacuum at 12 in. Hg.   ** Engine vacuum at 16 in. Hg.

calipers, frozen or seized pistons, and restricted brake lines or hoses. Check front end alignment, and look for suspension damage. Tires also affect braking; check tire pressures and condition.

4. *Brake squeal or chatter*—Check brake lining thickness and brake drum roundness. Check discs for excessive runout. Make sure the rear brake shoes are not loose. Clean away all dirt on shoes, pads, drum, and discs.

5. *Dragging brakes*—Check brake adjustment, including handbrake. Brake adjustment is an unlikely cause, since the brakes are self-adjusting, but it is a possibility. Check for broken or weak shoe return springs (rear brakes), worn piston seals (front brakes), swollen rubber parts due to improper brake fluid or contamination. Clean or replace defective parts.

6. *Hard pedal*—Check brake linings for contamination. Also check for restricted brake lines and hoses.

7. *High speed fade*—Check for distorted or out-of-round brake drums. Check discs for excessive runout. Be sure recommended brake fluid is installed. Drain entire system and refill if in doubt.

8. *Pulsating pedal*—Check for distorted or out-of-round brake drum. Check the discs for excessive runout.

STEERING AND SUSPENSION

The following symptoms indicate steering or suspension trouble:

a. Steering is hard

b. Car pulls to one side

c. Car wanders or front wheels wobble

d. Steering has excessive play

e. Tire wear is abnormal

Unusual steering, pulling, or wandering is usually caused by bent or otherwise misaligned suspension parts. This is difficult to check without proper alignment equipment. See Chapter Ten for repairs that you can perform, and those that must be left to a dealer or front end specialist.

If the trouble seems to be excessive play, check wheel bearing adjustment first. This is the most frequent cause. Total play in the steering mechanism should be no more than ⅜ in., measured at the steering wheel rim. If play is excessive, check steering linkage for worn parts. Check tie rod end ball-joints by shaking each tie rod. Check suspension ball-joints as described in Chapter Ten.

Tire wear may be caused by suspension troubles, but may have many other causes. See *Tire Wear Analysis* following.

TIRE WEAR ANALYSIS

Abnormal tire wear should always be analyzed to determine its causes. The most common causes are:

a. Incorrect tire pressure

b. Improper driving

c. Overloading

d. Bad road surfaces

e. Incorrect wheel alignment

Figure 9 identifies wear patterns and indicates the 6 most probable causes of tire wear, and their symptoms.

WHEEL BALANCING

All 4 wheels and tires must be in balance along 2 axes. To be in static balance (**Figure 10**), weight must be evenly distributed around the axis of rotation. (A) shows a statically unbalanced wheel. (B) shows the result—wheel tramp or hopping. (C) shows proper static balance.

To be in dynamic balance (**Figure 11**), the centerline of the weight must coincide with the centerline of the wheel. (A) shows a dynamically unbalanced wheel. (B) shows the result—wheel wobble or shimmy. (C) shows proper dynamic balance. A front-end specialist is best equipped to check wheel alignment and balance.

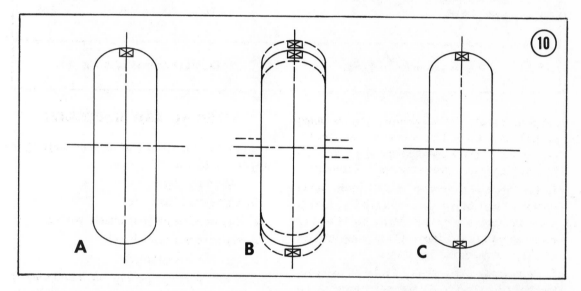

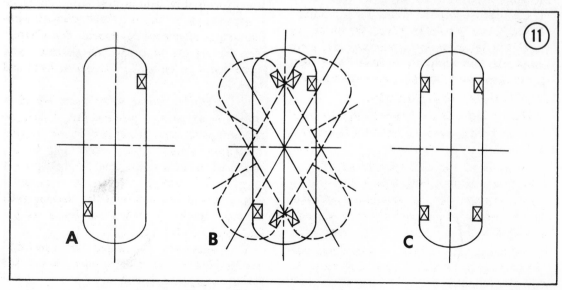

⑨

Underinflation—Worn more on sides than in center.

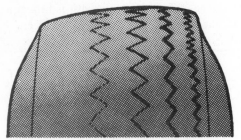

Wheel Alignment—Worn more on one side than the other. Edges of tread feathered.

Wheel Balance — Scalloped edges indicate wheel wobble or tramp due to wheel unbalance.

Road Abrasion—Rough wear on entire tire or in patches.

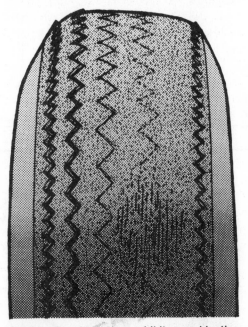

Combination—Most tires exhibit a combination of the above. This tire was overinflated (center worn) and the toe-in was incorrect (feathering). The driver cornered hard at high speed (feathering, rounded shoulders) and braked rapidly (worn spots). The scaly roughness indicates a rough road surface.

Overinflation—Worn more in center than on sides.

CHAPTER FOUR

ENGINE

Figure 1 gives left and right external views of the 4-cylinder, 140 cu. in. (2300cc) displacement overhead cam engine. Two versions of the basic engine are available. The standard powerplant has a Rochester single-barrel carburetor. A Rochester 2-barrel carburetor was optional equipment on 1971-1972 models. Models built in 1973 and later have been offered with an option of a 2-barrel Holley carburetor and a higher lift camshaft. Compression ratio for both single- and 2-barrel versions was 8.5:1 until 1973 when it was lowered to 8.0:1. Other engine differences between 1971 and 1975 are minor. In 1976 all Vega 140 cu. in. engines were equipped with hydraulic valve lifters (all previous models have mechanical lifters). This change also included shorter valves and valve springs, a revised camshaft, and different valve spring retainers. The cylinder head has been changed, including the addition of a check valve in the oil passage system to improve lubrication of the cam and lifters at start up. An improved oil pump (which can be used on earlier models as well) was also added.

The engine incorporates a die-cast aluminum and silicon block, a cast-iron cylinder head, and a 5-main bearing crankshaft. The cylinder walls are electro-chemically treated to etch away the surface aluminum, leaving a microscopic silicon riding surface for the iron-plating aluminum pistons. The intake manifold is water cooled.

An overhead valve, overhead cam design places all valves, tappets, and camshaft in the head assembly. Engine timing is achieved through a glass-fiber reinforced, cogged rubber belt and sprockets. Except for crankshaft and flywheel, all engine components can be removed with the engine in the vehicle. Therefore, the complete engine removal procedure is located at the end of this chapter.

Tables 1 and 2 (end of chapter) provide engine and torque specifications, respectively.

CRANKSHAFT PULLEY

Disconnect battery ground cable and loosen generator and air conditioning compressor. Remove drive belts. Pulley is secured by one bolt to the crankshaft and by 4 bolts to the timing sprocket. When replacing, align damper pin in the sprocket hole and pulley tang in the crankshaft key way.

TIMING BELT
AND WATER PUMP

1. See Chapter Five for diagnosis of faulty water pump or cooling system problems. Drain engine coolant and remove crankshaft pulley.

2. Remove fan, spacer, and engine front cover.

3. Remove lower cover, loosen water pump bolts, and remove timing belt.

4. Remove water pump.

5. When reassembling, refer to **Figure 2**. Align camshaft sprocket timing mark with notch on upper cover. Align crankshaft sprocket damper pin hole with cast rib on oil pump cover.

Later models have an alignment hole at the left rear of the camshaft sprocket cover and a hole in the camshaft sprocket. When these are aligned, the camshaft is timed for No. 1 cylinder at top dead center.

6. Install timing belt and adjust tension with tool J-23654 and a torque wrench as shown in **Figure 3**. Maintain 15 ft.-lb. torque, and tighten water pump bolts.

> NOTE: *Water pump bolts should be covered with an anti-seizing compound before installing.*

CAMSHAFT TIMING SPROCKET AND SEAL (1971-1974)

1. Remove front cover, loosen water pump, and remove timing belt.

2. Lock sprocket by inserting a socket through one of the sprocket holes onto the head of a bolt behind the procket. Remove camshaft sprocket retaining bolt.

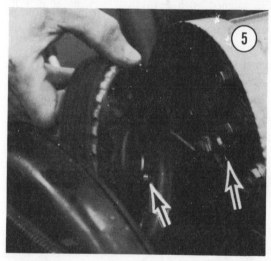

Tool hole

J-23654

3. Remove the 3 bolts holding the seal retainer and cover in place.

4. New seals should be installed flush with retainer.

5. When reassembling, align sprocket pin with hole in camshaft.

CAMSHAFT TIMING SPROCKET (1975-1977)

Removal

1. Disconnect negative cable at battery and remove alternator drive belt.

2. Remove bolts from upper timing belt cover and pull cover forward (**Figure 4**).

3. Remove the cam sprocket and timing belt.

Installation

1. Refer to **Figure 5** and install sprocket and timing belt together, making sure alignment pin on sprocket is aligned with hole in camshaft

hub. Also check to be sure timing belt is fitted to proper grooves in water pump pulley.

2. Replace timing belt cover.

3. Reinstall the alternator belt. If a strand tension gauge is available, adjust the belt tension to 100-140 lb.

> NOTE: *Adjustment of timing belt tension is not required.*

CRANKSHAFT SPROCKET AND SEAL

1. Remove crankshaft pulley, front cover, and timing belt.

2. Remove the 2 bolts from the crankshaft sprocket cover.

3. Remove the crankshaft sprocket with a suitable puller.

4. Using care not to damage seal housing or contact surfaces, pry old seal from housing. To facilitate removal, carefully drill 4 or 5 ⅛ in. holes about the perimeter of the seal to provide a grip for a suitable prying tool.

5. Clean and inspect the crankshaft surface for any nicks or wear.

6. Apply engine oil to lip of new seal and a suitable sealing compound to the outer circumference of the seal.

7. Slip new seal over crankshaft, seal lip leading edge facing engine, and tap into place.

When reassembling, sprocket timing mark should be facing outward, and key way should be aligned with crankshaft key as shown in Figure 2.

OIL PAN

To remove the oil pan, the front crossmember and braces must be removed, and the steering linkage must be dropped, as follows.

1. Raise car and drain engine oil.

WARNING
Use safety stands when working under the car. Never rely solely on hydraulic or mechanical jacks.

2. Using a suitable hoist, lift engine until weight is off front motor mounts so that there is no strain on engine mount supports when crossmembers and braces are removed.

3. Refer to **Figure 6** and remove crossmember and both braces.

4. Mark position of pitman arm to shaft. Remove arm with puller. Disconnect steering idler arm at frame side rail (at relay rod if equipped with air conditioning).

5. Remove flywheel (converter) cover and 18 oil pan retaining bolts (**Figure 7**). Tap pan lightly to break seal, and remove.

6. Remove bolt from center of pickup screen, 2 bolts from pickup screen support, and one bolt securing oil drain-back tube.

7. Baffle can now be removed by rotating it 90° toward left of engine.

8. Remove the 2 pickup tube mounting bolts, and carefully tap the tube on the inside of its 180° bend to release it from its press fit in the block.

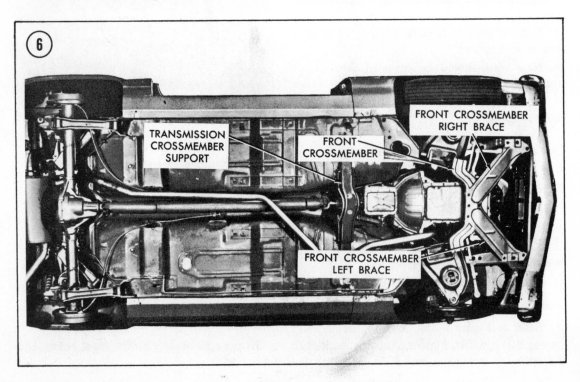

⑥

TRANSMISSION CROSSMEMBER SUPPORT

FRONT CROSSMEMBER

FRONT CROSSMEMBER RIGHT BRACE

FRONT CROSSMEMBER LEFT BRACE

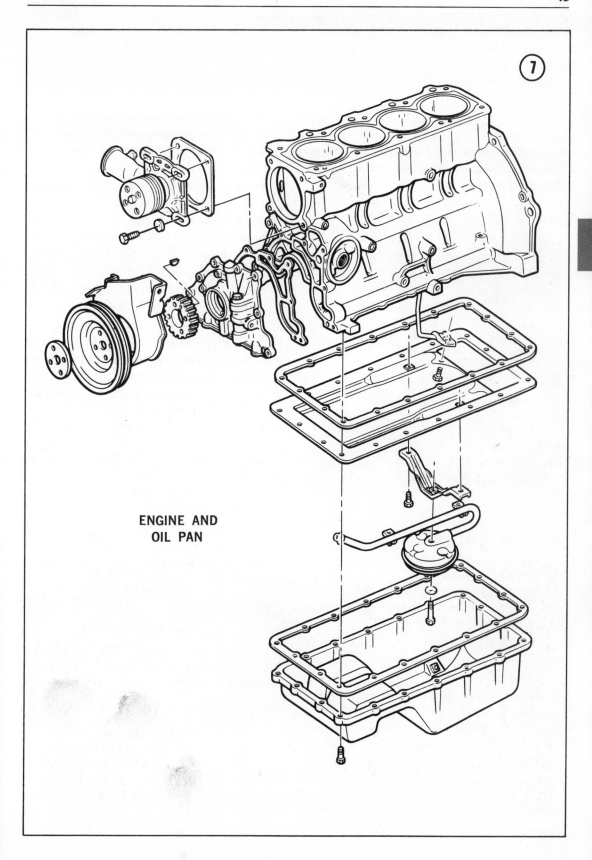

ENGINE AND
OIL PAN

NOTE: *In reinstalling the oil pickup tube, it is best to ensure adequate press fit by replacing the tube with a new one. However, a skillful mechanic might use the old tube after restoring the end to a correct press-fit size and applying a suitable sealing compound.*

9. Install refurbished, or new pickup tube by properly aligning brackets and seating tube as shown in **Figure 8**.

10. Apply a suitable anti-seizing compound to all retaining screws and bolts.

11. Clean all gasket surfaces and apply a suitable sealing compound.

12. Install new gasket between block and baffle. Temporarily secure baffle to engine block with 2 pan bolts.

13. Install drain-back tube bolt, pickup tube support, and screen-to-support bolt. Torque all bolts to specifications.

14. While supporting baffle, remove 2 screws temporarily securing baffle, put new gasket in place and install oil pan. Lightly tighten all pan bolts, then alternately torque to specifications.

15. Install flywheel (converter) cover, pitman arm, idler arm, crossmember, and braces. Torque all bolts to specifications.

16. Fill crankcase with oil, start engine, and check for leaks.

CRANKSHAFT REAR SEAL

Rear main bearing seal can be installed without complete engine disassembly, but the transmission must be removed. See Chapter Eight.

NOTE: *The following procedure does not require engine removal; however it actually might be easier to do so.*

1. Drain crankcase and remove oil pan, then slightly loosen all main bearing bolts, and remove rear main bearing cap.

2. Pry crankshaft down to relieve pressure against seal. Start old seal out of its seat with a brass drift punch until it can be gripped with a pair of pliers. Rotating the crankshaft slightly at the same time will facilitate removal.

3. Form a new upper seal in the bearing cap. Do not trim the seal yet.

4. Taper one end of the seal, and thread a piece of soft wire through it approximately ¼ in. from the end to assist in leading the seal around the crankshaft and into position. Special tools available at most automotive stores may make the job easier. Work the seal back and forth as it is pulled around the crankshaft to keep leading edge of seal slot from fraying the seal.

5. Tighten the first 4 main bearing caps to specification and trim top half of seal flush to the cap-to-block mating surface. Leave no raveled edges.

6. Seat the lower half of the seal in bearing cap and trim.

7. Check for proper seating of the seal by installing rear main bearing with gauging plastic, following directions on package.

8. After removing gauging plastic and torquing rear main bearing cap, seal sides of cap as shown in **Figure 9** following directions received with the sealing kit.

NOTE: *When installing sealant with engine in car, plug seal cavities for about one half hour until sealant cures.*

9. Reinstall oil pan, flywheel (converter) cover, pitman arm, and idle arm. Fill crankcase with oil, start engine and check for leaks.

← APPLICATOR

SEAL CAVITIES

OIL PUMP

Engine lubrication is accomplished by an externally mounted, crankshaft driven, eccentric gear oil pump and distribution system. Oil flows at 40-45 psi from the top of the gear set through the high pressure side of the regulator valve and into the full-flow oil filter. An oil filter bypass valve opens when 9-11 psi builds up in the filter.

Removal and replacement of the oil pump without removing the engine oil pan is not recommended.

> NOTE: *The 1976 oil pump was modified with a more precise regulator valve. This pump must be used on 1976 models with hydraulic valve lifters, and may be used as a replacement on all previous models.*

Removal

1. Remove engine front cover, crankshaft pulley, timing belt, crankshaft sprocket cover and sprocket, oil pan, and baffle.

2. Remove bolts and stud from oil pump and remove the assembly.

Cleaning and Inspection

1. Remove pressure regulator, clean all gasket surfaces, wash pump, and blow out all oil passages.

2. Examine pressure regulator. Make sure it operates freely in the housing.

3. Examine pump gears and check for the clearances given in **Table 3**.

CAUTION
Worn housing or gears must not be replaced individually. The entire unit must be replaced.

Table 3 PUMP GEAR CLEARANCES

Pump housing-to-driven gear	0.0038-0.0068 in.
Driven gear-to-crescent	0.0068-0.0148 in.
Drive gear-to-crescent	0.0023-0.0093 in.
Gear end-clearance	0.0009-0.0023 in.

4. Replace crankshaft oil seal if necessary.

5. Check oil filter bypass valve. Replace if necessary as shown in **Figure 10**.

Installation

Reverse removal procedure. Make certain the crankshaft key aligns with the pump driven gear, and that gears and seal lip have been lubricated with engine oil. Torque all bolts to specifications.

CAMSHAFT

A special tool (J-23591) is required to remove the camshaft, as shown in **Figure 11**. There is no substitute. If you are not equipped with this tool, the cylinder head can be removed, with the camshaft installed, and taken to your dealer for disassembly.

If a worn camshaft is suspected, check for worn camshaft lobes using a dial gauge. Remove spark plugs so that crankshaft can be turned easily. Set dial indicator at zero at the heel of the cam. Rotate the cam one complete turn, recording the highest dial reading. Make sure that the dial returns to zero, to confirm its accuracy, when one complete cam revolution is made.

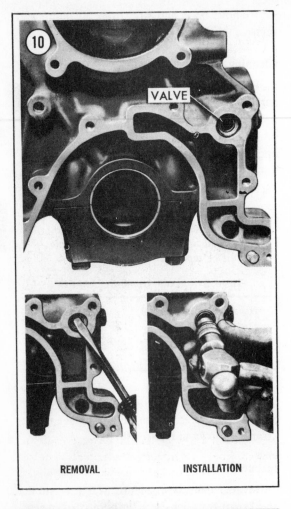

REMOVAL   INSTALLATION

Removal

1. Remove engine front cover, timing belt, and sprocket cover as previously described.

2. Remove distributor, idle solenoid, carburetor choke, coil rod assembly, and disconnect fuel line at carburetor.

3. Disconnect front engine mounts (**Figure 12**) and raise engine approximately 1½ in.

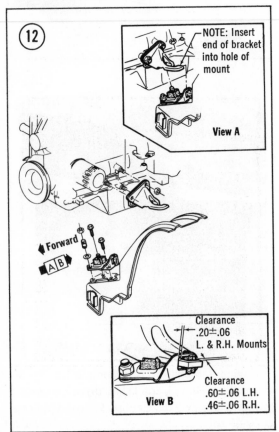

4. Install special tool J-23591 so that each lever depresses both the intake and exhaust valve for each cylinder.

5. Torque the tool attaching screws, making sure leverage screws are backed off so that levers do not press tappets prematurely.

6. Apply grease to the end of each leverage screw and tighten with a torque wrench to depress tappets. If more than 10 ft.-lb. torque is required to fully depress tappet, check for improper tool installation.

7. Once all tappets are fully depressed, slide out camshaft, being careful to guide it so bearings are not damaged by cam lobes.

8. If tappet removal is planned, release tool and remove the tappets at this point.

NOTE: *If the valve tappets are re-moved and disassembled, do not mix adjusting screws. (Adjusting screws are available in a range of sizes.) Tappet adjusting screws should be installed in the hole nearest the top of the tappet and positioned so that the flat side rides against the valve stem. See* **Figure 13**.

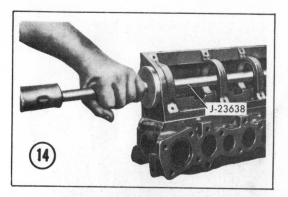

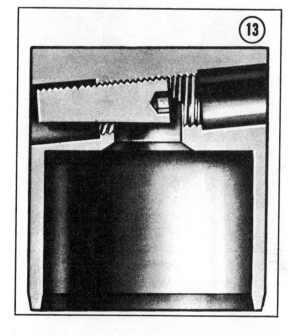

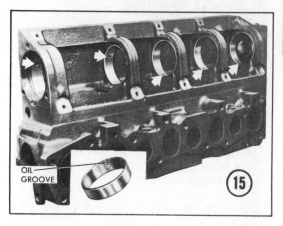

8. A camshaft generally should not exceed 0.001 in. out-of-round. Camshaft alignment should be checked by mounting in V-blocks and measuring at the center bearing with a dial gauge. If it is more than 0.0015 in. out of alignment, it should be replaced.

Bearing Replacement

1. Knock out bearings toward rear of engine with tool J-23638 or equivalent (**Figure 14**). Camshaft end plug need not be removed to remove the rear bearing.

2. Carefully tap rear bearing into distributor shaft housing, crush the bearing and remove housing. Take care not to unseat end plug.

3. Install new bearings from the front of the engine, beginning with the last bearing. Oil holes in the last 3 bearings should be aligned with those in the block as shown in **Figure 15**. The second and first bearings should be positioned

with the oil holes at the 11 o'clock position, viewed from the front of the engine. The oil groove in the front bearing should be pointed toward the front of the engine.

Installation

Reverse removal procedures, being sure to note the following.

1. After installing camshaft retainer plate and seal assembly, torque retaining bolts to specifications and measure camshaft end play with a dial indicator.

2. If end play is not within specifications (see table at end of the chapter), select a new retainer by measuring the required difference as shown in **Figure 16**. Camshaft retainers are available in 0.004 in. increments from 0.226-0.238 in.

VALVE SPRING AND OIL SEAL (1971-1975)

NOTE: *The following procedure does not require cylinder head removal, however, it might be easier to do so.*

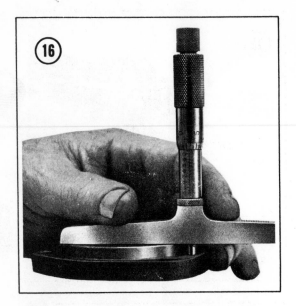

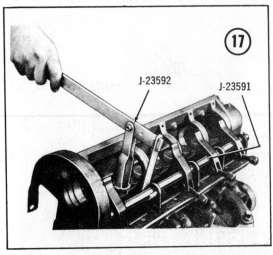

1. Remove camshaft and tappet as described previously.

2. Remove spark plug from the cylinder to be repaired and install an air hose adapter fitting (tool J-23590).

> NOTE: *An adaptor can be fashioned from an old spark plug by removing the insulator and welding a metal tire valve stem, or suitable airhose fitting, to the body.*

3. Turn crankshaft 90° from top dead center for the cylinder being repaired to avoid interference between valve and piston when valve is compressed.

4. Apply air pressure to hold valve in seated position.

5. Compress the valve spring with tool J-23592 as shown in **Figure 17**, remove valve keepers, and release to remove spring, damper, and oil seal.

> NOTE: *If air pressure is inadequate to hold valve in seated position for spring compression and keeper removal, cylinder head must be removed.*

6. Check spring free height. Check tension at specified compressed height. Automotive machine shops can do this for you. Replace if free height does not meet specifications, or if tension is not within 10 lb. of specification.

7. Using new seal, reassemble damper, spring, cap, and locks as shown in **Figure 18**. Measure valve spring installed height (**Figure 19**) from the spring seat to the top of the valve spring. If this measurement exceeds the specified height, a 1/16 in. thick shim should be added to the valve spring seat.

CAUTION
Do not shim spring to give an installed height under the minimum specified.

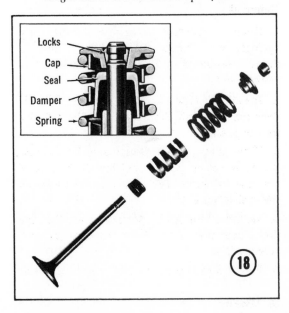

8. Reverse removal procedures to reassemble, and check valve adjustment as described in *Engine Tune-up*.

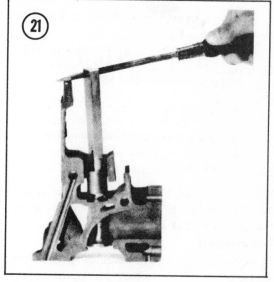

VALVE STEM OIL SEALS (1976-1977)

NOTE: *A special tool kit, J-26402, is required for this procedure. There is no readily available substitute. If you do not have access to this kit, take the cylinder head to your Chevrolet dealer for seal removal.*

Removal

1. Remove camshaft, valve lifters, valve caps, springs, and dampers as outlined above in Steps 1 through 5 of *Valve Spring and Oil Seal (1971-1975)*.

2. Install the pipe sleeve of tool kit J-26402 over the jaws and slide as far up the removal tool as possible.

3. While spreading the jaws, insert the tool into the valve spring pocket and install the lips of the jaws on either side and under the edge of the seal (**Figure 20**).

4. With the tool in this position, slide the pipe down over the seal to hold the jaws in place (**Figure 21**).

5. Pull straight up on tool to remove the seal.

Installation

NOTE: *A special installation/gauge tool is required for this procedure (tool J-26251).*

1. Place safety cap (provided with seal kit) over end of valve stem to prevent damage to seal.

2. Install new seal on valve stem, using a light coat of oil to prevent twisting of the seal.

3. Remove safety cap and use installation tool J-26251 to press the seal into place. The seal is in proper position when the upper white line, marked HYD, is aligned with the boss on the cylinder head (**Figure 22**).

4. Hold tool in place momentarily, then remove pressure. Recheck to make sure seal remains properly seated. Reinstall damper, spring, cap, and lifter.

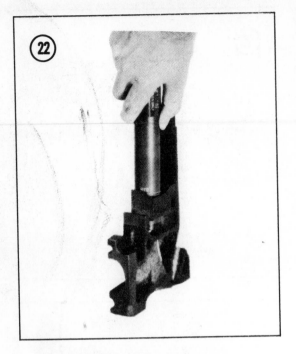

㉒

INTAKE AND EXHAUST MANIFOLDS

Exhaust manifold removal requires removal of intake manifold.

1. Disconnect battery ground cable and drain cooling system.

2. Disconnect heater hose at manifold and vent tube from air cleaner.

3. Remove air cleaner assembly.

4. Remove stove and tube assembly.

5. Disconnect choke coil rod at carburetor, PCV valve from cam cover, carburetor bowl vent line and fuel line from carburetor, throttle linkage, and transmission throttle valve linkage.

6. Loosen generator adjusting bolt, and—temporarily supporting generator—remove through bolt from thermostat housing for access to front intake manifold bolt. Remove manifold bolt, and temporarily remount generator by replacing through bolt. For cars equipped with power steering, disconnect pump brace at manifold.

7. Remove the remaining intake manifold bolts and the manifold with carburetor attached.

8. If exhaust manifold is to be removed, remove dipstick bracket bolt and 8 bolts securing manifold.

9. Disconnect exhaust pipe at manifold.

10. Reverse removal procedures to install, using new gaskets. Note that short bolts are used on the upper exhaust flange hole and longer bolts on the lower flange hole. Torque all bolts to specifications, fill cooling system, start engine, and check for leaks. Set ignition timing and adjust carburetor.

CYLINDER HEAD

Removal

1. Drain cooling system and remove radiator hose from thermostat housing.

2. Disconnect and remove distributor.

3. Remove generator, anti-pollution system (AIR) pump (for cars so equipped), engine front cover, camshaft cover, timing belt, camshaft sprocket, and intake and exhaust manifolds.

4. Remove 10 cylinder head bolts, cylinder head, and gasket.

CAUTION
Support head with blocks to avoid damaging open valves.

Disassembly

1. Referring to **Figure 23**, remove camshaft retainer and install tool J-23591, removing camshaft as described previously.

2. On 1971-1975 models, remove tappets and valve adjusting screws (keeping the 2 pieces matched, as screws come in different sizes). On 1976-1977 models, remove tappets. Identify tappet locations for reassembly.

3. Remove the valve springs as previously discussed under *Valve Spring and Oil Seal*. Remove valve, identifying their location for reassembly.

4. Remove spark plugs and thermostat housing.

5. Disconnect and remove anti-pollution system pump located on right front of head on some models.

Cleaning and Inspection

1. Prior to cleaning the head, stuff each cylinder with clean rags to keep dirt from lodging between piston and cylinder walls. Clean block surface and examine threads for damage.

2. Clean water jacket. Wash dirt and grime from external surfaces of cylinder head.

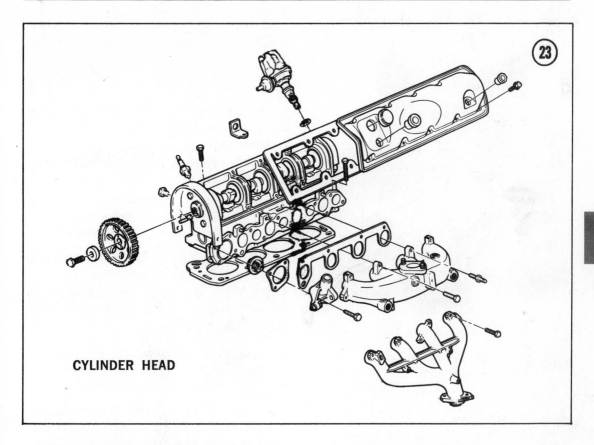

CYLINDER HEAD

3. Remove carbon from valve ports and combustion chambers. Clean head surface. Clean valve guides with a suitable tool to remove dirt and varnish deposits. Clean spark plug threads.

4. Inspect the cylinder head for cracks, pitting, broken valve guides, or damaged valve seats.

5. Wash tappets in solvent and dry with compressed air. Inspect adjusting screw surface, tappet surfaces, cylinder head tappet bore, and matching camshaft lobe for scuffs or wear.

6. Clean valves on stationary wire brush wheel.

7. Inspect valve stems for wear and valve faces for erosion and cracks. Measure valve stem clearance for each valve by mounting a dial indicator at right angle to the valve stem and moving stem from side-to-side in its guide. Reading should be taken with indicator stem contacting valve stem just above guide and valve head raised approximately 1/16 in. from valve seat. Valve guides must be reamed for oversized valve if clearance exceeds specifications.

8. Check valve spring tension as described previously under *Valve Spring and Oil Seal*.

9. Check camshaft bearings and camshaft alignment as described previously under *Camshaft*.

Repairs

1. If valve stem clearance exceeds specifications, replace with 0.003 in., 0.0015 in., or 0.030 in. oversized valves, after reaming guides to fit.

2. Valve seat and valve head refacing require special equipment available at automotive machine shops. The edge of the valve head must be not less than 1/32 in. thick after resurfacing or valve must be replaced.

> NOTE: *End of valve stem should be refinished in a valve resurfacing machine, but only enough to provide a smooth surface at right angles to the valve stem axis.*

3. On 1976-1977 models, measure the installed height of each valve stem (**Figure 24**). Use tool J-26480 or a similar gauge. Spring pad to valve tip specifications are: exhaust, 1.5695 ±0.0095 in.; intake, 1.5655 ±0.0095 in.

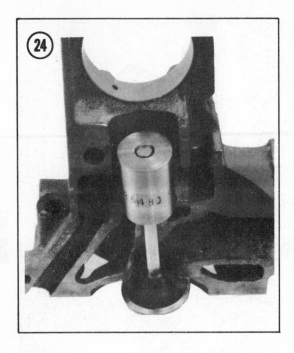

Reassembly

1. Install tool J-23591 (Figure 11), and replace valves in their respective locations, using valve spring compressing tool J-23592.

2. Check installed height of each valve spring as previously described under *Camshaft*.

3. Assemble valve tappets and adjusting screws. Coat with a thin film of light grease and insert tappets into their respective bores.

CAUTION
Continue assembly with head on blocks so that valves are not bent when they are opened by tool J-23591.

4. Depress tappets with tool J-23591 and carefully guide camshaft into place without nicking bearings. Using a new gasket, install camshaft retainer plate and seal assembly.

5. Check camshaft end play as described previously under *Camshaft*. Remove tool J-23591 and assemble camshaft sprocket to camshaft, making sure locater pin is aligned with hole in end of camshaft. Torque camshaft sprocket and camshaft seal retainer to specifications.

6. On 1971-1975 models, adjust tappets as outlined previously. Adjustment is not required on 1976-1977 models.

7. Clean, adjust, and install spark plugs.

8. If thermostat housing was removed, clean gasket surfaces and install housing with new gasket.

Installation

1. Make sure cylinders are clear of all foreign materials, and install cylinder head gaskets, smooth side up.

2. Coat cylinder head bolt threads with an anti-seize compound.

CAUTION
Do not drop cylinder head bolts into holes. Block threads damage easily.

3. Install short bolts on spark plug side, long bolts on manifold side, finger-tight.

4. Cinch the bolts in the sequence shown in **Figure 25**, then torque to specifications in the same sequence.

NOTE: *Repeat the torquing sequence until all bolts meet torque specifications through an entire sequence.*

5. Connect coolant hose, install manifold, timing belt, distributor, front cover, and camshaft cover as discussed previously.

6. Fill cooling system, start engine, and check for leaks.

ENGINE REMOVAL

1. Drain cooling system, disconnect heater hoses and coolant hoses from engine.

2. Disconnect and remove battery.

3. Disconnect PCV vacuum hose at manifold, remove PCV valve from cam cover; disconnect canister vacuum hose and bowl vent hose at carburetor.

4. Remove engine fan, spacer, shroud, and radiator (Chapter Seven).

5. Remove air cleaner and vent tube.

6. Remove engine ground strap at coil and all electrical leads from the following: TCS solenoid, TCS switch at transmission, generator, coil, starter solenoid, oil pressure switch, engine temperature switch.

7. Disconnect automatic transmission throttle valve linkage and accelerator cable at manifold.

8. Disconnect fuel line.

9. Disconnect air conditioning vacuum line and transmission vacuum modulator at the intake manifold.

10. Air conditioning compressor, if so equipped, should be disconnected at front and rear supports and rear lower bracket. Drive belt can then be removed, and compressor can be supported against frame forward brace (without bending hoses) and secured with a piece of rope or wire.

11. Without disconnecting power steering pump hoses, remove pump mounting bolts, and position pump so that it will not interfere with engine removal.

12. Disconnect exhaust pipe and remove flywheel (convertor) cover.

13. Remove convertor to flywheel retaining bolts on automatic transmission models.

CAUTION

Provide a means (for example, a safety wire) to hold the convertor on the transmission input shaft when engine is separated from converted housing,

especially if front of car is lower than rear; convertor could slip off the input shaft spline.

14. Remove flywheel housing (convertor housing) retaining bolts from engine block.

15. Loosen front engine mount bolts at frame.

16. Support transmission and connect hoist to engine.

17. Lift weight off engine mounts, and remove mount retaining bolts (Figure 12).

18. With engine now supported by hoist, pull it forward.

CAUTION

On standard transmission vehicles, depress clutch until engine is cleared of transmission input shaft to prevent clutch distortion; on automatic transmission vehicles, be certain convertor separates from flywheel and remains on transmission input shaft. As engine is removed, check occasionally to see that everything has been disconnected and that engine is clearing all other components in the engine compartment.

ENGINE DISASSEMBLY

1. Remove the following subassemblies, referring to previously described procedures: generator and brackets, crankshaft pulley, engine front cover, water pump, timing belt cover, timing belt, carburetor, distributor, starter, oil filter, engine oil dipstick and tube, thermostat housing, intake and exhaust manifolds, camshaft cover, cylinder head (putting it on block to prevent valve damage), crankshaft sprockets, oil pan, and oil pump.

2. Ream cylinder bore ridge if necessary.

3. Scribe each connecting rod and cap on the same side of the engine to identify its cylinder and correctly installed position. Piston skirts are already marked for correct position, but not necessarily for cylinder identification.

> NOTE: *Prior to removing connecting rod and piston assemblies, remove caps and inspect connecting rod bearings for wear. If the bearings look serviceable, check clearance with gauging plastic to determine whether there is excessive clearance. See specifications at end of this chapter.*

4. Remove connecting rod nuts (protect crankshaft journal from nicks by threads on connecting rod bolts). Push connecting rod and piston assembly out of block. If connecting rod bearings are to be reused, identify location of each for correct reassembly.

5. Scribe clutch pressure plate location on flywheel to ensure correct balance on reassembling.

6. Remove plate on left side of clutch housing. Disconnect clutch control cable and return spring.

7. Remove 6 bolts securing pressure plate to flywheel. Loosen each bolt a little at a time to avoid distorting clutch assembly.

8. Remove 6 flywheel-to-crankshaft retaining bolts. Knock flywheel off crankshaft flange with a soft, heavy hammer.

9. Inspect pilot bearing in end of crankshaft for wear. This is an oil impregnated bearing. It is a press fit in the crankshaft and requires a suitable puller to remove.

10. Check for excessive crankshaft end play by moving crankshaft to the extreme forward position and measuring clearance between No. 4 main bearing and bearing flange, as shown in **Figure 26**. Remove main bearing caps and inspect lower half for wear. If bearings appear serviceable, wipe oil from journals and check clearance with gauging plastic. If bearing clearances meet specifications, identify location of each for correct reassembly. Specifications are at the end of this chapter.

11. Remove rear main bearing oil seal.

CYLINDER BLOCK

Cleaning and Inspection

1. Remove oil passage plugs with a sharp punch, or by drilling. Wash cylinder block in a non-caustic cleaning solvent. Clean and inspect all gasket surfaces.

2. Wash cylinders with hot water and detergent; dry and coat with a thin film of light engine oil. *Do not clean cylinder with gasoline or kerosene.*

3. Check and record cylinder taper and roundness with a dial indicator. If bores are badly tapered or out-of-round, the cylinder block must be reconditioned.

NOTE: *Reboring and honing proce-dures for the Vega aluminum-silicon block are the same as those for cast iron blocks, except for final finishing by a silicon lapping process. Manufac-turers of reboring and honing equip-ment can supply information and material for this mandatory step.*

4. Clean crankshaft and blow out oil passages.

5. Measure and record main bearing and connecting rod journals for taper, roundness, and undersize.

6. Support crankshaft at front and rear main bearing journals and measure for possible bend or distortion with a dial indicator.

7. Recondition or replace the crankshaft if measurements do not meet specifications.

8. Inspect main and connecting rod bearing for etching, chips, and other obvious signs of wear.

NOTE: *Main bearings will show great-est wear on the bottom half; connecting rod bearings on the top half. If it be-comes necessary to replace a main bearing cap, tapered shims may be re-quired for correct bearing clearance. Do not file bearing cap mating faces to aid fit. Shims should not be used with original bearing caps to attain specified clearances. Occasionally, in production, one half of a standard insert will be combined with a 0.001 in. undersize half (but this practice is not recom-mended for overhaul). Always replace both bearing halves. Bearings are avail-able in 0.001 in., 0.002 in., 0.010 in., and 0.020 in. undersize.*

PISTON AND CONNECTING ROD

Disassembly

1. Clasp connecting rod between your knees (or lightly in a vise, protecting the connecting rod with a rag), cup hands around piston and ex-pand top ring with middle fingers and remove. Remove the rest of the rings in the same manner.

WARNING
Edges of old rings are sharp. Use care not to cut hands.

2. Press pin from piston. A deep socket of suit-able outside diameter may be used.

CAUTION
Piston pins are a snug fit in the piston boss and a medium fit on the rod. Pins and pistons are matched sets. Do not mix.

Cleaning and Inspection

1. Wash rods, pins, and pistons. *Do not wire brush pistons.*

2. Remove varnish from piston skirts with a strong cleaning solvent. Clean ring grooves and oil ring holes. If groove cleaning tool is not available, break an old piston ring and carefully scrape the varnish and foreign material from the ring groove with finished end of the piston ring.

3. Inspect the piston for scuffed or cracked skirts, burred or broken ring lands, damaged pin bosses, or eroded tops.

4. Blow out connecting rod oil passages, and check for bent, twisted, nicked, or cracked rods. Any connecting rod that is badly nicked should be checked for alignment at a machine shop.

5. Measure piston pin and bore, for each piston, against specifications at the end of this chapter. Replace both piston *and* pin for any sets not meeting specifications.

6. Measure piston diameter at right angles to pin bore, and compare to cylinder bore diameter measurement taken 2½ in. from the top of the cylinder bore. If cylinder bore taper and round-ness are within specifications, but piston-to-cylinder clearance does not meet specifications, replace with a new piston and pin set. New pis-tons are available in the size ranges found in **Table 4**. Be sure to measure each new piston for its exact diameter to ensure best fit in cylinder bore. Mark each new piston with cylinder identification.

Table 4 PISTON SIZES

3.4977 in. to 3.4982 in.
3.4982 in. to 3.4987 in.
3.4987 in. to 3.4992 in.
3.4992 in. to 3.4997 in.

7. Always replace piston rings. Check for ring freedom and general fit in the ring groove for each piston by rolling ring around circumference of piston.

8. Slip the top compression ring into the cylinder bore. Position ring squarely in bore approximately ¼ in. into cylinder and measure gap.

> NOTE: *If cylinder wall has been cut because of improper ridge reaming, ring gap measurement should be taken at deeper levels in the bore, as well as the ¼ in. level.*

9. If ring gap is too small, *minor* adjustments can be made by dressing the gap with a fine stone. If such an adjustment is necessary, all ring gaps should be checked in their cylinders.

Reassembly

1. Lubricate the pin, piston boss, and connecting rod.

2. Match each piston, pin, and connecting rod for each cylinder. Assemble so that scribe marks on connecting rod will be located in their original position when installed and so that the "F" on the piston face (**Figure 27**) will be toward the front of the engine. Be certain that pin is centered in piston without either end extending beyond rim of piston boss.

3. Lubricate ring grooves and install piston rings, beginning with the lowest ring and working upward. Ring should be installed with gaps located as shown in **Figure 28**. Begin with oil ring spacer, then follow by lower steel oil ring rail (making sure spacer ends are butted). Install upper steel oil ring rail.

4. Install second and third compression rings, marked side up.

5. Measure ring clearance in grooves using a feeler gauge. If clearance exceeds specifications, piston and pin must be replaced. Check to see that rings compress freely in groove. If binding occurs, remove ring and carefully dress ring groove at binding point with a fine toothed file.

ENGINE REASSEMBLY

1. Install new oil passage plugs.

2. Install top half of rear main seal in block

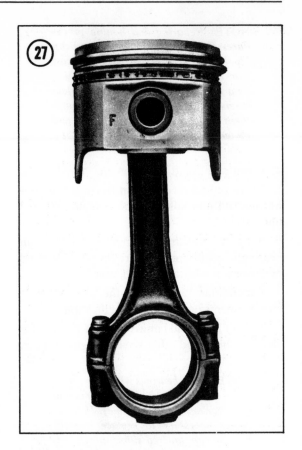

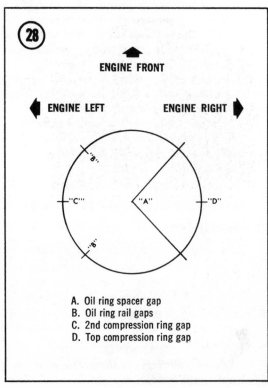

A. Oil ring spacer gap
B. Oil ring rail gaps
C. 2nd compression ring gap
D. Top compression ring gap

and lower half in cap as discussed previously under *Crankshaft Rear Seal*.

3. Install and lubricate main bearings.

> **CAUTION**
> *Be certain there is no foreign material or burrs on back of bearings or on bearing seats. Pay particular attention to sides of the No. 4 main bearing, seat, and journal so that crankshaft end play will be 0.002-0.007 in.*

4. Lubricate crankshaft main bearing journals and carefully set crankshaft in place. Check main bearing clearance with gauging plastic as described previously. Install main bearing caps with letter "F" facing front of engine.

5. Tap crankshaft rearward to seat bearings, then to extreme forward position and check end play clearance at front of No. 4 bearing as shown in Figure 26.

6. Rear main bearing cap-to-block interface should receive a thin coat of oil sealant as shown in **Figure 29**. After installation, apply sealant as shown in Figure 9.

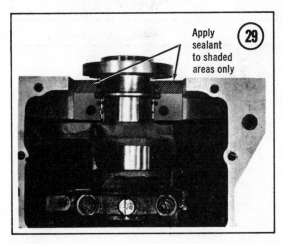

Apply sealant to shaded areas only (29)

7. Clean surfaces on flywheel-to-crankshaft interface, making sure there are no burrs. Install flywheel, aligning dowel. Torque the bolts to specifications.

8. Put pressure plate in place with long end of disc spine facing flywheel as shown in **Figure 30**.

9. Insert a suitable alignment tool (an old main shaft, or a deep socket), and—with the pressure plate properly indexed against the flywheel—install the 6 mounting bolts, tightening them a little at a time until pressure plate is seated. Torque bolts to specifications at the end of this chapter.

10. Apply a little graphite grease to the clutch fork fingers and sockets, and install clutch housing. Torque bolts to 25 ft.-lb.

11. Lubricate connecting rod bearings and install in rods and caps. Lubricate pistons and cylinder walls with light engine oil.

12. With the ring gaps located as shown in Figure 28, install the ring compressor tool and tool J-23267 (or lengths of plastic tubing) on connecting rod bolts to protect journals. Insert piston and connecting rod assembly into the correct cylinder, with "F" on piston facing the front of engine.

13. Holding the ring compressor firmly against the block, tap the top of the piston with a hammer handle until it is completely inserted in the cylinder. Be certain connecting rod straddles journal and is properly aligned to it.

14. Check connecting rod clearance with gauging plastic. *Do not shim bearings or rod-to-cap interface to obtain correct clearance.*

15. After installation of rod caps, lightly tap each rod to check side-to-side movement on journals. Measure side clearance.

16. Install the oil pump, pickup tube, baffle, and oil pan.

17. Install crankshaft sprocket.

18. Install exhaust and intake manifolds to cylinder head.

19. Install assembled cylinder head, using new gasket and making certain cylinders are clean.

20. Install the following: oil dipstick and tube, oil filter, thermostat housing and thermostat, starter and brace, carburetor, distributor and spark plug wires, timing belt, lower sprocket cover, water pump, front cover, generator, crankshaft pulley and belts.

ENGINE INSTALLATION

1. Lower engine into vehicle, keeping it free of other components and parts in the engine compartment.

2. Align the engine with the transmission input gear. Remove means of retaining convertor in-

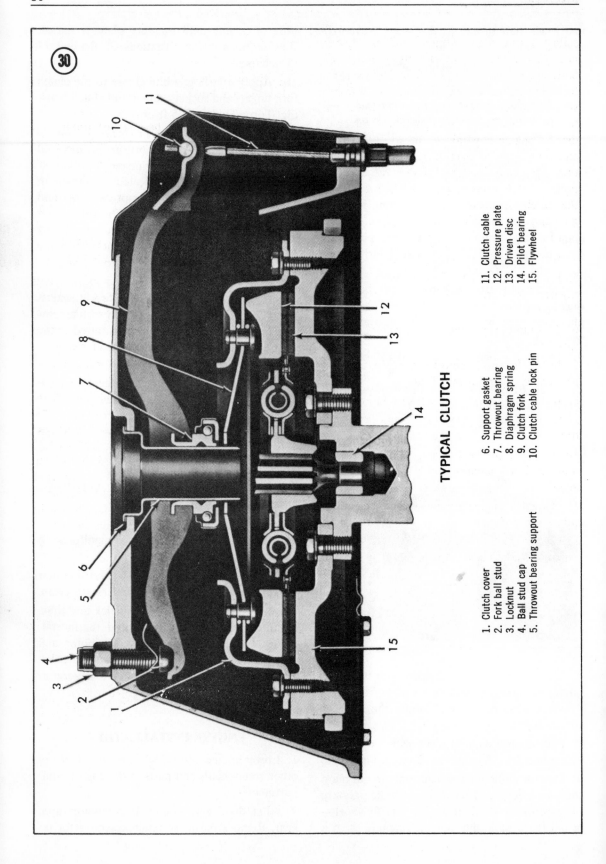

TYPICAL CLUTCH

1. Clutch cover
2. Fork ball stud
3. Locknut
4. Ball stud cap
5. Throwout bearing support

6. Support gasket
7. Throwout bearing
8. Diaphragm spring
9. Clutch fork
10. Clutch cable lock pin

11. Clutch cable
12. Pressure plate
13. Driven disc
14. Pilot bearing
15. Flywheel

stalled during engine removal. (Cock engine if necessary to align flywheel housing bolt holes.) Slide engine into place. If difficulty is encountered in the final mating of engine to transmission on standard transmission vehicles, it may be caused by a slight misalignment of the clutch disc. If engine is within ½ in. to ¾ in. of the clutch housing, connect the clutch cable and depress the cluch to allow disc to align, or loosen pressure plate bolts enough to take pressure off the clutch disc.

3. Connect the engine front mounts, leaving bolts loose.

4. Install engine-to-housing bolts.

5. Install converter-to-flywheel mounting bolts (tighten pressure plate bolts if they were loosened).

6. Torque housing and engine mount bolts to specifications.

7. Install flywheel (convertor) cover and connect exhaust pipe at manifold.

8. Install compressor and power steering pump.

9. Connect accelerator cable and automatic transmission throttle valve linkage at manifold.

10. Connect air conditioning vacuum line and transmission vacuum modulator line at inlet manifold.

11. Connect engine ground strap at cowl and connect fuel line.

12. Make the following electrical connections: generator, coil, starter, oil pressure switch, engine temperature switch, TCS switch at transmission, TCS solenoid.

13. Install air cleaner. Connect vent tube at base of air cleaner, bowl vent at carburetor, PCV valve at cam cover, and vacuum line at inlet manifold. Install canister vacuum hose at carburetor.

14. Install radiator, shroud, fan, and spacer.

15. Connect battery cables, heater hoses, and coolant hoses.

16. Fill cooling system, start engine and check for leaks.

MAIN BEARING REPLACEMENT WITHOUT ENGINE REMOVAL

The technique of installing main bearings without crankshaft removal is accepted practice. A cotter pin with a flattened head can be used, but an inexpensive special tool can be purchased at any automotive store for this purpose.

With the main bearing cap removed, insert the tool (or a cotter pin with a flattened head) into the crankshaft journal oil hole, and rotate the shaft clockwise, in its normal direction, to roll the upper bearing out of the block. Oil the replacement bearing half, and start the unnotched end into place between the notched side of the block and the crankshaft journal. Insert the tool in the oil hole and rotate the bearing into place. Lubricate the lower bearing half, and seat it in the bearing cap. Install cap with the letter "F" facing the front of the engine, and torque to specifications found in Table 2.

Table 1   ENGINE SPECIFICATIONS

Designation	Standard (1 bbl.)		Optional (2 bbl.)	
Design	4-cylinder, inline, overhead cam		4-cylinder, inline, overhead cam	
Displacement	140 cubic inches		140 cubic inches	
Horsepower/rpm				
1971-1972	90/4,800		110/4,800	
1973	72/4,400		85/4,800	
1974	75/4,400		85/4,400	
1975	78/4,200		87/4,400	
1976-1977	69/4,000 (all)		80/4,000 (Calif.)	
			87/4,400 (Fed.)	
Torque/rpm				
1971-1972	136/2,400		138/3,200	
1973	100/2,000		115/2,400	
1974	115/2,400		122/2,400	
1975	120/2,000		122/2,800	
1976-1977	113/2,400 (all)		116/2,800 (Calif.)	
			122/2,800 (Fed.)	
Compression ratio				
1971-1972	8.5:1		8.5:1	
1973-1977	8.0:1		8.0:1	
Firing order	1-3-4-2		1-3-4-2	
Stroke	3.625 in.		3.625 in.	
Bore	3.4996-3.5024 in.		3.4996-3.5024 in.	
Out-of-round, maximum	0.002 in.		0.002 in.	
Taper, maximum	0.005 in.		0.005 in.	
Piston/cylinder clearance				
1971-1975	0.0018-0.0050 in.		0.0018-0.0050 in.	
1976	0.0018-0.0028 in.		0.0018-0.0050 in.	
Piston size range	3.4977-3.4997 in.		3.4977-3.4997 in.	
Size range groups	3.4977 in.	3.4982 in.	3.4987 in.	3.4992 in.
	to	to	to	to
	3.4982 in.	3.4987 in.	3.4992 in.	3.4997 in.
Ring gap				
Compression	0.009-0.020 in.		0.015-0.026 in.	
Oil	0.010-0.031 in.		0.010-0.031 in.	
Ring groove clearance				
Compression	0.0012-0.0028 in.		0.0012-0.0028 in.	
Oil	0.000-0.005 in.		0.000-0.005 in.	
Piston/pin diameter	0.9270-0.9273 in.		0.9270-0.9273 in.	
Piston/pin clearance	0.0003-0.001 in.		0.0003-0.001 in.	
Rod/pin clearance	0.0008-0.0021 in.		0.0008-0.0021 in.	

(continued)

Table 1   ENGINE SPECIFICATIONS (continued)

Designation	Standard (1 bbl.)	Optional (2 bbl.)
Crankshaft journals		
Main diameter	2.2983-2.2993 in.	2.2983-2.2993 in.
Out-of-round, maximum	0.001 in.	0.001 in.
Taper, maximum	0.001 in.	0.001 in.
Connecting rod diameter	1.000-2.000 in.	1.000-2.000 in.
Out-of-round	0.001 in.	0.001 in.
Taper	0.001 in.	0.001 in.
Bearing clearance		
Main, maximum	0.002 in.	0.002 in.
Connecting rod	0.0007-0.0004 in.	0.0007-0.0004 in.
Crankshaft end play	0.002-0.007 in.	0.002-0.007 in.
Connecting rod side clearance	0.0085-0.0135 in.	0.0085-0.0135 in.
Camshaft		
Lift		
Intake, 1971-1975	0.4179-0.4219 in.	0.4345-0.4348 in.
Intake, 1976-1977	0.3980-0.4020 in.	0.3980-0.4020 in.
Exhaust, 1971-1975	0.4281-0.4321 in.	0.4345-0.4385 in.
Exhaust, 1976-1977	0.4130-0.4170 in.	0.4130-0.4170 in.
Journal diameter	2.2812-2.2822 in.	2.2812-2.2822 in.
Runout, maximum	0.0015 in.	0.0015 in.
End play	0.004-0.012 in.	0.004-0.012 in.
Valves		
Intake		
Face angle	45°	45°
Seat angle	46°	46°
Seat runout, maximum	0.002 in.	0.002 in.
Seat width	$3/64$-$1/16$ in.	$3/64$-$1/16$ in.
Stem clearance	0.0010-0.0028 in.	0.0010-0.0028 in.
Valve damper free length	1.84 in.	1.84 in.
Exhaust		
Face angle	45°	45°
Seat angle	46°	46°
Seat runout, maximum	0.002 in.	0.002 in.
Seat width	$3/64$-$5/64$	$3/64$-$5/64$
Stem clearance	0.0010-0.0029 in.	0.0010-0.0029 in.
Valve damper free length	1.84 in.	1.84 in.
Valve spring		
Free length	2.03 in.	2.03 in.
Installed height	$1\,3/4 \pm 1/32$ in.	$1\,3/4 \pm 1/32$
Pounds force, valve closed	71-79	71-79
Pounds force, valve open		
1971-1975	179-193	183-197
1976-1977	183-197	183-197

Table 2   TORQUE SPECIFICATIONS

Size	Usage	Torque ①
¼-14	Engine front cover	50 in.-lb.
¼-20	Cam cover	35 (80) in.-lb.
	Oil screen-to-support	50 in.-lb.
	Clutch housing dust cover	80 in.-lb.
	Convertor housing underpan	95 in.-lb.
	Oil screen support-to-baffle	50 in.-lb.
	Oil drain back tube-to-baffle	50 in.-lb.
⁵⁄₁₆-18	Fan blade to pump	20 ft.-lb.
	Clutch pressure plate-to-flywheel	20 ft.-lb.
	Oil pick-up tube-to-case	25 ft.-lb.
	Crankshaft damper/pulley-to-sprocket	15 ft.-lb.
	Oil pump-to-case (bolt)	15 ft.-lb.
	Water pump-to-case	15 ft.-lb.
	Oil pan-to-case	15 ft.-lb.
	Cam retainer	15 (18) ft.-lb.
⁵⁄₁₆-24	Exhaust gas recirculation valve to manifold	20 ft.-lb.
¹¹⁄₃₂-24	Connecting rod cap	35 ft.-lb.
⅜-16	Oil pump to case (stud)	30 ft.-lb.
	Distributor clamp nut	25 ft.-lb.
	Water outlet-to-head	30 ft.-lb.
	Manifold (bolts)	30 ft.-lb.
	Clutch housing-to-case	25 ft.-lb.
	Clutch pressure plate-to-flywheel	35 (30) ft.-lb.
⅜-18	Inlet manifold-to-head (stud)	30 ft.-lb.
⁷⁄₁₆-14	Engine mount stud-to-block	20 ft.-lb.
	Main bearing caps	65 ft.-lb.
	Cylinder head	60 ft.-lb.
⁷⁄₁₆-20	Flywheel-to-crank	60 (65) ft.-lbs.
½-13	Cam sprocket-to-cam	80 ft.-lb.
	Damper/pulley-to-crank	80 ft.-lb.
½-20	Oil pan drain plug	20 ft.-lb.
1.00-12	Oil filter connector-to-case	30 ft.-lb.
	Oil filter	Handtight
14mm	Spark plug	15 (20) ft.-lb.

① Figures in parentheses are for 1976 models only.

CHAPTER FIVE

COOLING, HEATING, AND VENTILATION

The Vega engine is liquid cooled by a pressurized, thermostatically controlled system. The heating system for the interior of the car makes use of the heat supplied by the engine coolant. The coolant is routed through a heater core mounted on the dash and enclosed by a duct assembly as shown in **Figure 1**. Cars equipped with air conditioning have a different arrangement that includes the air conditioning evaporator shown in **Figure 2**.

The air conditioning system makes use of the heating and ventilation ducts. Special tools and equipment, as well as knowledge of refrigeration principles and systems, are required for service or overhaul of the air conditioning system. Any air conditioning repair that requires opening the system should be left to a dealer or an experienced air conditioning mechanic. Chapter Two includes some minor checks that can be made without opening the system.

The optional rear window defogger is discussed in Chapter Seven.

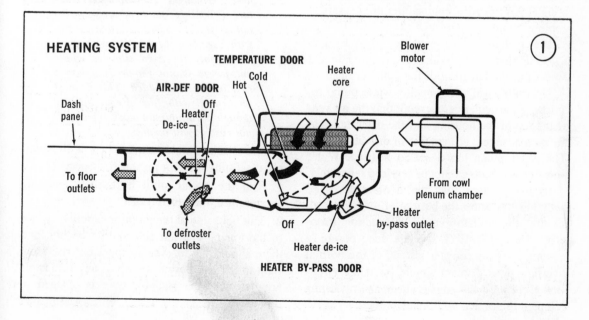

HEATING SYSTEM

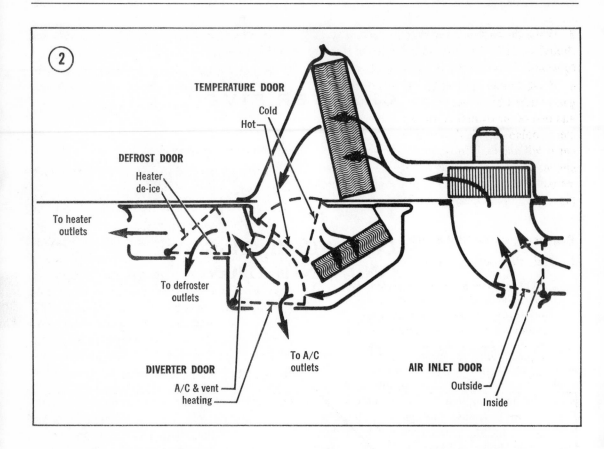

TEMPERATURE DOOR
Cold
Hot
DEFROST DOOR
Heater de-ice
To heater outlets
To defroster outlets
DIVERTER DOOR
A/C & vent heating
To A/C outlets
AIR INLET DOOR
Outside
Inside

ENGINE COOLING SYSTEM

The pressurized engine cooling system uses a 15 psi radiator filler cap. With the system operating at this pressure, engine operation is safe at cooling liquid temperatures up to 247°F.

The system is designed to operate with a 195°F thermostat, which is mounted in the housing at the left front of the cylinder head.

The centrifugal vane impeller water pump requires no particular care, except that the air vent at the top of the housing and the drain holes at the bottom should be kept free of dirt and grease. The water pump has a sealed bearing. Water pump components cannot be serviced separately.

It is important that the coolant level be kept 3 inches below the bottom of the filler neck so that the radiator cap will function properly. The 1973-1977 models incorporate a coolant recovery canister instead of the normal overflow pipe. Coolant should be at the FULL-HOT mark with the engine at normal operating temperature or add additional coolant.

CAUTION
Drain and flush cooling system with fresh water every 2 years. Refill with new permanent coolant/water mixture (−20°F coolant minimum). Do not reuse old coolant as it deteriorates with use. Do not operate with fresh water only (even in climates where anti-freeze is not required) unless a rust inhibitor is added. This is most important with the Vega because though the aluminum block engine will not rust, it will oxidize.

Two checks should be made before disassembly if a faulty cooling system is suspected.

1. Run the engine until it reaches operating temperature, then turn it off.

2. The right side of the radiator should be warm to the touch. The left side should be hot, and there should be an even temperature rise from right to left and bottom to top. If any cold spots are detected, the radiator core is clogged in that area.

3. While the engine is running, a pressure surge should be felt when the upper radiator hose is squeezed. Check pump for a plugged vent hole.

4. If substantial coolant loss is noted, the head gasket might be blown between the water jacket and one of the cylinders. In extreme cases, sufficient coolant will leak into a cylinder when the car is left standing for several hours so that the engine cannot be turned by the starter. White smoke (steam) might also be observed at the tailpipe when the engine is running.

Radiator Removal/Installation

1. Drain the cooling system.

> NOTE: *There is no radiator drain plug or engine drain plug on 1972 models; the system can be partially drained by removing the lower radiator hose connection. Remaining water must be siphoned from the block. Later models have a drain petcock.*

2. Remove fan shroud and coolant recovery and radiator hoses.

3. Remove upper radiator mounting bracket or panel and lift radiator out of lower brackets.

4. Installation is reverse of these steps.

Thermostat Replacement

1. Drain radiator, and remove the upper radiator hose.

2. Remove generator mounting bolt, thermostat housing bolts, and housing.

3. Remove thermostat from housing (**Figure 3**). To test thermostat, prepare 2 pans of water. Heat until the water in one pan is approximately 15°F above the temperature stamped on the valve and the water in the other pan is 10°F below. The valve should open and close completely when alternately submerged in the 2 pans of water.

4. Install by reversing these steps.

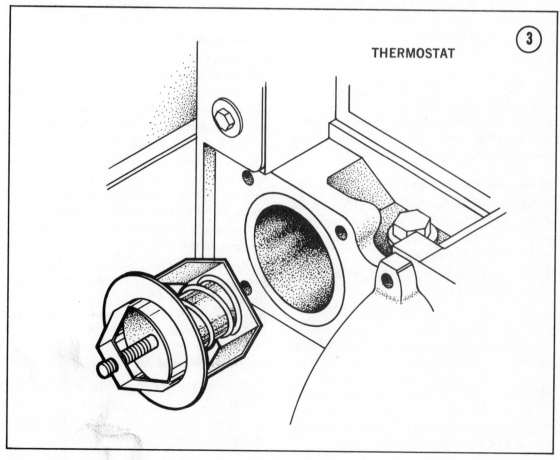

THERMOSTAT

③

Water Pump Removal/Installation

1. Drain engine coolant and remove crankshaft pulley.

2. Remove fan, spacer, and engine front cover.

3. Remove lower cover, loosen water pump bolts, and remove timing belt.

4. Remove water pump.

5. When reassembling, align camshaft sprocket timing mark with notch on upper cover. Align crankshaft sprocket damper pin hole with cast rib on oil pump cover.

> NOTE: *Later models have an alignment hole at the left rear of the camshaft sprocket cover and a hole in the camshaft sprocket. When these are aligned, the camshaft is timed for No. 1 cylinder at top dead center.*

6. Install timing belt and adjust tension with tool J-23654 and a torque wrench. Maintain 15 ft.-lb. torque, and tighten water pump bolts.

> NOTE: *Water pump bolts should be covered with an anti-seizing compound before installing.*

HEATING AND VENTILATION

The heating and ventilation system uses outside air only. (Air conditioned models use outside or inside air.) Do not rewire the blower switch to provide an OFF position.

Blower Motor Replacement

Before replacing blower motor check operation of blower switch. If high speed operates properly, but not low speed, check resistor (right side of floor air distributor).

1. Disconnect the battery ground cable and the blower motor lead wire.

2. Scribe the position of the motor flange on the case, and remove the blower.

3. Separate the motor and blower wheel by removing the retaining nut.

Heater Core and Hoses (Without Air Conditioning)

1. Disconnect the battery ground cable and the blower motor lead wire.

2. Carefully disconnect hoses from the heater. (If the hoses are stuck to the heater connection, they should be cut away and replaced.) Secure the ends of the hoses in a raised position to save coolant.

3. Remove coil bracket from dash panel.

4. Remove the blower inlet.

5. Remove core retaining strip screws and core.

Heater Core and Hoses (With Air Conditioning)

1. Disconnect battery ground cable and heater hoses at the core. If hoses are stuck, cut them from the connections. Tie the hose ends in an upright position to save coolant.

2. Remove the selector duct mounting nuts from the engine side of the dash panel.

3. Disconnect the left dash outlet hose from the center distributor duct (**Figure 4**). Remove the right dash outlet assembly, the instrument cluster bezel and outlet, the ashtray and retainer, the radio, the cigarette lighter, and the control assembly-to-instrument panel screws. Lower the control assembly.

4. Remove the screw from the right end of the instrument panel carrier reinforcement.

5. Remove center distributor duct by removing clip retaining it to the instrument panel and screws connecting it to the selector duct.

6. Remove the selector duct-to-panel screws and screw connecting the selector and defroster duct. Pull duct to the rear and disconnect all electrical wires, vacuum lines, and bowden cables. Remove selector duct assembly.

7. To replace the heater core, remove the temperature door bell crank.

8. Remove the screws from the backing plate and the temperature cable retainer, then remove the heater core and backing plate and the temperature cable retainer. Remove the heater core and backing plate as an assembly.

Air Ducts (Without Air Condtioning)

1. Remove the heater core as described previously.

2. Remove the floor outlet (**Figure 5**), and disconnect the defroster duct (**Figure 6**).

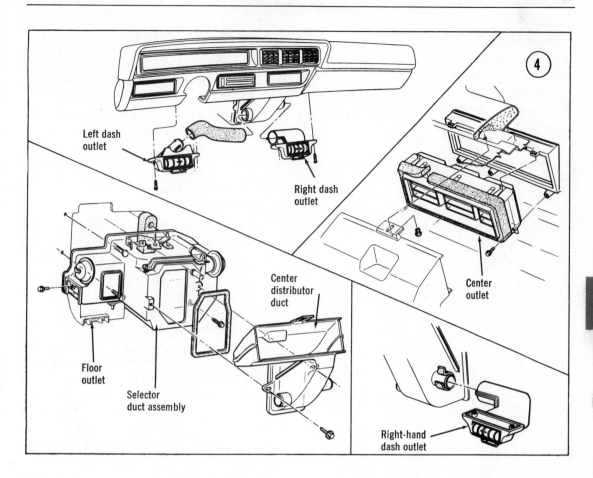

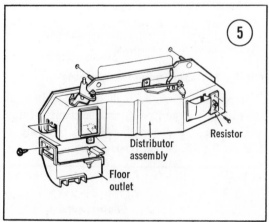

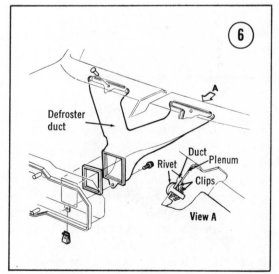

3. Unplug the resistor, and remove the air-defrost and temperature door cables. Distributor duct can now be removed.

Defroster Duct

1. Disconnect the battery ground cable and lower the steering column by removing the toe pan screws in the 2 steering column brackets-to-instrument panel nuts.

2. Remove the instrument panel bezel and cluster mounting screws.

3. With the cluster pulled rearward, remove the clips from the defroster duct to plenum panel rivets (see view A in Figure 6).

4. Disconnect the defroster duct from the distributor duct and remove defroster duct.

Controls (Without Air Conditioning)

1. Disconnect the battery ground cable and remove the instrument panel bezel.

2. Referring to **Figure 7**, remove the control retaining screws, and push the control forward and down enough to disconnect the cables and electrical leads.

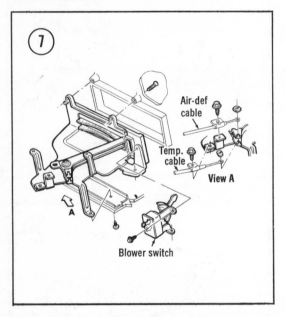

3. The blower switch can now be removed.

4. To remove control assembly completely, remove the bowden cable retaining clips and attaching screws (view A, Figure 7).

5. When reassembling, the air-defrost and temperature doors can be adjusted by the screw on top of the distributor duct. Adjust the air-defrost door while the upper control lever is set at HEATER. Adjust the temperature door while the lower control lever is at COLD. The air-defrost door, when properly adjusted, should seal at the rear side of the duct and have a ¼ in. to ⅛ in. gap at the forward side. The temperature door is properly adjusted if it seals at the forward side of the duct when the temperature lever is at the COLD position.

Controls (With Air Conditioning)

1. Disconnect battery ground cable and left dash outlet retaining screws. Move dash outlet, with the flexible hose connected, to the floor.

2. Remove the intrument panel bezel and the controls-to-instrument panel screws.

3. Push the controls forward and down, then disconnect cables, leads, and hoses (**Figure 8**).

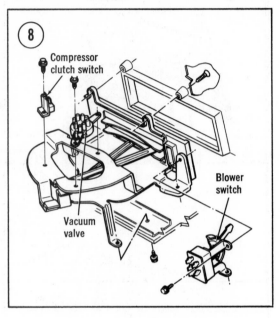

4. The blower switch and compressor clutch switch can now be removed.

Other Air Conditioning Components

Replacement of the high blower switch, air inlet door, vacuum tank, and ambient pressure switch can be accomplished by referring to **Figures 9 through 12**, respectively.

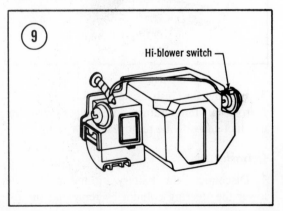

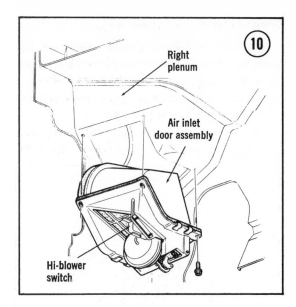

Right plenum

Air inlet door assembly

Hi-blower switch

10

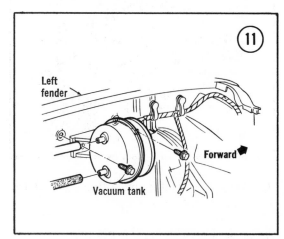

Left fender

Forward

Vacuum tank

11

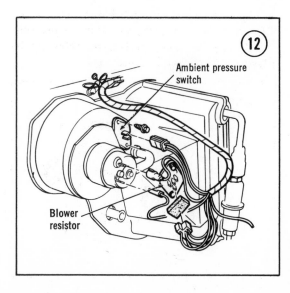

Ambient pressure switch

Blower resistor

12

Air Conditioner Control Switches and Relays

There are various switches that control the operation of the air conditioner (A/C) compressor. The compressor discharge and thermostatic switches prevent A/C operation below 45°F ambient or below 42 psi at the compressor outlet. If compressor will not operate, check the following for continuity (refer to **Figures 13**, **14**, **and 15**).

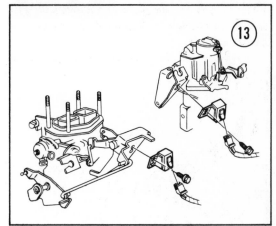

13

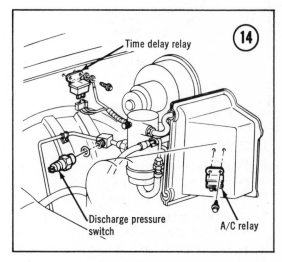

Time delay relay

Discharge pressure switch

A/C relay

14

1. Compressor discharge pressure switch.
2. Master switch (on control head).
3. Wide-open throttle cut-off switch (on carburetor).
4. Time delay relay (on right fender skirt).
5. Thermostatic switch (on evaporator cover).
6. A/C fuse (in junction block).

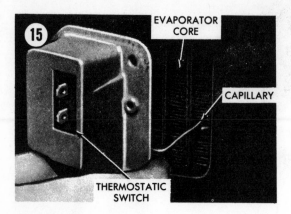

EVAPORATOR CORE

CAPILLARY

THERMOSTATIC SWITCH

False Compressor Seizure

If the air conditioning system has been inactive for a period of time (one month or longer) check for false compressor seizure. This can sometimes be loosened without removing the compressor from the car. Use a wrench on the compressor shaft locknut to rock the shaft back-and-forth several times. This should free the shaft so it can be turned by hand. Start the engine and run air conditioner for several minutes.

CHAPTER SIX

FUEL, EMISSION CONTROL, AND EXHAUST SYSTEMS

This chapter presents repair and replacement procedures for the fuel tank, fuel pump, carburetors, exhaust pipe, muffler, and tailpipe. Additional emission control devices, including those required for 1973 and later Vegas, are described. Carburetor adjustments performed on a routine basis are found in the *Tune-up* section of Chapter Two.

There are 3 basic carburetors found on the 1971-1977 Vegas; one 1-barrel, Rochester MV, and 2 different 2-barrels. The Rochester 2 GV 2-barrel was used for 1971-1972 models and was replaced in 1973 by the Holley 5210-C 2-barrel carburetor. Minor variations (mostly external) for transmission, air conditioning, and emission control requirements are identified by different carburetor numbers. For specifications, see the **Tables 1 and 2** at the end of this chapter. **Figure 1** shows the location of the part number on basic carburetors.

The 11 gallon (16 gallon for 1974-1977) fuel tank incorporates an electric fuel pump, the fuel gauge sending unit, and the vapor separator assembly for the fuel evaporation control system.

Engine exhaust is routed from the combustion chambers through a 4-port manifold, equipped with a stamped metal carburetor heat stove. A single exhaust pipe leads to a single transverse mounted muffler. The muffler is fitted with a

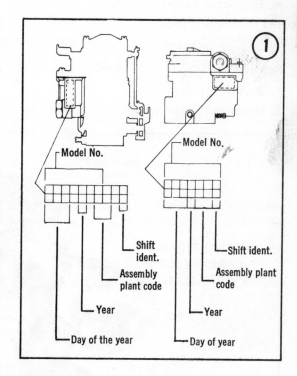

short tailpipe which terminates behind the left rear wheel.

ROCHESTER MV CARBURETOR

The Rochester model MV is a single bore, down draft design. It uses a triple venturi and a plain tube nozzle. The main venturi diameter measures 7-7/32 in., and the throttle bore measures 1-7/16 in.

In 1973, several modifications were made to the basic design. A new automatic choke with a new vacuum break diaphragm assembly is externally mounted. For engines with air conditioning, a hot idle compensator to maintain smooth idle with high under-hood temperatures was added. The MV carburetor has been recalibrated for 1974 engine requirements. **Figures 2 and 3** present opposing views of this carburetor. **Figure 4** shows the version used in 1975-1976 models. **Figure 5** (page 78) is an exploded view of the basic MV carburetor.

The MV carburetor used on 1975-76 models is similar to the 1974 version, except that an auxiliary vacuum diaphragm unit, which is attached to the air hose with 2 screws, has been added. With this exception, removal, disassembly, reassembly, and installation procedures are identical.

Removal

1. Remove air cleaner.
2. Disconnect fuel line, vacuum line, choke rod, accelerator linkage, and throttle valve linkage (automatic transmission).
3. Remove the mounting nuts and solenoid assembly.
4. Carefully remove carburetor from engine so as not to disturb fuel in carburetor bowl. When disassembling, take note of any contamination (dirt, water, etc.) in the float bowl.

Disassembly

Refer to Figure 5 for this procedure.

1. Remove fast idle cam and choke rod.
2. Remove choke coil rod lever.
3. Remove air horn (3 long and 3 short screws).
4. Remove the vacuum break diaphragm cover (Figure 2, 1971-1972). Remove vacuum break assembly (Figure 3, 1973-1974). Remove auxiliary vacuum break unit (Figure 4, 1975-1976).
5. Remove the vacuum break diaphragm and plunger rod by holding the choke valve wide open and pushing the rod up until the looped end releases from the wire lever attached to choke valve.
6. If the choke valve is to be removed, file the staking on the 2 screws before removing. (Note 2

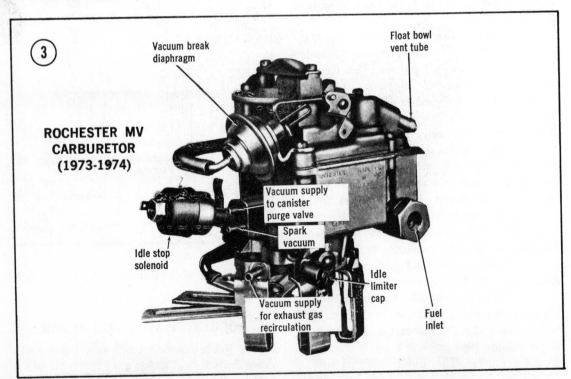

③ ROCHESTER MV CARBURETOR (1973-1974)

Vacuum break diaphragm

Float bowl vent tube

Vacuum supply to canister purge valve

Spark vacuum

Idle stop solenoid

Idle limiter cap

Vacuum supply for exhaust gas recirculation

Fuel inlet

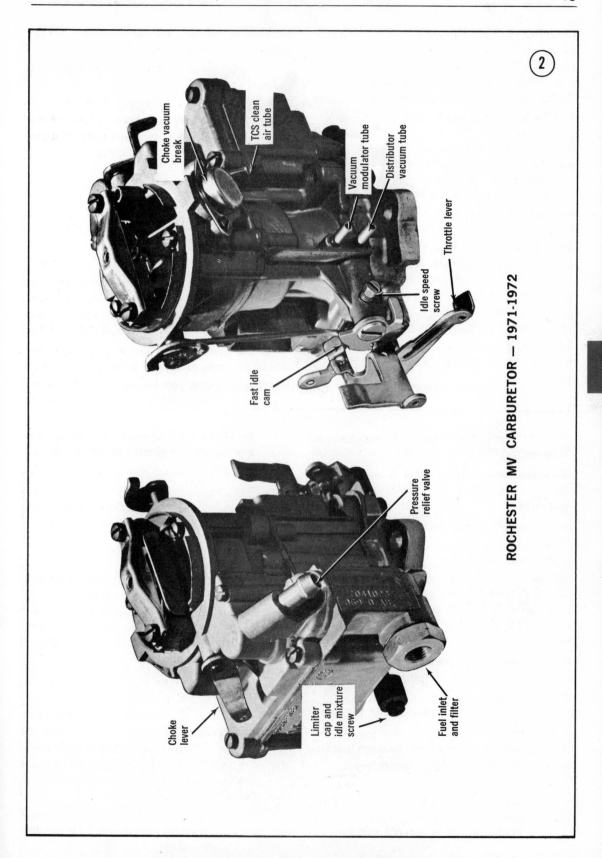

Choke vacuum break

TCS clean air tube

Vacuum modulator tube

Distributor vacuum tube

Throttle lever

Idle speed screw

Fast idle cam

Pressure relief valve

Choke lever

Limiter cap and idle mixture screw

Fuel inlet and filter

ROCHESTER MV CARBURETOR — 1971-1972

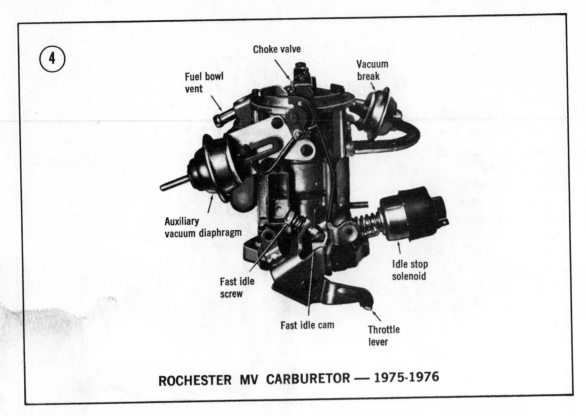

④

Choke valve

Vacuum break

Fuel bowl vent

Auxiliary vacuum diaphragm

Fast idle screw

Fast idle cam

Idle stop solenoid

Throttle lever

ROCHESTER MV CARBURETOR — 1975-1976

plastic washers between the choke valve and air horn wall.)

7. If the pressure relief valve is defective, the air horn and valve must be replaced as an assembly.

8. Remove float, float needle, and seat.

9. Remove fuel inlet nut, gasket, filter element, and pressure relief spring. Discard filter.

10. With needle-nose pliers, remove the pump discharge guide. Ball and spring may now be removed by inverting the assembly. The idle tube and power valve can also be removed in this fashion.

11. Disconnect accelerator pump lever on throttle shaft, and remove the plunger. Remove the return spring.

12. Remove main metering jet and idle speed stop screw.

13. Remove the throttle body-to-bowl attaching screws, and separate the 2 assemblies.

NOTE: *If idle mixture needles are replaced and no* CO *reading equipment is available, bottom the old mixture*

needles (counting the number of turns) and install new needles in that same position.

14. Check to see that the throttle valve screws are tight and staked in place. Do not remove the valve or shaft. These are precision fitted parts.

Cleaning and Inspection

Clean all castings in an appropriate carburetor cleaning solution. Blow out passages and jets. Do not use drills or wires to clean jets and passages. Check all parts for wear and replace if necessary. Replace fuel filter element. Check springs for distortion.

Assembly

1. If the plastic idle mixture needle limiter cap or the needle itself has been removed, reinstall to the original adjustment by counting the number of turns from the bottomed position to equal the number of turns which the needle was set when disassembled.

If the throttle body is being replaced, and a CO meter is available, install the idle mixture needle 4 turns from the bottomed position. This preliminary setting can be refined later.

2. Using a new gasket, install throttle body to the bowl.

3. Install idle adjustment screw, main metering jet, pump return spring, pump plunger, and drive link. The drive link ends should point toward the carburetor bore.

4. Install the pump actuating lever so that the offset faces the throttle body and aligns with the pump plunger shaft.

5. Pushing downward on pump assembly, align the lever and throttle shaft flats, and install the retaining screw.

6. Install idle tube so that it is flush with the top of the float bowl casting.

7. Install pump discharge ball, spring, and retainer so that the latter is flush with the top of the bowl casting.

8. Install fuel filter spring and a new filter, with open end facing the hole in the fuel inlet nut. Install nut and gasket.

9. Install float needle seat and gasket, needle valve, power valve, and float.

10. Adjust float level to specifications as shown in **Figure 6,** with bowl gasket removed.

11. Install choke shaft, valve, and vacuum break lever. Be certain that the 2 plastic washers are installed between the choke shaft and the air horn casting. Also make sure that the choke valve is aligned before tightening and staking the retaining screws.

12. Install the vacuum break diagraphm and plunger. Hold choke valve in open position and slide the plunger rod eyelet over the end of the vacuum break lever.

13. After seating the vacuum break diaphragm over the sealing bead, install the diaphragm cover and the 2 retaining screws.

14. Assemble air horn to float bowl with new gasket.

15. Assemble choke rod so that upper end of rod points away from the air horn casting.

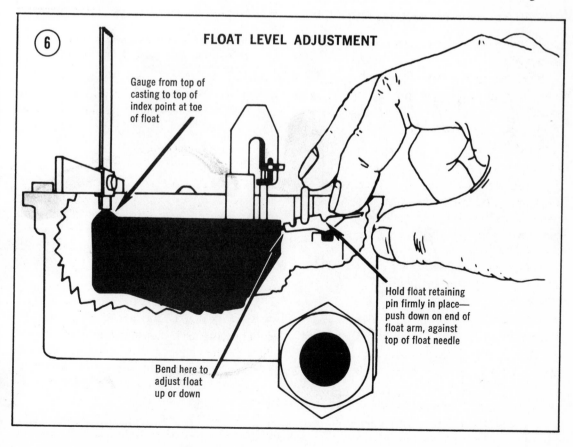

6 FLOAT LEVEL ADJUSTMENT

Gauge from top of casting to top of index point at toe of float

Hold float retaining pin firmly in place— push down on end of float arm, against top of float needle

Bend here to adjust float up or down

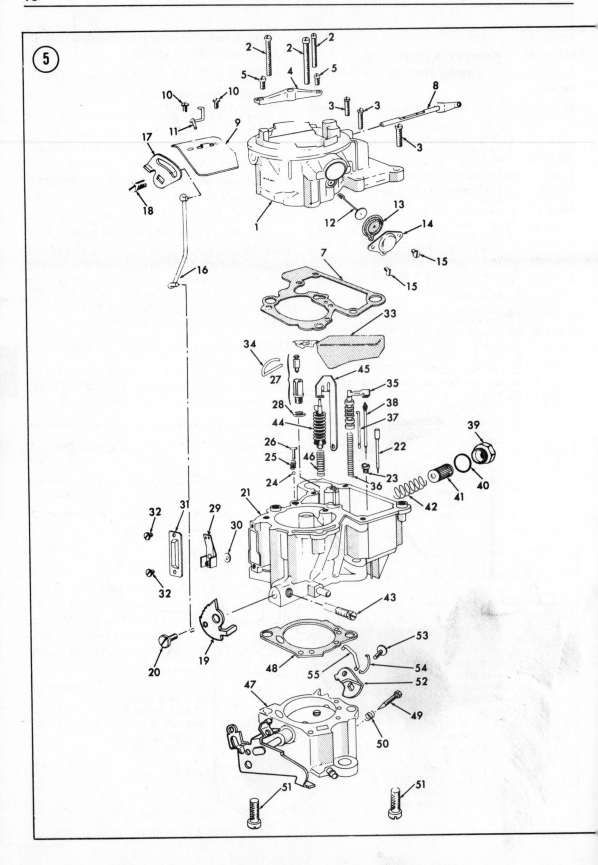

BASE ROCHESTER MV CARBURETOR

1. Air horn assembly
2. Long air horn screw
3. Short air horn screw
4. Air cleaner stud bracket
5. Bracket attaching screw
7. Air horn gasket
8. Choke shaft and lever assembly
9. Choke valve
10. Choke valve screw
11. Vacuum break link lever
12. Vacuum break link assembly
13. Vacuum break diaphragm
14. Vacuum break cover
15. Cover screw
16. Choke rod
17. Choke lever
18. Choke lever screw
19. Fast idle cam
20. Cam attaching screw
21. Float bowl assembly
22. Idle tube assembly
23. Main metering jet
24. Pump discharge ball
25. Pump discharge spring
26. Pump discharge guide
27. Needle and seat assembly
28. Needle seat gasket
29. Idle compensator assembly
30. Idle compensator gasket
31. Idle compensator cover
32. Cover screw
33. Float assembly
34. Float hinge pin
35. Power piston assembly
36. Power piston spring
37. Power piston rod
38. Metering rod and spring assembly
39. Fuel inlet filter nut
40. Filter nut gasket
41. Fuel inlet filter
42. Fuel filter spring
43. Slow idle screw
44. Pump assembly
45. Pump actuating lever
46. Pump return spring
47. Throttle body assembly
48. Throttle body gasket
49. Idle needle
50. Idle needle spring
51. Throttle body screw
52. Pump and power rods lever
53. Lever attaching screw
54. Power piston rod link
55. Pump lever link

16. Hook fast idle cam onto lower end of choke rod and fasten to float bowl.
17. Install choke coil rod lever.

Idle Stop (Anti-dieseling) Solenoid Adjustment

1. Adjust carburetor idle screw. See *Tune-up,* Chapter Two.

2. Connect the wire terminal to the anti-dieseling solenoid (Figures 2, 3, and 4) and open the throttle for a second.

3. Turn the plunger adjusting screw with a ⅜ in. wrench until the specified engine rpm is reached. Check specification decal for proper rpm setting. Generally it will be 1,000 rpm for manual transmission, 750 rpm for automatic transmission-equipped vehicles.

Fast Idle Adjustment

Carburetor idle screw and idle stop solenoid must be properly adjusted. See *Tune-up* and *Idle Stop Solenoid.*

1. Refer to **Figure 7**.

2. Open throttle, and close it against the high step of the fast idle cam.

3. Adjust fast idle by bending the cam follower tang extending from the throttle lever. Refer to rpm specifications at the end of this chapter or the tune-up specification sticker.

Choke Rod Adjustment

1. Refer to **Figure 8**. Cam follower must be held on second highest step, and the choke coil rod lifted to its highest position. This can be accomplished by first setting the cam in position, then holding the choke closed as far as possible with firm pressure.

2. Check clearance between air horn wall and center *bottom* edge of the choke valve.

3. Adjust to clearance specified for your carburetor by bending the choke rod.

Unloader Adjustment

1. Refer to **Figure 9**.

2. Hold throttle valve wide open.

3. Hold choke valve closed as far as possible.

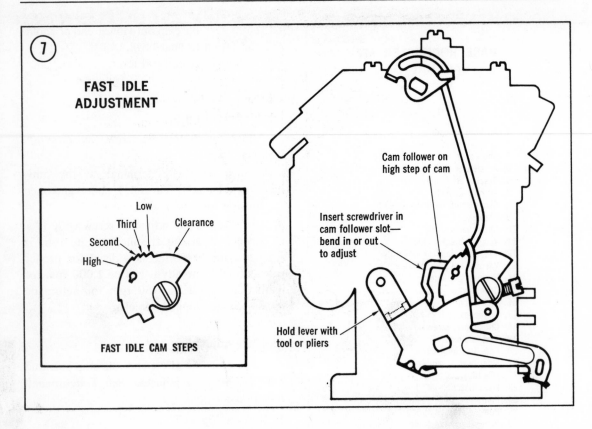

⑦

FAST IDLE ADJUSTMENT

Low

Third   Clearance

Second

High

FAST IDLE CAM STEPS

Cam follower on high step of cam

Insert screwdriver in cam follower slot— bend in or out to adjust

Hold lever with tool or pliers

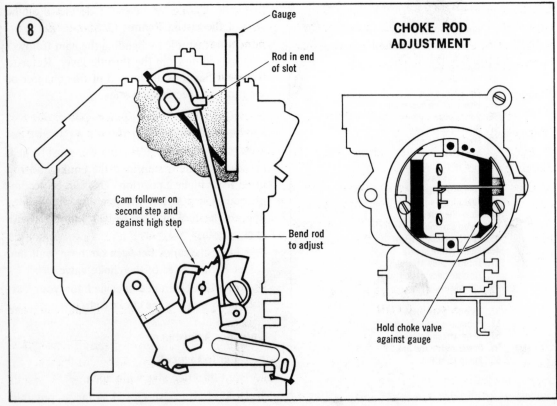

⑧

Gauge

CHOKE ROD ADJUSTMENT

Rod in end of slot

Cam follower on second step and against high step

Bend rod to adjust

Hold choke valve against gauge

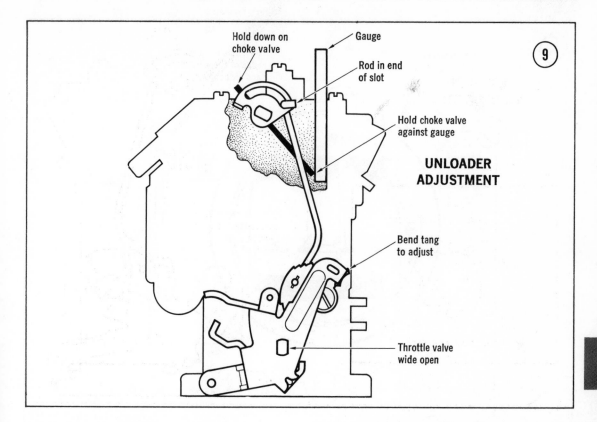

Hold down on choke valve

Gauge

Rod in end of slot

Hold choke valve against gauge

UNLOADER ADJUSTMENT

Bend tang to adjust

Throttle valve wide open

4. Check clearance between the center *bottom* edge of the choke valve and the air horn wall.

5. Adjust to clearance specified for your carburetor by bending the unloader tang.

Vacuum Break

1. Hold choke valve closed with rubber band (**Figure 10**).

2. Push in vacuum break plunger until the diaphragm seats.

3. Check clearance between the center *bottom* edge of the choke valve and the air horn wall.

4. Adjust to clearance specified for your carburetor by bending the tang on the end of the vacuum break lever.

2-BARREL ROCHESTER 2GV CARBURETOR

All fuel metering is located in a cluster in front of the main venturi. The cluster includes the main well tubes, idle tubes, mixture passages, air bleeds, and pump jets. Each of the 2 barrels is fitted with a venturi and a separate fuel feed. **Figure 11** gives 2 side views of the 2GV carburetor. **Figure 12** shows the component parts.

Removal

1. Remove air cleaner.

2. Disconnect fuel line, vacuum line, choke rod, accelerator linkage, and throttle valve linkage (automatic transmission).

3. Remove the mounting nuts and solenoid assembly.

4. Carefully remove carburetor from engine so as not to disturb fuel in carburetor bowl. When disassembling, take note of any contamination (dirt, water, etc.) in the float bowl.

Disassembly

1. Remove the pump rod, fast idle cam, and choke rod.

2. Remove choke vacuum diaphragm hose, fuel filter nut, filter, and pressure relief spring.

3. Remove choke coil rod lever from end of choke shaft.

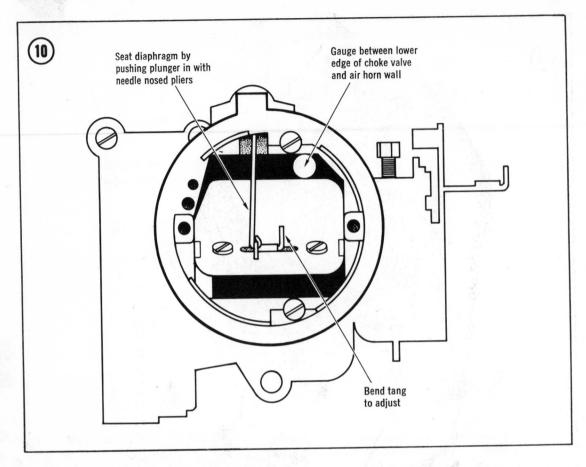

(10)

Seat diaphragm by
pushing plunger in with
needle nosed pliers

Gauge between lower
edge of choke valve
and air horn wall

Bend tang
to adjust

4. Remove the choke vacuum break diaphragm assembly from the air horn (**Figure 13**).

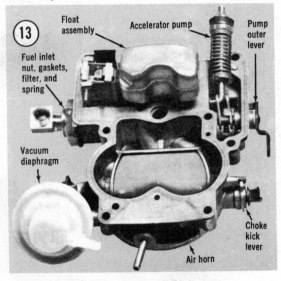

(13)

Float
assembly

Accelerator pump

Pump
outer
lever

Fuel inlet
nut, gaskets,
filter, and
spring

Vacuum
diaphragm

Choke
kick
lever

Air horn

5. Remove the air horn (8 screws).

6. Remove float, needle, seat, and gasket.

7. Note plastic washer between the outer pump lever and air horn, then remove pump assembly and inner pump arm by loosening the setscrew on the inner pump arm.

8. If the choke shaft or valve needs replacement, first remove the staking by filing the valve screws, then disassemble.

9. Refer to **Figure 14** and remove the accelerator pump spring and the power valve.

10. Remove the 3 cluster retaining screws (note the fiber sealing gasket on the center one), and remove cluster, gasket, and main well inserts.

11. Remove the pump check ball by first removing the retainer at the bottom of the pump well with a pair of needlenose pliers, then inverting the bowl.

12. Remove the 2 throttle body-to-bowl attaching screws and separate the throttle body from the carburetor bowl.

13. Break the limiter caps to remove the idle mixture screws. Before removing them, count

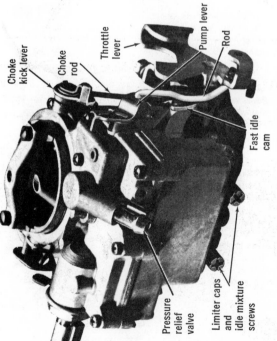

Fuel inlet and filter

Choke lever

Distributor vacuum tube

Idle speed screw

TCS clean air tube

Choke vacuum break

Choke kick lever

Choke rod

Throttle lever

Pump lever

Rod

Fast idle cam

Pressure relief valve

Limiter caps and idle mixture screws

ROCHESTER 2GV CARBURETOR

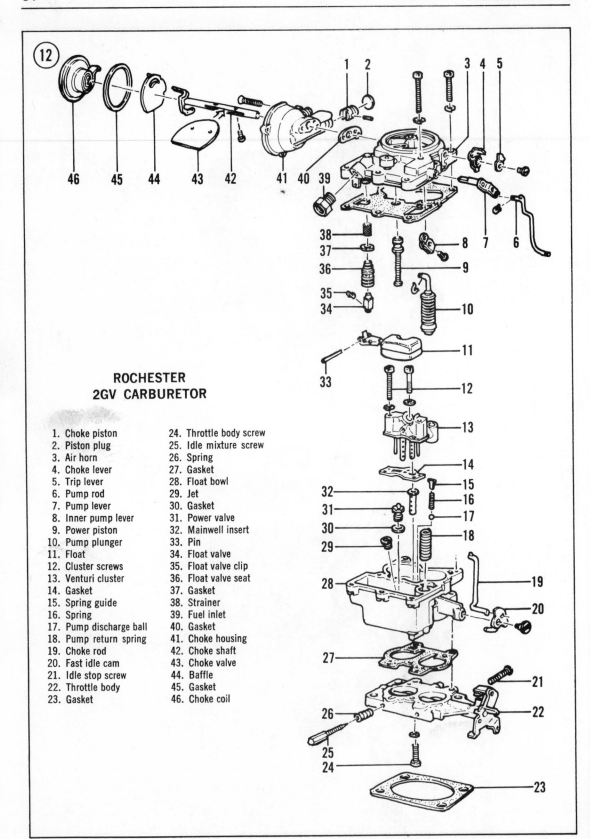

**ROCHESTER
2GV CARBURETOR**

1. Choke piston
2. Piston plug
3. Air horn
4. Choke lever
5. Trip lever
6. Pump rod
7. Pump lever
8. Inner pump lever
9. Power piston
10. Pump plunger
11. Float
12. Cluster screws
13. Venturi cluster
14. Gasket
15. Spring guide
16. Spring
17. Pump discharge ball
18. Pump return spring
19. Choke rod
20. Fast idle cam
21. Idle stop screw
22. Throttle body
23. Gasket

24. Throttle body screw
25. Idle mixture screw
26. Spring
27. Gasket
28. Float bowl
29. Jet
30. Gasket
31. Power valve
32. Mainwell insert
33. Pin
34. Float valve
35. Float valve clip
36. Float valve seat
37. Gasket
38. Strainer
39. Fuel inlet
40. Gasket
41. Choke housing
42. Choke shaft
43. Choke valve
44. Baffle
45. Gasket
46. Choke coil

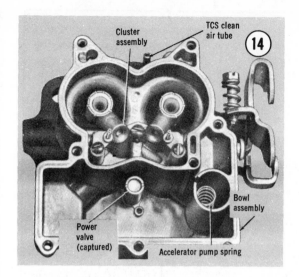

and record for reassembly the number of turns required to bottom them.

Cleaning and Inspection

Wash all carburetor castings in a suitable carburetor cleaning solvent. Blow out passages. Do not clean jets or passages with wire or drills. Inspect all parts for wear and replace as necessary. Make certain that the power enrichment valve is clean. The valve should move freely inside the assembly.

Assembly

1. If the plastic idle mixture needle limiter caps or the needles have been removed, reinstall to the original adjustment by counting the number of turns from the bottomed position to equal the number of turns at which the needles were set when disassembled.

If the throttle body is being replaced, and a co meter is available, install the idle mixture needles 4 turns from the bottomed position. This preliminary setting can later be refined.

2. Assemble throttle body to float bowl with new gasket.

3. Install the 3/16 in. steel pump discharge ball and retainer.

4. Install the main well inserts, gasket, and cluster assembly. Include the sealing gasket for the center screw.

5. Install the main metering jets, power valve, and gasket.

6. Install pump return spring.

7. Assemble the choke shaft, lever, collar, and valve. Before tightening valve screws, make certain there is 0.020 in. clearance between the lever and collar. Stake choke valve screws.

8. Install the plastic bearing washer, pump lever, and shaft assembly into the air horn.

9. Hook the pump plunger assembly onto the inner pump lever, with the end of the plunger shaft toward the carburetor bore.

10. Install air horn gasket, float needle seat and gasket, and needle.

11. Adjust float level to specifications as shown in **Figure 15**.

12. Adjust float drop to specifications as shown in **Figure 16**.

13. Assemble air horn to bowl, making certain that pump enters well and that inner pump lever slides over flat on pump shaft. Tighten inner lever retaining screw.

14. Attach pump rod to pump lever and throttle lever. Assemble cam to the lower end of the rod, and install cam on bowl. The rod offset end should be toward the fast idle cam.

15. Install choke vacuum break diaphragm and vacuum break rod, then install the coil rod lever on the choke shaft.

16. Attach vacuum hose to vacuum diaphragm and throttle body.

Choke Rod Adjustment

1. Adjust fast idle stop screw until it barely touches the bottom step of the fast idle cam; then turn it one complete revolution clockwise (**Figure 17**).

3. Move cam to the second step so that the fast idle screw is against the shoulder leading to the high step.

4. Check clearance between the air horn wall and the center *upper* edge of the choke valve.

5. Adjust to clearance specified for your carburetor by bending the upper choke lever tang.

Unloader Adjustment

1. Refer to **Figure 18**.

2. Hold throttle valves wide open.

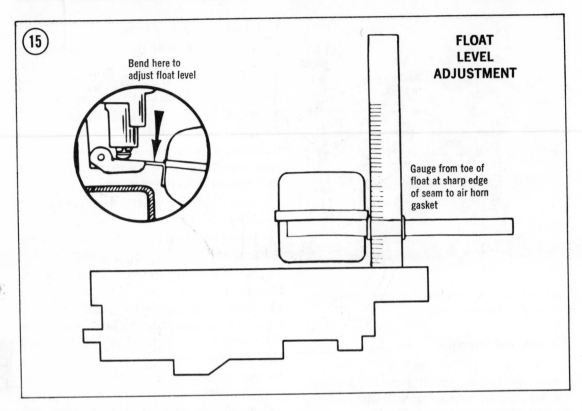

15

Bend here to
adjust float level

**FLOAT
LEVEL
ADJUSTMENT**

Gauge from toe of
float at sharp edge
of seam to air horn
gasket

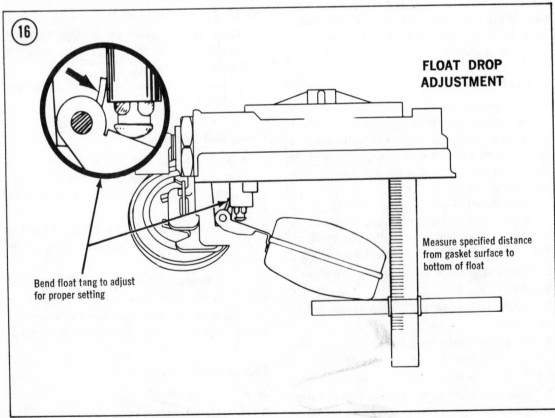

16

**FLOAT DROP
ADJUSTMENT**

Measure specified distance
from gasket surface to
bottom of float

Bend float tang to adjust
for proper setting

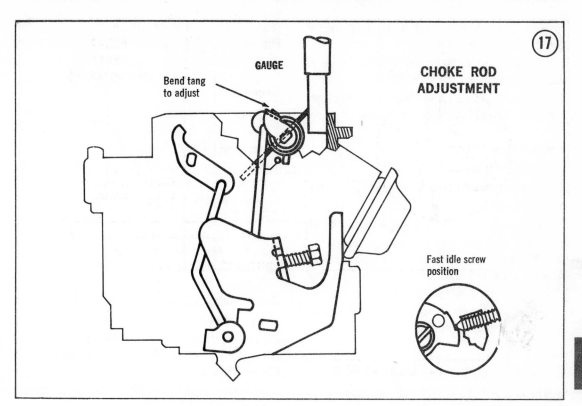

GAUGE

Bend tang
to adjust

**CHOKE ROD
ADJUSTMENT**

Fast idle screw
position

17

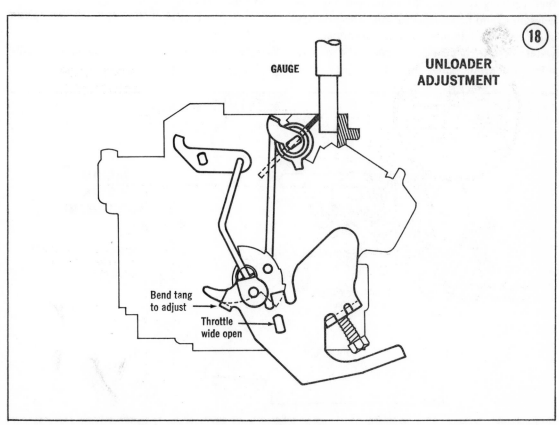

GAUGE

**UNLOADER
ADJUSTMENT**

Bend tang
to adjust

Throttle
wide open

18

6

3. Hold choke valve closed as far as possible. Use of a rubber band helps.

4. Check clearance between the *upper* edge of the choke valve and the air horn well.

5. Adjust to clearance specified for your carburetor by bending the unloader tang.

Vacuum Break

1. Refer to **Figure 19**.

2. Push in vacuum break plunger until diaphragm seats.

3. Hold choke valve closed with a rubber band.

4. Check clearance between the *upper* edge of the choke valve and the air horn wall, making sure the vacuum break rod is at the bottom end of the choke lever slot as shown.

5. Adjust to clearance specified for your carburetor by bending the rod.

HOLLEY 5210-C CARBURETOR

The Holley 5210-C carburetor utilizes 4 basic fuel metering systems: idle, main metering, accelerating, and power enrichment. The primary stage is smaller in size than the secondary. A water heated bimetallic thermostatic choke housing is another unique feature of this carburetor. Refer to **Figure 20** for 2 views of the Holley 5210-C. **Figure 21** is an exploded view of the 5210-C.

Removal

1. Remove air cleaner.

2. Disconnect fuel line, vacuum line, choke heater hoses, choke rod or choke water cover, accelerator linkage, and throttle valve linkage (automatic transmission).

3. Remove mounting nuts or bolts.

4. Carefully remove carburetor from engine so as not to disturb fuel in carburetor bowl. When disassembling, take note of any contamination (dirt, water, etc.) in the float bowl.

Disassembly

1. On 1975-1977 models, remove retaining clip, then remove 2 screws. Remove choke pull-off solenoid and bracket from carburetor. See **Figure 22**.

2. Remove choke rod, the 5 air horn hold-down screws, and lift off air horn.

3. Unscrew fuel inlet nut, remove filter, clean filter recess.

4. Remove float shaft, float, fuel inlet needle valve, seat, and gasket.

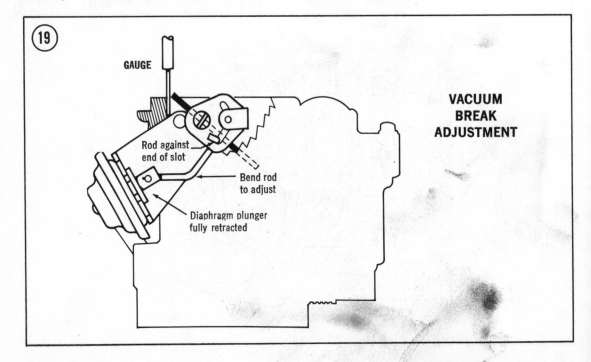

(19)

GAUGE

Rod against end of slot

Bend rod to adjust

Diaphragm plunger fully retracted

VACUUM BREAK ADJUSTMENT

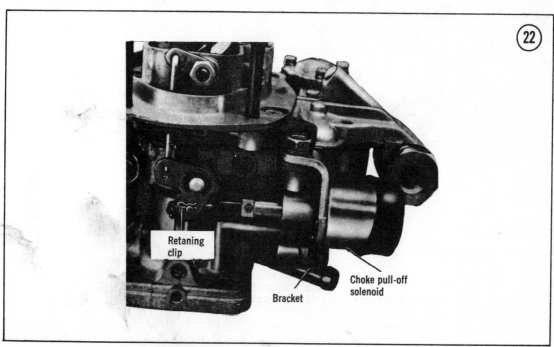

Choke water cover

20

Bowl vents

Accelerator pump

Bowl vent

Choke housing

Choke diaphragm

Fuel inlet

Vent tube

HOLLEY 5210-C CARBURETOR

Primary shaft

Secondary shaft

Idle stop solenoid

6

22

Retaning clip

Bracket

Choke pull-off solenoid

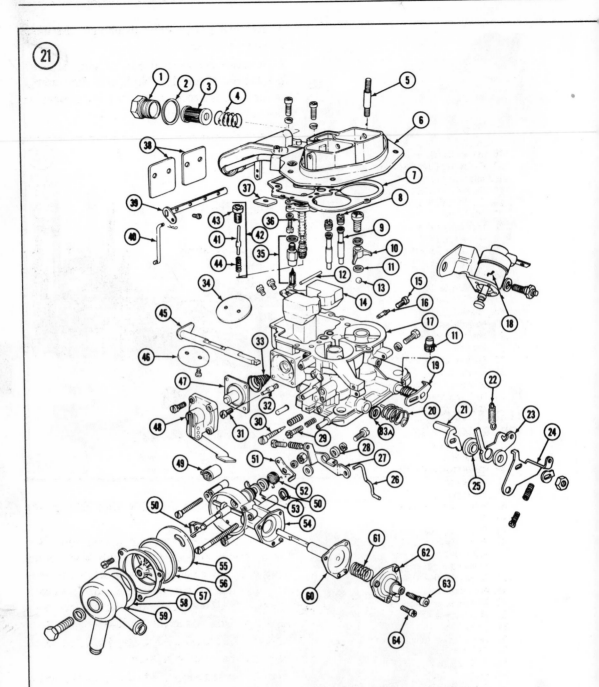

HOLLEY 5210-C CARBURETOR

1. Fuel inlet nut
2. Gasket
3. Filter
4. Spring
5. Studs, air cleaner attachment

6. Air horn
7. Gasket
8. High speed bleed
9. Main well tube
10. Pump discharge nozzle

11. Gasket
12. Float shaft
13. Discharge check ball
14. Float
15. Retainer

16. Secondary idle jet
17. Carburetor body assembly
18. Idle stop solenoid
19. Secondary throttle lever
20. Throttle return spring
21. Idle lever
22. Secondary operating lever
     return spring
23. Secondary operating lever
24. Throttle lever
25. Bushing
26. Fast idle rod
27. Fast idle lever
28. Bushing
29. Low idle screw
30. Fuel mixture screw
31. Retainer
32. Primary idle jet
33. Return spring
34. Secondary throttle plate
35. Fuel inlet needle
     and seat assembly
36. Power valve
     economizer assembly
37. Choke rod seal
38. Choke plates
39. Choke shaft and lever
40. Choke rod
41. Power valve
42. Power valve assembly
43. Seat
44. Spring
45. Primary throttle shaft
     and lever assembly
46. Primary throttle plate
47. Accelerator pump
48. Accelerator pump cover
49. Mixture screw limiter cap
50. Choke housing shaft
51. Choke lever
52. Fast idle cam spring
53. Fast idle cam
54. Choke housing
55. Gasket
56. Thermostatic housing
57. Retainer
58. Gasket
59. Water cover
60. Diaphragm and shaft
61. Return spring
62. Choke diaphragm cover
63. Hex head screw
64. Cover screw

5. Remove power valve diaphragm assembly and choke rod seal.

6. Remove evaporation control system (ECS) diaphragm (**Figure 23**). No further disassembly of air horn is necessary unless there is damage to choke plates, shaft, or lever.

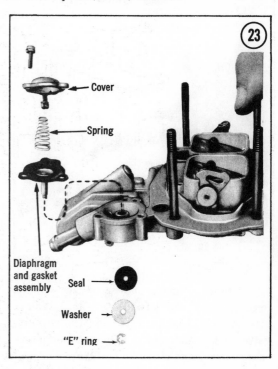

7. Remove choke assembly after disengaging fast idle rod.

8. Remove accelerator pump assembly. Remove pump diaphragm assembly and return spring. Remove pump discharge screw and nozzle assembly, discharge nozzle, and 2 gaskets (**Figure 24**). Be careful not to lose check ball. Invert carburetor and catch ball as it rolls out.

9. Disassemble choke assembly including small O-ring from vacuum passage.

10. Remove idle mixture limiter caps and screw mixture screws in until they lightly bottom in the seat. Count the number of turns required to nearest 1/16 of a turn.

11. Remove primary and secondary high speed bleeds and main well tubes. See **Figure 25**. Note that primary refers to right-hand bore when float bowl faces you. Record sizes of air bleed restrictions and main well tubes so they can be reinstalled in original positions.

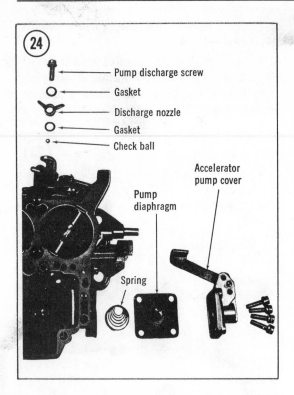

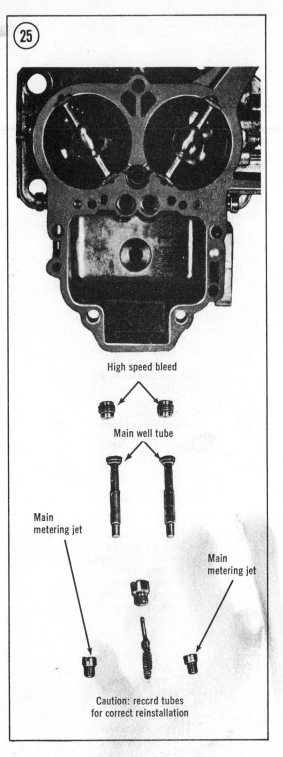

Caution: record tubes
for correct reinstallation

12. Remove primary and secondary idle jet retainer plugs and jets (**Figure 26**). Remove main metering jets. Record sizes. Remove power valve gasket and spring. Remove pump discharge nozzle and check balls (**Figure 27**).

13. Disassemble and remove throttle lever assembly. Observe how return spring is hooked over idle adjusting lever and body. Do not remove throttle valve because of close tolerance fit involved.

14. Remove idle adjusting lever spring and washer. Remove idle speed screw and spring from lever. Remove secondary throttle stop screw (**Figure 28**).

Cleaning and Inspection

Clean all metal parts in a suitable carburetor cleaning solvent. Do not immerse any plastic or rubber parts in solvent. Blow out passages. Inspect all parts for wear. It is a good idea to obtain a carburetor rebuild kit for parts subject to wear and deterioration. Make sure power enrichment valve is clean and operates freely. Inspect accelerator pump diaphragm for wear. Fast idle cam should be replaced if steps are worn.

Assembly

1. Install secondary throttle adjusting screw, idle speed screw, spring, and lever.

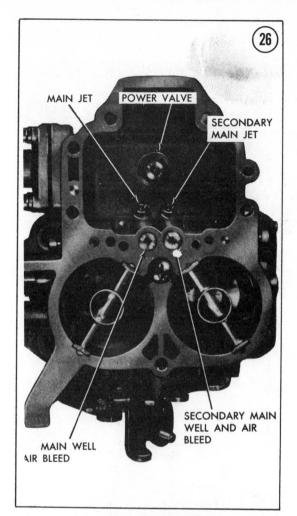

MAIN JET POWER VALVE
SECONDARY MAIN JET
SECONDARY MAIN WELL AND AIR BLEED
MAIN WELL AIR BLEED

2. Install idle mixture needles and springs to same number of turns as when removed. Install idle jets and plugs. *Do not interchange primary and secondary.*

3. Install power valve, primary and secondary main jets, main well tubes, and high speed bleeds. Install ECS diaphragm.

4. Install pump discharge check ball, gasket, nozzle, and screw. Assemble accelerator pump diaphragm and cover. Start the 4 screws by hand and align diaphragm gasket. Tighten screws in rotation.

5. Reassemble the choke assembly. Replace vacuum passage O-ring.

6. Install inlet needle, seat, and gasket.

7. Depress spring and install power diaphragm assembly. Install float.

8. On 1971-1975 models, adjust float level to specifications shown in Figure 6. Rochester and Holley carburetors set the same way. Bend float tang to adjust.

> NOTE: *On 1976-1977 models, adjust float as shown in* **Figure 29**. *With air horn inverted and float tang resting lightly on inlet needle, insert gauge (see Table 2) between air horn and float. Bend tang on float if adjustment is required.*

9. On 1971-1975 models, adjust float drop to specifications as shown in Figure 16.

> NOTE: *On 1976-1977 models, adjust secondary throttle stop screw (see* **Figure 30**) *after assembly. Back off screw until secondary throttle is completely seated in bore. Then turn in screw until it just touches tab on secondary throttle lever, plus an additional ¼ turn.*

10. Install choke rod seal and rod. Install air horn gasket, choke link into choke lever, attach retaining clip. Install air horn, new fuel filter, gasket, spring, and inlet plug.

11. Adjust secondary throttle stop screw until throttle plate seats in bore. Turn in ¼ turn.

12. Adjust choke setting so index is aligned with second mark past center in clockwise direction.

Idle speed screw and spring

Secondary throttle stop screw

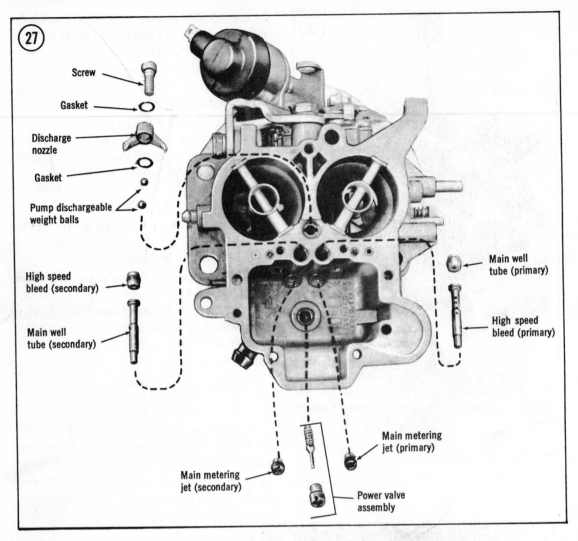

(27)

Screw

Gasket

Discharge
nozzle

Gasket

Pump dischargeable
weight balls

High speed
bleed (secondary)

Main well
tube (secondary)

Main well
tube (primary)

High speed
bleed (primary)

Main metering
jet (primary)

Main metering
jet (secondary)

Power valve
assembly

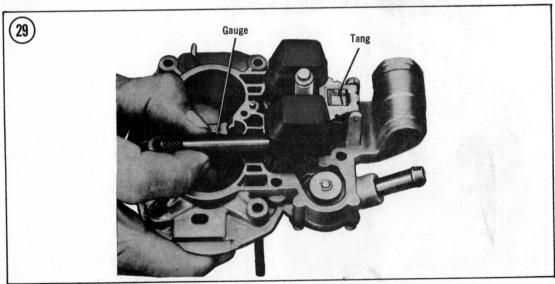

(29)

Gauge

Tang

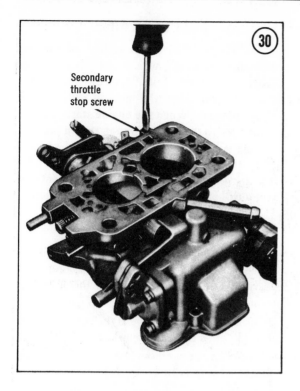

Secondary
throttle
stop screw

(30)

2. Place a drill or wire gauge (see Table 2 for size) between choke plate and side of air horn. Hold choke plate down with finger.

3. Adjust by bending choke lever tang.

Choke Adjustment

Loosen 3 screws holding choke cover and rotate cover index ⅛ in. counterclockwise until it lines up with the small punch mark on choke housing. Retighten holding screws.

Choke Plate Vacuum Pull-down

1. Remove the 3 choke cover screws and retaining ring. Do not remove choke water housing screw if adjusting on car.

2. Refer to **Figure 31** and push diaphragm stem against stop. Place gauge (Table 2) between primary choke plate and air horn. Hold linkage tight with finger. Adjust with 5/32 in. Allen wrench as shown.

13. Attach all vacuum hoses, throttle linkage, and choke water tubes. Install choke pull-off solenoid.

Fast Idle Cam Adjustment

1. Set fast idle screw on the *second* step of fast idle cam.

IDLE MIXTURE ADJUSTMENT (ALL CARBURETORS)

Idle mixture adjustments have been made at the factory and should be readjusted only after major carburetor overhaul, at 24,000-mile intervals, or when a poor idle cannot be smoothed out by a complete tune-up and emission control

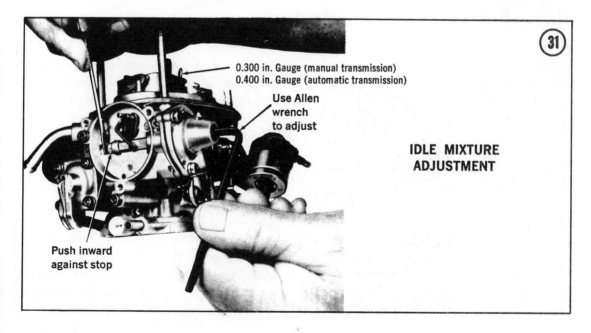

(31)

0.300 in. Gauge (manual transmission)
0.400 in. Gauge (automatic transmission)

Use Allen
wrench
to adjust

**IDLE MIXTURE
ADJUSTMENT**

Push inward
against stop

checks. A tachometer is required and a reliable CO meter is recommended for this adjustment. If a CO meter is unavailable, follow the lean drop mixture adjustment procedure.

Adjustment With CO Meter

1. Set parking brake, block wheels, warm engine to operating temperature, and turn off air conditioner. Leave manual transmission in NEUTRAL, automatic transmission in DRIVE.

2. Disconnect and plug vacuum advance hose at distributor. Disconnect fuel vent hose from EEC canister.

3. On manual transmissions, disconnect the TCS solenoid lead.

4. Set curb idle speed (associated with idle stop solenoid; see Chapter Two) to maximum rpm specified on "Solenoid Adjustment De-energized" line of tune-up decal. Make sure air cleaner is in place.

5. Connect CO meter to exhaust.

6. Break off tab on idle mixture limiter caps with needle-nose pliers to permit adjustment. Do *not* remove caps.

7. While an assistant observes the CO meter, adjust the idle mixture for smoothest idle without exceeding emission specifications (0.5% CO maximum). Reset idle speed if necessary.

8. Shut off engine; unplug and reconnect all hoses. Reconnect lead to TCS solenoid.

Adjustment Without CO Meter (Lean Drop Idle Speed Method)

1. Perform Steps 1 through 4 of the previous method.

2. Adjust curb idle speed (idle solenoid, single-barrel; or idle stop screw, 2-barrel) to maximum lean drop idle mixture rpm.

3. Back out mixture screw(s) until maximum smoothest idle is obtained. Reset curb idle rpm as necessary.

4. Turn idle mixture screw(s) in until lower lean drop idle mixture rpm is reached.

5. Shut off engine; unplug and reconnect all hoses. Reconnect wire to TCS solenoid.

FUEL PUMP

The electric fuel pump is part of the fuel metering assembly, which also includes the gauge sending unit. Initially, electricity is fed to the fuel pump when the ignition key is in the START position. When the engine starts, current is supplied to the pump through the oil pressure safety switch when there is 2 psi (0.14 kg/cm^2) or more of pressure. If oil pressure drops below 2 psi, the pump stops. An inefficient fuel pump will affect high speed engine operation.

Pressure and Delivery Check

1. Unplug the oil pressure safety switch located on left front of the engine block.

2. Insert a jumper wire across the 2 outside terminals in the plug.

3. Disconnect the fuel line at the carburetor and direct it into a one pint container.

4. Turn on the ignition switch. The container should fill within 30-45 seconds.

5. Connect a pressure gauge to the fuel line and operate the pump again. If the battery is supplying the required 12.6 volts or more, the gauge should read 3-4½ psi (0.21-0.31 kg/cm^2).

If there is fuel in the tank, but none is delivered by the pump, check both the electric fuel fuse (20 amp) and gauge fuse (10 amp) in the fuse panel under the dash. Before reconnecting the fuel line, install a new filter.

Replacement

1. Disconnect battery ground cable and remove gauge sending unit as previously described.

2. Remove the flat conductor from the fuel pickup tube plastic clip.

3. Release the clamp and slide the pump back about ½ in.

4. Disconnect wire from terminals, and remove pump from tank unit.

5. With rubber isolator and saran strainer attached to the new fuel pump, slide it through the circular support bracket so that it rests against the rubber coupling.

6. Connect the pump terminal wires, with the flat conductor on the terminal located away from the float arm.

7. Complete pump installation by pushing it into the rubber coupling, and connect the wire conductor to the plastic clip on the fuel tube.

POSITIVE CRANKCASE VENTILATION (PCV) SYSTEM

Crankcase vapors resulting from combustion blow-by are removed and fresh air is drawn in from a connection to the air cleaner. These combustible vapors are mixed with the normal air/fuel mixture from the carburetor in the intake manifold and are burned. The PCV valve varies the amount of flow through the system depending on engine load and also protects the engine from internal damage in case of backfire.

Replacing the PCV valve is a normal routine maintenance procedure (Chapter Two). Improper operation of the PCV valve usually results in one or more of the following symptoms:

1. Rough idle
2. Oil present in air cleaner
3. Oil leaks
4. Excessive oil sludging or dilution

Check also for deteriorated hoses that need replacing.

EXHAUST GAS RECIRCULATION SYSTEM

Exhaust gas recirculation is used to reduce emission oxides of nitrogen by lowering combustion temperatures. Under normal operating load (cruising speed) a small amount of inert exhaust gas is returned to the intake manifold. This is controlled by the EGR valve (**Figure 32**) on top of the intake manifold. At idle, recirculation is not required and a leaky EGR valve sometimes appears as a rough idle.

EGR Valve Inspection

1. Remove EGR valve by disconnecting vacuum line and removing nuts and washers securing the unit.

2. Manually depress valve diaphragm to check for freedom of movement. If sticky or immovable, clean valve.

3. Apply vacuum to vacuum line and check for leaks. If leaky, rebuild or replace unit.

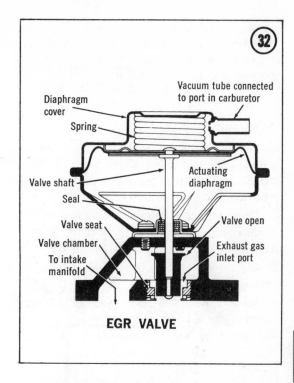

EGR VALVE

4. Inspect valve and seat and remove any deposits. Avoid getting particles into valve seat or intake manifold. A commercial abrasive spark plug cleaner is a convenient means of removing large deposits.

> CAUTION
> *Avoid using solvents or degreasers to clean valve assembly or diaphragm may be damaged.*

5. Inspect vacuum line and manifold gasket. Replace as necessary.

EVAPORATION CONTROL SYSTEM

This system, shown in **Figure 33**, consists of a vapor separator located on the fuel tank and an evaporative canister in the left front corner of the engine compartment (**Figure 34**). The canister absorbs and temporarily stores vapors from the fuel tank and carburetor fuel bowl. The stored vapors are drawn into the combustion chambers, through the carburetor, after the engine is running.

> NOTE: *A pressure-vacuum fuel tank cap is required for this system to function properly.*

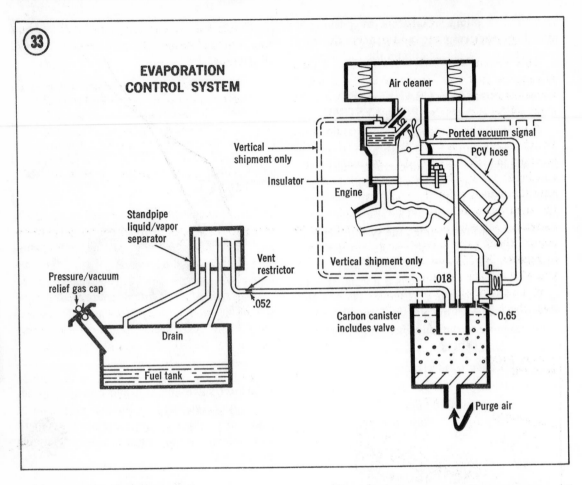

(33)

EVAPORATION CONTROL SYSTEM

Air cleaner

Ported vacuum signal

PCV hose

Vertical shipment only

Insulator

Engine

Standpipe liquid/vapor separator

Vent restrictor

Vertical shipment only

.018

Pressure/vacuum relief gas cap

.052

Carbon canister includes valve

0.65

Drain

Fuel tank

Purge air

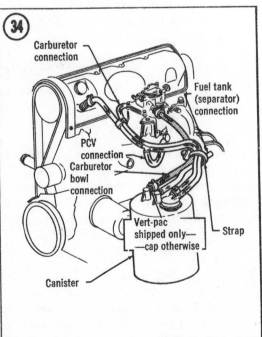

(34)

Carburetor connection

Fuel tank (separator) connection

PCV connection

Carburetor bowl connection

Vert-pac shipped only— cap otherwise

Strap

Canister

Replace the filter located in the bottom of the canister every 12 months or 12,000 miles (30,000 miles on 1975-1977 cars). The canister must be disconnected and removed from its mounting to replace the filter (**Figure 35**). When replacing the canister filter, examine all hose connection openings for obstruction. Apply vacuum to the small hose leading to the cap of the canister purge valve. If it does not hold vacuum, snap off the cap (slowly, as it is under spring tension) and replace necessary parts.

(35)

TRANSMISSION CONTROLLED SPARK (TCS)

This system eliminates distributor vacuum advance in first and second gears on standard transmissions and low gear on Torque Drive and Powerglide, except when the engine is cold.

A vacuum advance solenoid is controlled by 2 switches; one on the transmission energizing the solenoid in high, the second a temperature override below 93°F. The TCS system tends to aggravate the tendency for the engine to diesel with the ignition switch off, so an idle stop (anti-dieseling) solenoid is used on the carburetor to control the throttle valve closing. The diagrams in **Figures 36, 37, and 38** will help familiarize you with the TCS system.

If the engine surges or hesitates on acceleration, check TCS system operation as follows.

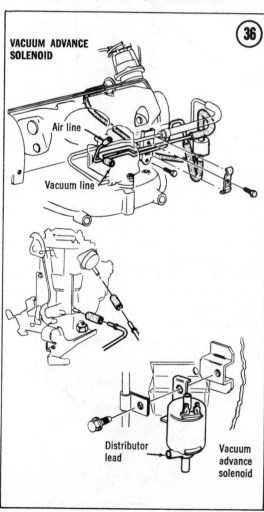

1. Connect a vacuum gauge into the vacuum line running between the TCS solenoid and the distributor.

> NOTE: *Engines equipped with standard transmissions will not show full vacuum, at this connection, in the high gears when the engine is idling (rear wheels are off the ground). Engines equipped with the automatic transmission must be driven to shift into high gear.*

2. If the gauge registers vacuum in all gears, check for blown fuse, wire disconnected at transmission switch or solenoid, and faulty transmission or TCS solenoid switch. If this does not locate the trouble, unplug the wire from the temperature sending unit located on the right side of the block between No. 1 and No. 2 spark plugs. This disconnects the temperature override switch. Replace the switch if the gauge now registers vacuum when required.

3. If the gauge registers no vacuum in the high gears, check for wrong connection of clean air line and vacuum line at the solenoid, leak in vacuum hoses, grounded transmission switch or lead wire, and broken plunger return spring.

AIR INJECTION REACTOR (AIR) SYSTEM

This system consists of an air pump (driven by the engine via a belt), air diverter valve, check valve, air hose, and a signal pipe. See **Figure 39**. The air pump compresses air and injects it into the exhaust system near the exhaust valves. This promotes further burning of the exhaust gases and in this way reduces the amount of contaminants emitted from the exhaust pipe.

Air Pump Inspection

The AIR pump, except for filter replacement, is non-repairable and must be replaced as a unit if defective. To check the air pump, start engine, disengage air hose, and accelerate to about 1,500 rpm and note the flow of air from the pump. If air flow increases as engine speed increases, pump is functioning properly. If air speed does not increase, proceed with inspection.

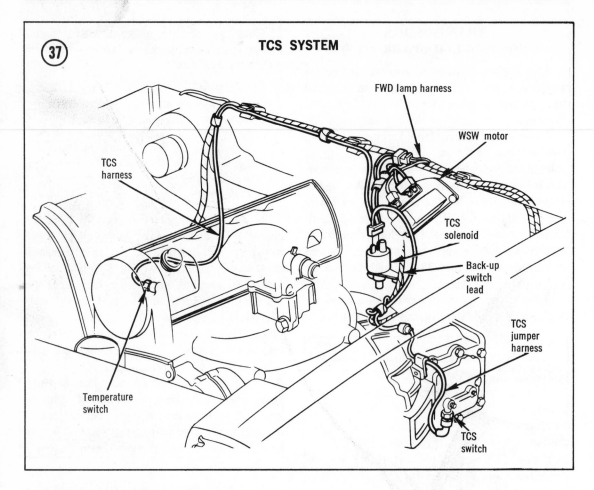

TCS SYSTEM

(37)

FWD lamp harness

WSW motor

TCS harness

TCS solenoid

Back-up switch lead

TCS jumper harness

Temperature switch

TCS switch

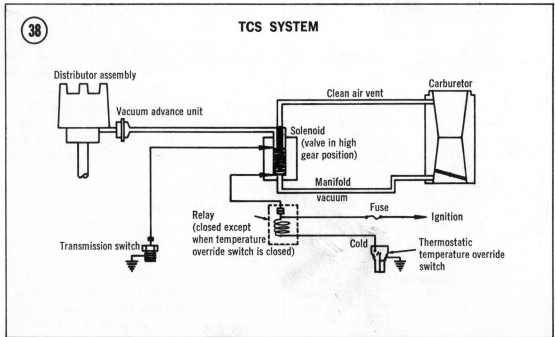

TCS SYSTEM

(38)

Distributor assembly

Clean air vent

Carburetor

Vacuum advance unit

Solenoid (valve in high gear position)

Manifold vacuum

Fuse

Ignition

Relay (closed except when temperature override switch is closed)

Transmission switch

Cold

Thermostatic temperature override switch

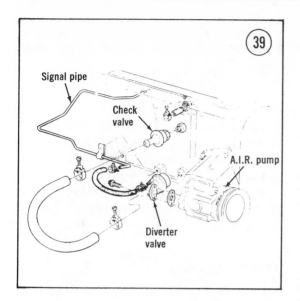

Signal pipe

Check valve

A.I.R. pump

Diverter valve

1. Check drive belt for proper tension.

2. Check the diverter valve for a leaky relief valve. If this valve is leaking, escaping air will be heard. In this case, replace diverter valve.

3. If excessive noise appears to be originating from the pump (some noise is normal), remove the drive belt and operate the engine. If the noise continues, it is not coming from the pump.

4. If the noise stops after performing Step 3, check for a seized pump. If pump seems OK, check hoses and connections for leaks and proper routing. Also check the pump for proper mounting. If noise still persists, replace pump.

Air Pump Replacement

1. Compress drive belt to hold pulley from turning, then loosen pump pulley bolts.

2. Loosen alternator mounting bolt at thermostat housing and loosen bolt at adjustment bracket, then remove drive belt.

3. Remove pulley bolts, then remove pulley.

4. Disconnect hoses at pump.

5. Remove pump mounting bolts and remove pump.

6. Installation is the reverse of the above steps. Torque pump pulley bolts to 25 ft.-lb. (3.4 mkg). Drive belt tension should be 50-75 lb. (22.7-39.0 kg) for a used belt or 120-130 lb. (54.5-59.0 kg) for a new belt, as measured with a strand tension gauge.

Pump Filter Replacement

1. Remove air pump and pulley as outlined in *Air Pump Replacement*.

2. Pry the filter fan outer disc loose and remove.

3. Pull off remainder of filter with pliers (**Figure 40**).

NOTE: *Don't allow filter fragments to enter the pump air intake port.*

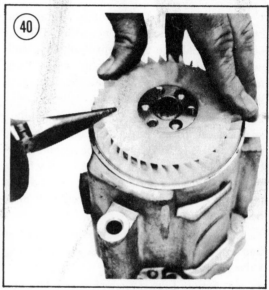

4. Use the pump pulley and attaching bolts as a tool to press the new filter into place. Apply torque evenly to all bolts, using a crisscross alternating pattern. Make sure outer edge of filter slips into housing of pump.

NOTE: *A slight amount of interference between the filter and housing can be expected. Squealing may also be heard after a new filter has been installed. This is normal and should disappear after a short time of operation.*

AIR System Hose Inspection/Replacement

1. With engine running, check all AIR system hoses and connections with a soapy water solution. If bubbles result, replace faulty hose or tighten leaking connection.

2. When replacing hose, use only hose designed for AIR system high temperatures. No substitutes should be made.

AIR Check Valve

The check valve is non-repairable and defective valves must be replaced as a unit. To inspect the check valve, remove hose and blow through valve toward engine. Then attempt to suck air back through the valve. If the latter is possible, the valve is defective and must be replaced.

Diverter Valve Inspection/Replacement

1. Check routing and condition of all lines and connections and correct as necessary. Disconnect the signal line at the diverter valve and, with the engine running, check line with a finger for presence of a vacuum signal. Replace signal line if no signal is present.

2. With the engine running at normal idling speed, check to see if air is escaping from the diverter valve muffler. This can be accomplished by manually opening the valve to discharge through the muffler for a second or two and then closing the valve. If valve is defective, it must be replaced.

3. Remove valve by first removing signal line and air hose. Then remove screws attaching valve to pump.

4. Installation is the reverse of Step 3. Use new gasket and torque attaching screws to 85 in.-lb. (78.3 cmkg). After installing signal line and air hose, check all connections for leaks.

CATALYTIC CONVERTER
(1975-1977)

All 1975 and some 1976-1977 Vegas are equipped with exhaust systems that include catalytic converters. These converters cause exhaust gases to flow through beads which are coated with a catalytic material containing palladium and platinum. The interaction of the gases with these materials causes further combustion and reduces the emission of air pollutants.

Catalytic converters do not require periodic maintenance. Catalytic materials may lose their effectiveness, however, and require replacement. As high temperatures are produced in the converter, the container may also eventually require replacement. Testing of catalysts, and replacement of catalysts or converters, require equip-ment and skills not readily available except at a dealer or authorized exhaust system repair shop.

FUEL TANK

The fuel tank is secured to the vehicle with 2 retaining straps. The fuel gauge and the fuel pump assembly are retained in the tank as shown in **Figure 41**.

Part of the Evaporation Control System (ECS) connections are located at the fuel tank as shown in **Figure 42**.

Tank Replacement

Disconnect battery ground cable. Drain tank with a siphon hose. Disconnect gauge wire, fuel line at gauge unit, tank vent lines to vapor separator, and ground wire from under body floor pan. Remove tank strap bolts and tank.

Gauge Sending Unit Replacement

Remove tank as described previously. Remove cam lock (use tool J-22554 as shown in **Figure 43**, if available). Remove sending unit and gasket, being careful not to damage the screen at the end of the pickup pipe. Use a new gasket when reinstalling.

EXHAUST SYSTEM

Figure 44 shows the general layout of the exhaust system. Note that the exhaust pipe travels from the left-hand side of the car, under the drive shaft, to the right side where it attaches to the transverse mounted muffler. The exhaust pipe and muffler are clamped together, but the muffler and tailpipe are welded together in production.

To replace the tailpipe, it must be cut from the muffler. Allow ½ in. for attachment of a replacement tailpipe, using clamps. **Figure 45** shows the muffler exhaust and the tailpipe hanger details.

When replacing exhaust system parts, leave all clamps loose, and adjust system to clearances shown in Figure 44, then tighten clamps securely.

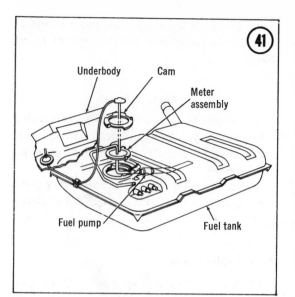

(41)

Underbody   Cam

Meter assembly

Fuel pump

Fuel tank

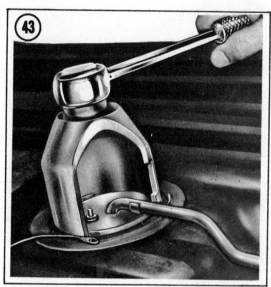

(43)

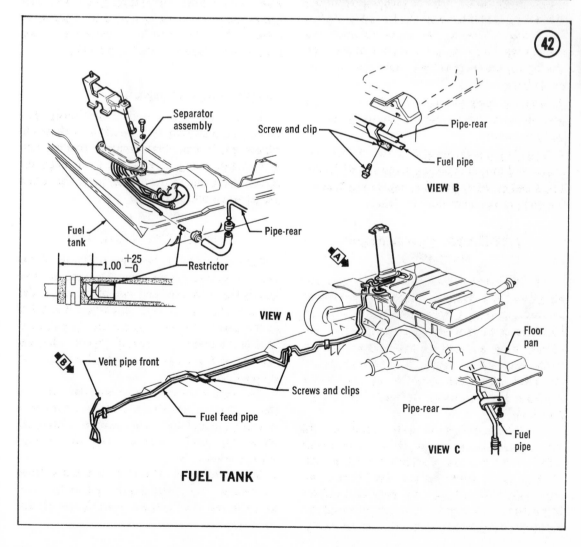

(42)

Separator assembly

Screw and clip

Pipe-rear

Fuel pipe

VIEW B

Fuel tank

Pipe-rear

Restrictor

$1.00 {+25 \atop -0}$

VIEW A

Floor pan

Vent pipe front

Screws and clips

Fuel feed pipe

Pipe-rear

Fuel pipe

VIEW C

FUEL TANK

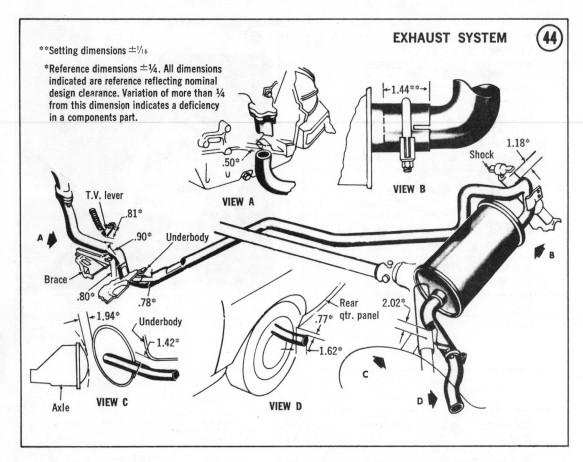

EXHAUST SYSTEM ④④

**Setting dimensions ±1/16

*Reference dimensions ±¼. All dimensions indicated are reference reflecting nominal design clearance. Variation of more than ¼ from this dimension indicates a deficiency in a components part.

VIEW A

1.44**

Shock

1.18*

VIEW B

T.V. lever

.81*

A

.90* Underbody

Brace

.80*

.78*

1.94*

Underbody

1.42*

Axle VIEW C

Rear qtr. panel

.77*

1.62*

2.02*

C

B

D

VIEW D

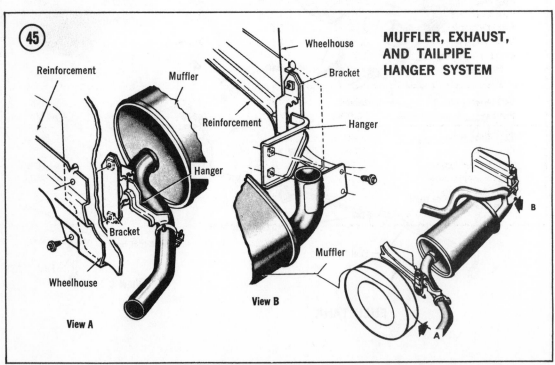

④⑤ MUFFLER, EXHAUST, AND TAILPIPE HANGER SYSTEM

Reinforcement

Muffler

Wheelhouse

Bracket

Reinforcement

Hanger

Hanger

Bracket

Muffler

Wheelhouse

B

View B

View A

A

Table 1 ROCHESTER CARBURETOR ADJUSTMENTS

Carburetor Number:	7041023	7041024	7042023 7042993	7041182
Float level	1/16 in.	1/16 in.	⅛ in.	⅝ in.
Float drop				1¾ in.
Pump rod				1⅜ in.
Fast idle (bench)	0.110 in.	0.110 in.	0.110 in.	
Choke rod	0.080 in.	0.120 in.		0.080 in.
Vacuum brake	0.140 in.	0.200 in.		0.120 in.
Unloader	0.350 in.	0.350 in.		0.180 in.

Carburetor Number:	7042106 7042107 7042822 7042827	7044023 7044033 7044323 7044333	7044024 7044034 7044324 7044334	7045025 7045029 7045024 7045028	17056023 17056027 17056022 17056026
Float level	19/32 in.	1/16 in.	1/16 in.	⅛ in.	⅛
Float drop	1⅞ in.				
Pump rod	1-1/16 in.				
Choke rod		0.080 in.	0.080 in.	0.080 in.	0.045
Vacuum brake		0.130 in.	0.130 in.	0.100 in.	0.060prim/ 0.450 sec.
Unloader		0.375 in.	0.375 in.	0.450 in.	0.215

Table 2 HOLLEY CARBURETOR ADJUSTMENTS

Carburetor Number:	338179 338181	338168 338170	348659 348663	348661 348665	348660 348664
Float drop	0.420 in.	0.420 in.	0.420 in.	0.420 in.	0.420 in.
Float level	1.0 in.	1.0 in.	1.0 in.	1.0 in.	1.0 in.
Fast idle cam index	0.140 in.	0.140 in.			0.110 in.
Choke vacuum break	0.300 in.	0.400 in.	0.325 in.	0.275 in.	0.300 in.
Choke index setting (notches rich)	2½	3½	3	3	4

Carburetor Number:	348662 348666	366829 366831	366833 366841	366830 366832	366834 366840
Float drop	0.420 in.	0.420 in.	0.420 in.	0.420 in.	0.420 in.
Float level	1.0 in.				
Fast idle cam index	0.110 in.	0.320 in.	0.320 in.	0.320 in.	0.320 in.
Choke vacuum break	0.275 in.	0.313 in.	0.268 in.	0.288 in.	0.268 in.
Choke index setting (notches rich)	4	2	2	3	3

CHAPTER SEVEN

ELECTRICAL SYSTEM

This chapter includes information on battery, fusing, alternator/regulator, starter, distributor and coil, lights, instruments, and electrical accessories. Electrical specification tables are located at the end of this chapter.

The heart of the Vega 12-volt electrical system is a 10-S1 Series Delcotron AC generator (alternator), which includes a solid state regulator within its frame. In addition to providing electricity for the starter, ignition, instruments, lighting, and conventional accessories, the generator—coupled with a power rated (rather than ampere-hour rated) storage battery—services the electric windshield wiper motor, the electric fuel pump, the optional rear window defogger, and numerous small devices and switches.

Electrical circuits in the Vega are protected by a fuse block (located on the fire wall just above the dimmer switch), a circuit breaker in the headlight switch, and fusible links in the wiring at the points shown in **Table 1**. Fusible links can be replaced by splicing. Obtain replacement links at dealer.

Cars equipped with air conditioning include a 30 amp fuse in the wire running from the horn relay to the air conditioning relay. Other fuse specifications can be found in **Table 2**.

Table 2   FUSE SPECIFICATIONS

Turn flasher, fuel gauge instrument panel warning lights, seat belt warning, heat gauge, tachometer, back-up lights, TCS idle stop sol. (gauges)	20A
Electric fuel run	10A
Radio	10A
Wiper	25A
Heater or air conditioner	25A
Instrument panel lights, radio light	4A
Traffic hazard flasher, stop lights	20A
Tail lights, marker lights, park lights	20A
Clock, dome, lighter, courtesy	20A
Electric fuel start	10A

BATTERY

The classification of the original equipment battery in the Vega is identified by a measurement called peak watt rating. The product of the maximum current and maximum voltage determine the peak watt rating value, which is embossed on the battery case. Batteries are usually classified by ampere-hours, which is, typically, the amperage furnished for a period of 20 hours at a specified cell voltage. When

Table 1　　FUSIBLE LINKS—In Engine Compartment

Starter solenoid	14 gauge wire on BAT side 20 gauge wire on IGN side
Ammeter	20 gauge wire at junction block (circuit 106) 14 gauge wire at junction block (circuit 2)
Molded splice(s) at solenoid BAT terminal (with Electro-Clear) to horn relay	14 gauge brown wire
Molded splice located at the horn relay to bulkhead connector	16 gauge black wire
Molded splice in ammeter circuit (both sides of meter)	20 gauge orange wire
Molded splice between horn relay control timer	10 gauge red wire

replacing a battery, do not confuse the ampere-hour rating with the peak watt rating.

Refer to the *Tune-up* section in Chapter Two for battery maintenance.

Often, a perfectly good battery will fail because of inadequate charging. Causes include a slipping alternator drive belt, slow speed, short duration driving, a faulty Delcotron unit, or low voltage regulator setting.

There is a simple test to determine whether a short exists in the electrical system when the car is parked with the ignition off. Disconnect the battery ground cable at the battery terminal, making sure the ignition key and all lights and accessories are turned off. If there is a short in the system, sparking will occur when the battery ground terminal is struck with the end of the grounding cable.

CAUTION

Disconnect battery positive (+) terminal before working on vehicle electrical system.

Battery Testing

After visual inspection, perform an instrument test. Follow the testing instrument manufacturer's directions. If tests indicate that a battery is good, but it becomes discharged after a short time in service, conduct a hydrometer test.

NOTE: *Do not take the hydrometer reading immediately after water has been added to the battery. Charge first at a relatively high rate for 15-20 minutes.*

NOTE: *Freedom Batteries used in late models are sealed and the hydrometer test cannot be performed on them.*

A full charge is indicated by a hydrometer reading of 1.270 after correcting for temperature. Lower readings indicate an undercharged or defective battery; higher readings indicate that the cells have not been properly filled or serviced.

Unless the electrolyte temperature is 80°F, the hydrometer reading must be adjusted 4 specific gravity points (0.004) for every 10°F variation. Add 4 points for every 10°F above 80°F; subtract 4 points for every 10°F below 80°F.

If you have no battery testing instruments, but do have a hydrometer, conduct a specific gravity cell comparison. This test can be performed without regard to the amount of charge in the battery. Measure and record the specific gravity of each cell. If there is a difference of 50 points (0.050) or more, the battery is defective.

Battery Charging

Avoid possible damage to the charging circuit by disconnecting battery before charging. Charging rate and time depend on the age and condition of the battery, temperature of the electrolyte, electrical capacity, and the state of charge. Charging should be stopped (or the charging rate reduced) if the electrolyte temperature exceeds 125°F, or if gassing causes spewing of the electrolyte.

NOTE: *When the charge indicator on a Freedom Battery becomes light, do not attempt to charge or "jump" the battery. The battery must be replaced.*

If the green dot fails to appear on a Freedom Battery charge indicator after the battery has been fully charged on a constant voltage charger, it may be necessary to tip the battery from side to side a few times to cause the dot to appear.

STARTER

Refer to the sectional view (**Figure 1**) and the exploded view (**Figure 2**) of the starting motor and solenoid switch. In addition to the starting circuit test (Chapter Two, *Engine Tune-up*), the following checks can be made with the starter installed.

Solenoid Check

If no solenoid action is observed when the starting switch is closed, measure the voltage drop between the switch and battery terminals on the solenoid; it should not exceed 3.5 volts. If the solenoid meets this test, measure the volt-age at the switch terminal of the solenoid. The solenoid should pull in if 7.7 volts are measured at the switch terminal. If the solenoid is warm, a slightly higher voltage will be required. If the solenoid does not pull in, and low voltage is measured, check the solenoid control circuit for high resistance.

If the solenoid does not pull in and greater than 7.7 volts is measured, the starter will have to be removed to check for solenoid current draw, starting motor pinion clearance, and freedom of shift linkage. If the solenoid engages and disengages rapidly, but does not hold in, there may be an open circuit in the solenoid winding.

Neutral Start Switch

All models contain a neutral start switch. The switch is activated by the shift lever on cars equipped with automatic transmissions and by the clutch for standard transmission cars.

Refer to **Figure 3** for replacement on the automatic transmissions. The shift lever should be in NEUTRAL when removing and replacing the switch. New switches have a plastic pin to index the switch during installation. After the switch is installed, the plastic pin is sheared by moving the shift lever out of NEUTRAL.

Figure 4 shows the clutch-operated neutral start switch. Remove by simply depressing the switch shaft barb retainer and pushing the shaft out of the hole in the clutch arm. Then slide switch off its pivot.

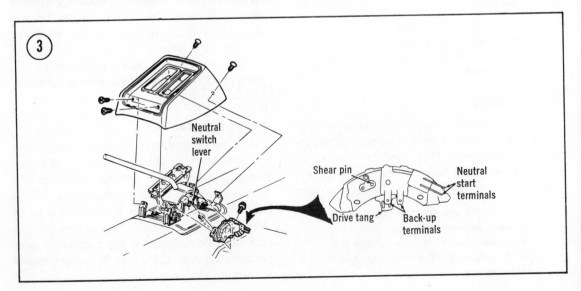

Neutral switch lever

Shear pin

Drive tang

Back-up terminals

Neutral start terminals

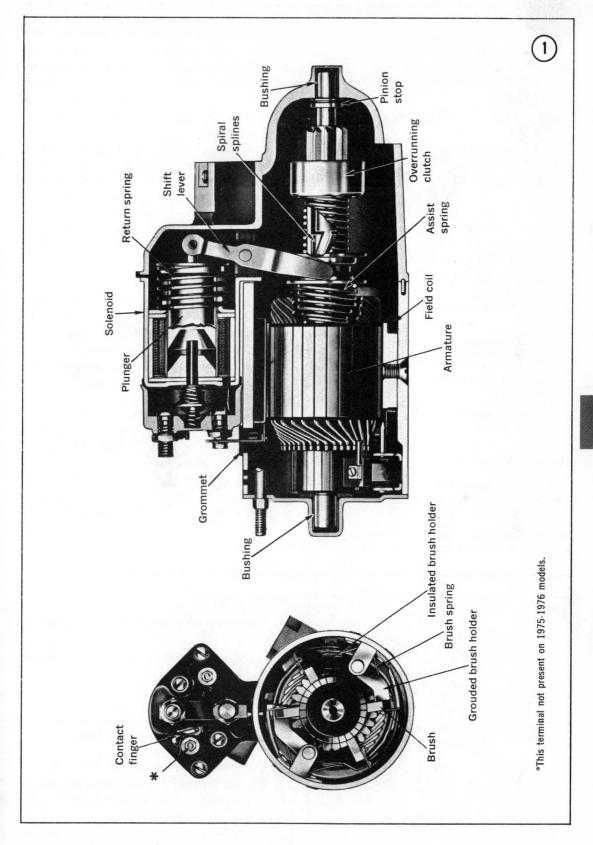

1

Bushing

Pinion stop

Spiral splines

Shift lever

Return spring

Overrunning clutch

Assist spring

Solenoid

Field coil

Plunger

Armature

Grommet

Bushing

Insulated brush holder

Brush spring

Grouded brush holder

Contact finger

Brush

*

*This terminal not present on 1975-1976 models.

7

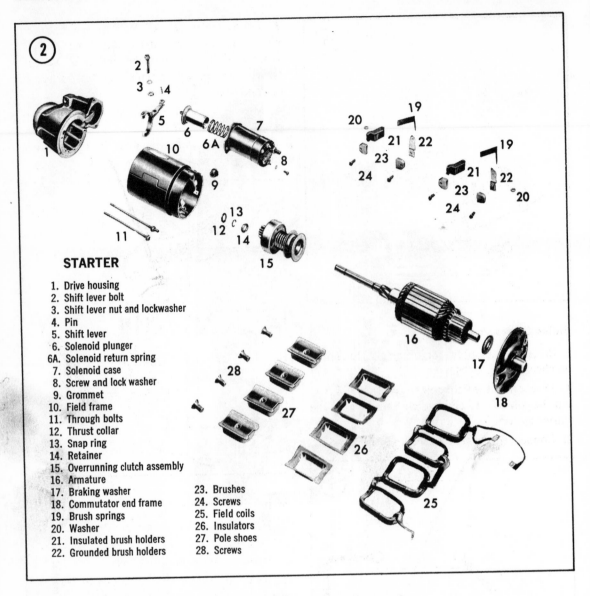

STARTER

1. Drive housing
2. Shift lever bolt
3. Shift lever nut and lockwasher
4. Pin
5. Shift lever
6. Solenoid plunger
6A. Solenoid return spring
7. Solenoid case
8. Screw and lock washer
9. Grommet
10. Field frame
11. Through bolts
12. Thrust collar
13. Snap ring
14. Retainer
15. Overrunning clutch assembly
16. Armature
17. Braking washer
18. Commutator end frame
19. Brush springs
20. Washer
21. Insulated brush holders
22. Grounded brush holders
23. Brushes
24. Screws
25. Field coils
26. Insulators
27. Pole shoes
28. Screws

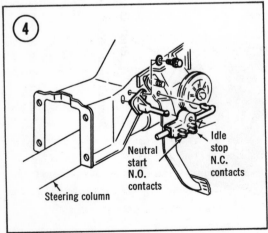

Starter Removal

1. Disconnect the ground cable from the battery terminal.

2. Disconnect all wires and cables from the solenoid switch.

> NOTE: *Wiring cable terminals at the solenoid may have different thread sizes. Use care in replacing nuts.*

3. Loosen the front bracket bolt (**Figure 5**).

4. Remove the front bracket bolt at the engine, rotate the bracket, and lower the starter from its mounting, front end first.

Pinion Clearance Check

Before disassembly, pinion clearance should be checked if possible.

1. Disconnect the field coil strap. This will permit the solenoid to activate without turning the starter motor.

2. Connect the battery as shown in **Figure 6**.

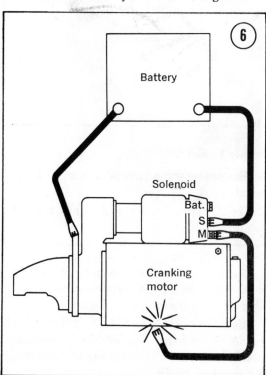

3. Connect the jumper lead to the solenoid motor terminal and strike the other end to ground. This will shift the pinion to its full travel where it will remain until the battery is disconnected.

4. Measure the clearance as shown in **Figure 7** (0.010-0.140 in./0.25-3.55mm). Excessive clearance indicates wear in the shifting mechanism and should be corrected.

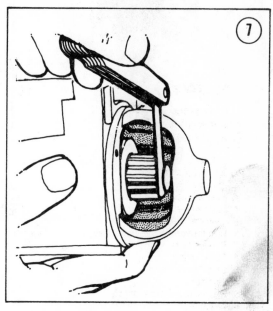

Starter Disassembly

1. Remove the field strap terminal nut from the solenoid.

2. Remove starter through bolts.

3. Remove drive housing from assembly, and remove thrust washers from the shaft if they do not come off with the housing.

4. Remove the pinion stop/retainer by sliding a short length of ½ in. pipe onto the shaft, as shown in **Figure 8**, and tapping the retainer toward the armature to reveal the snap ring.

5. Remove snap ring and slide retainer and clutch from the shaft.

6. Remove commutator end frame. Disconnect brushes by releasing the V-springs from the brush holders, removing the support pins, and lifting out holders, brushes, and springs as a unit.

7. Disconnect leads from each brush.

8. Withdraw armature.

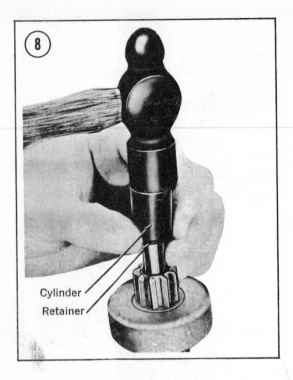

Cylinder

Retainer

NOTE: *Do not remove field coils unless replacement is necessary.*

Cleaning and Inspection

CAUTION
Do not use grease-dissolving solvent when cleaning the armature, field coils, or overrunning clutch.

1. The overrunning clutch should lock in the cranking direction and run freely in the overrunning direction. Examine the pinion teeth for excessive wear, chipping, and cracks. Examine the spring and collar for wear. This unit can be disassembled by forcing the collar toward the clutch and removing the lock ring (**Figure 9**).

2. Examine brush holders, and make sure brush slides freely through them.

3. Replace brushes if excessively pitted or worn.

4. Check for worn armature shaft bushings.

5. Check for out-of-roundness or a rough commutator.

Testing

1. Use a growler to check the armature for a short circuit. If a short circuit is indicated, clean between the commutator bars and recheck.

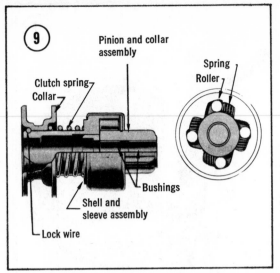

Pinion and collar assembly

Clutch spring

Collar

Spring

Roller

Bushings

Shell and sleeve assembly

Lock wire

NOTE: *Commutators with molded insulation should not be undercut.*

2. Check the armature for ground by placing one growler lead on the armature core or shaft and the other on the commutator as shown in **Figure 10**.

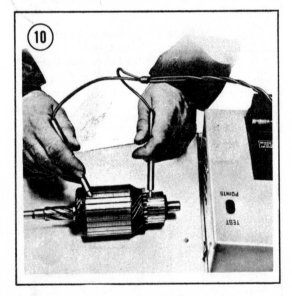

3. Test for field coil continuity by placing one growler lead on the field connector bar and the other on an *insulated* brush (**Figure 11**).

4. Disconnect the shunt coil (if equipped) and test for a grounded field coil by placing one growler lead on a connector bar and the other on a *grounded* brush.

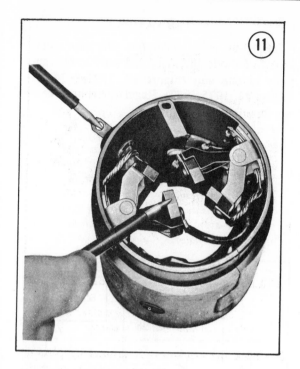

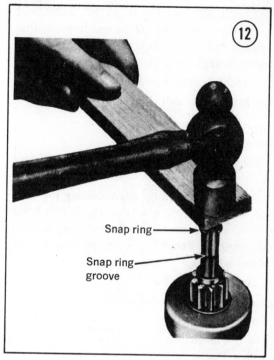

Commutator Repair

1. A rough or out-of-round commutator should be turned in a lathe. Use care not to cut into the armature-to-commutator leads.

2. Undercut insulation (unless molded insulation is used 1/32 in. (0.8mm) deep and the full width of the insulation, but no wider. Clean the slots after cut, and finish the commutator with No. 00 sandpaper.

3. Check again for short circuits.

Starter Assembly

1. Reassemble and connect brushes.

2. Apply silicone lubricant to the armature shaft drive end.

3. Install clutch assembly.

4. Install retainer with flat face toward pinion.

5. Force the snap ring over the shaft as shown in **Figure 12**, and slide it into shaft groove.

6. Install thrust collar, and force retainer over snap ring as shown in **Figure 13**.

7. Apply a silicone lubricant to the drive housing bushing. Slide the assembled armature and clutch into the drive housing, with the shift lever properly engaged in the collar.

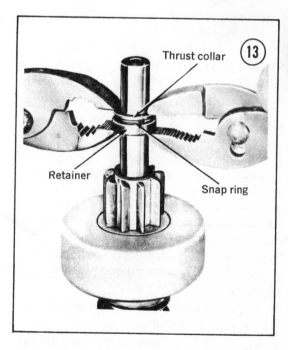

8. Slide the field frame over the armature, guiding the brushes over the commutator. Engage the index pin in the drive housing, and seat the assembly.

9. Install the leather brake washer on the armature shaft.

10. Apply silicone lubricant to the commutator end frame bushing. Install the end frame so that through bolt holes are correctly positioned. Install through bolts.

11. Recheck pinion clearance.

12. Install field coil strap terminal nut.

Solenoid Repair

Solenoid repair consists primarily of contact cleaning or replacement.

1. Remove solenoid by disconnecting the field coil strap terminal, removing the 2 mounting screws, and twisting the solenoid clockwise to disengage the flange key from the keyway slot in the housing.

2. Refer to **Figure 14**.

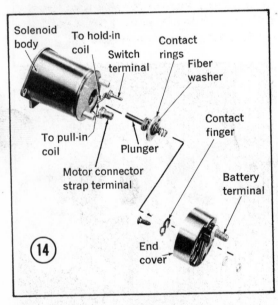

3. Remove nuts and washers from terminals along with the 2 cover retaining screws, and remove cover.

4. Remove battery terminal, resistor bypass terminal, and contact finger.

5. Remove field coil connector strap terminal and replace, soldering in position.

6. Install new battery terminal.

7. Install the contact finger and resistor bypass terminal.

8. Reinstall cover and mount solenoid, referring to Step 1 above.

ALTERNATOR

The 10-SI series Delcotron alternator combines a 6-diode alternator and solid state regulator in one unit (**Figure 15**, 1971-1974, or **Figure 16**, 1975-1977). Regulator voltage cannot be adjusted.

> NOTE: *The alternator used in 1975-1977 models is identical to that used in previous years except that a 40 ohm resistor has been added to the warning indicator circuit. See Figure 16. This resistor ensures a definite warning light in the event of an open field circuit in the alternator.*

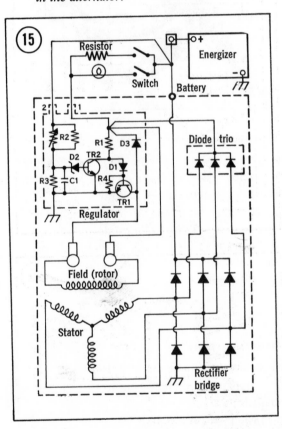

The charging circuit is protected by a fusible link in the 10-gauge wire running from the battery terminal on the starter solenoid to the horn relay. **Figure 17** shows the basic charging circuit.

CAUTION
Never polarize the alternator, nor operate it with battery (output) terminal disconnected. Do not ground or short across any charging circuit terminals.

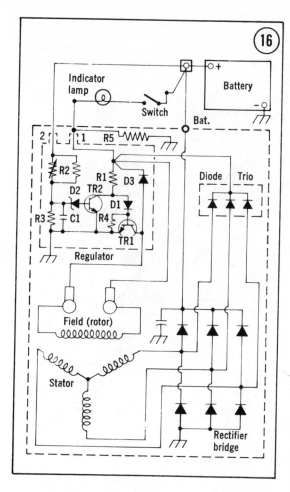

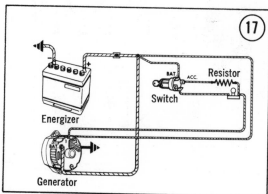

Indicator Light Circuit Check

This check does not apply to vehicles equipped with an ammeter.

1. If indicator light remains on with the ignition switch turned off, disconnect No. 1 and No. 2 alternator terminals (**Figure 18**). Check for a short between the 2 disconnected leads if the light stays on. If the light goes out, the rectifier bridge must be replaced.

2. If the indicator light stays off with the engine stopped and the switch on, check first for a burned out light bulb. Check for reversal of No. 1 and No. 2 leads. If neither of these checks reveals the trouble, there is an open circuit. Connect a voltmeter between ground and alternator terminal No. 2. No reading indicates an open circuit between the battery and the terminal.

3. Turn on switch and disconnect No. 1 and No. 2 terminal leads; *use care not to ground* No. 2 lead. Ground No. 1 lead. If indicator light remains off, and both the fuse and the fusible link are good, check for an open circuit in the No. 1 lead.

4. If light goes on, disconnect ground, and reconnect the 2 leads at the alternator. Ground alternator winding by pushing tab in end frame test hole with screwdriver (**Figure 19**).

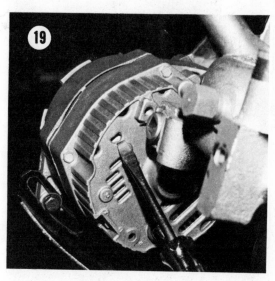

5. If light remains off, alternator must be removed to check field winding, slip rings, and brushes.

6. If light goes on, regulator must be replaced.

7. If indicator light stays on with engine running, and previous checks (drive belt tension, etc.) do not reveal the source of the trouble, check for an open circuit between the battery and alternator. Connect the voltmeter from the alternator battery terminal to ground; from the alternator No. 1 terminal to ground; and

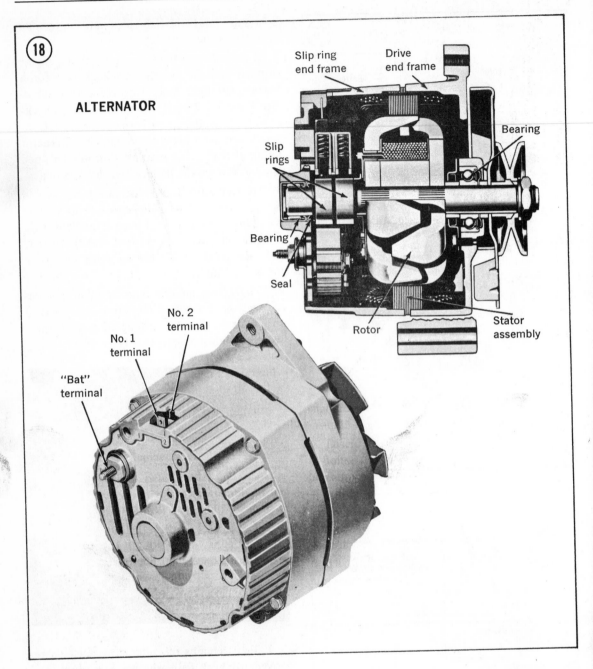

ALTERNATOR

Slip ring end frame

Drive end frame

Bearing

Slip rings

Bearing

Seal

Rotor

Stator assembly

No. 2 terminal

No. 1 terminal

"Bat" terminal

from alternator No. 2 terminal to ground. No reading at any of these points indicates an open circuit.

Alternator Check

1. Disconnect ground cable at battery, and battery lead from alternator terminal.

2. Reconnect battery ground cable and turn on all of the electrical accessories such as headlights, radio, windshield wipers, blower (high speed), etc.

3. With a carbon pile (variable load) connected across the battery terminals, accelerate the engine to 1,500-2,000 rpm and adjust carbon pile to achieve maximum current output.

4. If current output is not within 10% of specifications, ground the alternator (Figure 18) and readjust carbon pile for maximum output.

5. If output now meets specifications, replace regulator. If it does not, further tests must be made after alternator is removed.

Alternator Removal

Refer to **Figure 20**.

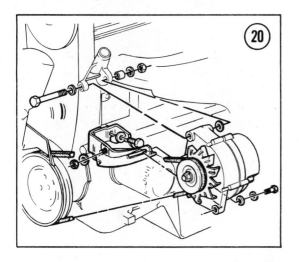

1. Disconnect the ground cable from the battery terminal.

2. Disconnect leads from alternator, and remove alternator adjusting bolt and nut from alternator mounting bolt.

3. Lift alternator, remove fan belt, and withdraw mounting bolt.

Alternator Disassembly

1. Remove the alternator pulley, holding shaft with 5/16 in. Allen wrench.

2. Remove 4 through bolts, and separate the alternator housing.

3. Disconnect the 3 stator leads, and remove stator from end frame.

> NOTE: *Without further disassembly, rotor, rectifier bridge, stator and diode trio brush lead clip can be checked* (*see* Testing).

4. Disconnect diode trio from brush holder assembly and remove the attached nuts from the 3 terminals.

5. Remove the battery terminal screw and the rectifier bridge attaching screw. Disconnect the capacitor lead.

6. Remove the brush holder attaching screws.

7. Remove capacitor.

8. Withdraw rotor and spacers from the drive end frame.

Cleaning and Inspection

Clean all metal parts, except stator, rotor, and slip ring end frame bearing in kerosene or solvent.

1. Remove bearing retainer plate from drive end frame. Remove bearing, wipe clean, and inspect. Do not relubricate bearing.

2. Clean rotor slip rings with 400-grain polishing cloth and inspect.

3. Out-of-round slip rings may be trued to within 0.001 in. (0.025mm) in a lathe. Slip rings are not replaceable.

4. Inspect brushes, springs, and holders for signs of wear.

Testing

Some of the following tests require an ohmmeter with a 1½-volt cell. Use the lowest range scale.

1. To each slip ring, connect a lead from a 110-volt test light or an ohmmeter. Rotor field windings are open if ohmmeter is high or light does not go on.

2. Check for shorted rotor field windings by connecting an ammeter in series with the 2 slip rings, using a 12-volt battery source. If the field amperage draw is above specifications, the windings are shorted.

3. Using a 110-volt test lamp or an ohmmeter, test for grounded stator windings (test light goes on, or ohmmeter reads low) and open stator windings (test light stays off, or ohmmeter reads high) by referring to the connections (**Figure 21**).

> NOTE: *Special test equipment is required to locate short circuits in the stator windings. Suspect a short if there are discolorations from heat on the winding or if all other electrical checks fail to locate the trouble.*

4. Using an ohmmeter, check between the brush lead and each of the 3 connectors of the diode

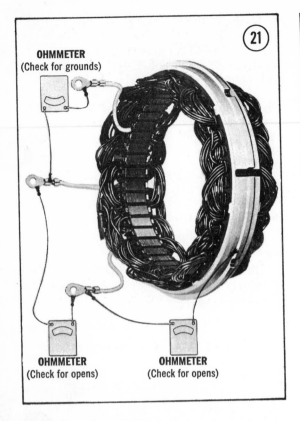

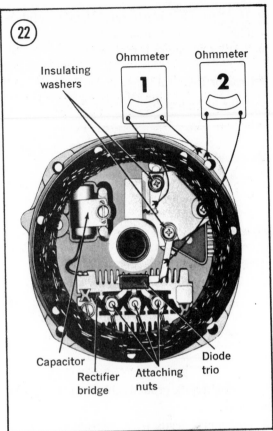

trio unit, reversing the test leads at every connector. A good unit will give one high and one low reading for each connector. Replace the unit if both readings are the same on any connector.

5. Check for a grounded brush lead before disassembly by connecting an ohmmeter as shown in **Figure 22**. Note the reading and reverse the leads. A ground is indicated if both readings are zero. Ground will be caused by a damaged or missing insulator sleeve, or by a defective regulator.

6. Check the rectifier bridge by referring to the ohmmeter connection in **Figure 23**. Check each of the 3 terminals on both the insulated and grounded side of the heat sink, reversing the leads at every terminal. One high and one low reading should be obtained each time the leads are reversed; if a pair of readings are the same, replace the entire bridge.

Slip Ring End Frame
Bearing Replacement

Unless there is adequate grease supply, this bearing should be replaced. Do not relubricate.

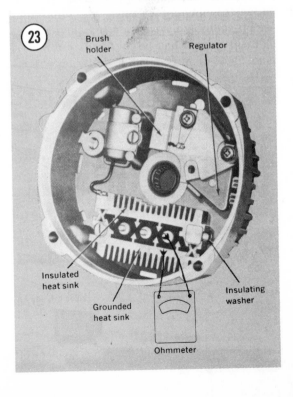

1. Bearing should be pressed out toward inside of housing.

2. Install new bearing from outside of housing. Put a plate over the bearing and support the bearing bore from the inside with a socket of suitable size. Make sure the bearing is properly aligned, and press it in until the plate is flush with the outside of the bearing bore.

Alternator Reassembly

1. If drive end bearing has been cleaned, refill ¼ full with high temperature bearing grease.

2. Press the assembled bearing and slinger (**Figure 24**) into end frame. Replace retainer plate if felt seal is worn, and install retainer plate, staking bolts to plate.

> NOTE: *Stake by punching the casting with a diamond- or center-point punch so that part of casting is raised against the bolt head or other item to be locked in place.*

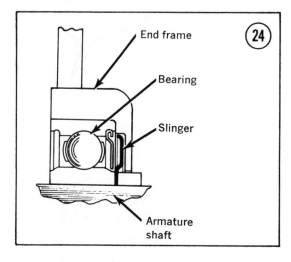

3. Install the rotor, and attach spacer, fan, and pulley.

4. Install washer and nut. Tighten to 40-50 ft.-lb. (5.5-6.9 mkg), using an Allen wrench and torque wrench with crowfoot attachment.

5. Mount capacitor in slip ring end frame.

6. Install the regulator and brush holder assemblies, using the 2 screws with special insulating sleeves.

7. Install the rectifier bridge with the attaching screw and the battery terminal screw.

8. Insert the diode trio and connect the brush lead clip. This finishes installation of the brush holder and regulator assemblies.

9. Install the stator and connect the leads to the rectifier bridge.

10. Lift brushes and insert toothpick at opening in slip ring end frame to hold brushes.

11. Install the slip ring end frame to the drive end frame.

12. Install 4 through bolts and remove toothpick from brush holder.

IGNITION

Refer to *Engine Tune-up* section for on-the-car ignition operations—such as replacing points and spark plugs—and certain distributor tests.

COIL AND CONDENSER

Various instruments are available for coil and condenser tests. Failure of either of these 2 components probably will stop engine operation completely and will severely affect performance in any case.

7

DISTRIBUTOR (1971-1974)

If a dwell meter shows a variation in cam angle reading greater than 3° between engine idle and 1,750 rpm, the distributor should be disassembled and inspected for wear. See **Figure 25**.

Removal

1. Disconnect distributor primary lead from coil and remove distributor cap.

2. Scribe the distributor body and engine in line with the rotor, noting the relative position of the vacuum advance chamber.

3. Remove distributor clamp and distributor from the engine.

> NOTE: *If engine is not rotated while distributor is out, distributor may be reinstalled in its original position by referring to the scribe mark on the body and engine block.*

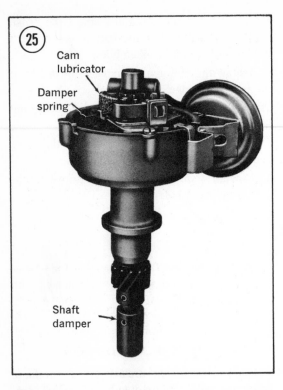

㉕

Cam lubricator

Damper spring

Shaft damper

Disassembly

1. Refer to **Figure 26**. Remove rotor, vacuum advance assembly, points, and condenser.

2. Remove the 2 breaker plate attachment screws, and lift the plate from the housing. Do not disassemble breaker plate.

3. Punch out the damper cup roll pin, and the gear roll pin. Slide both from the shaft. Now separate the shaft from the body.

4. Remove the screws from the break cover, and complete the disassembly by removing the weight springs, weights, and cam.

Cleaning and Inspection

1. Except for the vacuum advance assembly, breaker plate assembly, condenser, rotor, and distributor cap, all parts can be cleaned with solvent.

2. Inspect all parts for wear, and replace where necessary. Weights should move freely on the pivot pins. Shaft-to-body and cam-to-shaft bear-

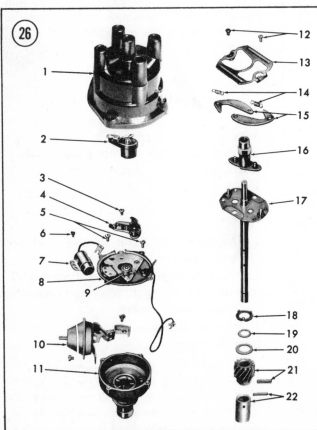

㉖

DISTRIBUTOR (1971-1974)

1. Distributor cap
2. Rotor
3. Contact point attaching screw
4. Contact point assembly
5. Breaker plate attaching screws
6. Condenser attaching screw
7. Condenser
8. Breaker plate assembly
9. Cam lubricator
10. Vacuum advance control assembly
11. Distributor housing
12. Weight cover attaching screws
13. Weight cover
14. Weight springs
15. Advance weights
16. Cam assembly
17. Distributor main shaft
18. Tanged washer
19. Wave washer
20. Flat washer
21. Drive gear and roll pin
22. Damper and roll pin

ing surfaces should be smooth. Shaft, cam, and body mating surfaces should fit freely, but without side play.

3. Shaft runout should not exceed 0.002 in. (0.05mm).

4. The distributor cap, rotor, points, condenser, and vacuum chamber should be checked according to tune-up procedures. Clean distributor cap high tension terminals with steel wool.

Assembly

1. Lubricate main shaft bearing surfaces with high temperature bearing grease, and slide cam onto shaft.

2. Install weights, springs, and weight cover.

3. Slide shift into distributor body and install washers, gear, and damper cup. Insert gear and damper cup roll pins.

> NOTE: *The damper cup fits into a cavity, which receives full engine oil pressure. The cap must be installed or engine oil pressure will drop below specifications.*

4. Install breaker plate, points, condenser, and vacuum advance assembly.

5. Adjust points, and check spring tension as described in *Engine Tune-up,* Chapter Two. Install rotor.

Installation

1. If crankshaft has not been rotated, omit Steps 2 and 3. Align rotor with scribe marks on distributor body and engine block.

2. If crankshaft has been rotated with the distributor removed, place finger on No. 1 plug hole and turn crankshaft clockwise until compression is felt. Continue turning until the pulley timing mark reaches 8° before top dead center.

3. Referring to **Figure 27**, insert distributor with vacuum advance unit pointing toward front of engine, and rotor pointing toward No. 1 distributor cap terminal.

4. With one hand holding distributor body in correct position, turn rotor clockwise about ⅛ turn so that gears will mesh and permit distributor to seat.

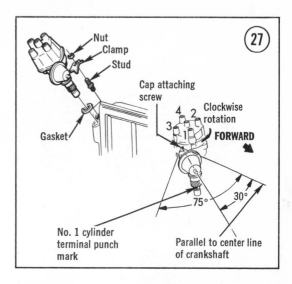

5. Slightly rotate distributor until points just begin to open. Rotor now should be aligned with No. 1 terminal (or scribe marks on the distributor body and block).

> NOTE: *Final adjustments will be accomplished with a timing light, thus absolute precision is not necessary.*

6. Tighten clamp, install cap and spark plug wires, and connect the primary and secondary coil wires.

7. Make final ignition timing adjustment as described in *Engine Tune-up,* Chapter Two.

DISTRIBUTOR (1975-1977)

All 1975-1977 Vegas are equipped with High Energy Ignition (HEI) systems. See **Figure 28**.

The HEI is a pulse-triggered, transistor controlled, inductive discharge system. Conventional breaker points are not used. Principal system elements are the ignition coil, electronic module, pickup assembly, and the centrifugal and vacuum advance mechanisms (**Figure 29**).

Ignition Coil

The HEI coil operates in basically the same way as a conventional coil, but is smaller in size and generates higher secondary voltage when the primary circuit is broken. The coil is the only HEI component not built into the distributor.

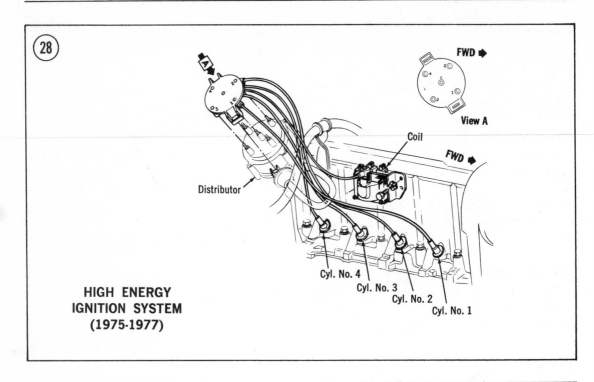

FWD ➡

View A

Coil

FWD ➡

Distributor

Cyl. No. 4
Cyl. No. 3
Cyl. No. 2
Cyl. No. 1

**HIGH ENERGY
IGNITION SYSTEM
(1975-1977)**

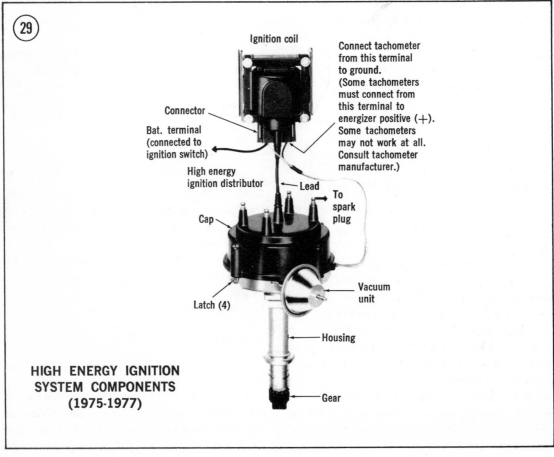

Ignition coil

Connect tachometer
from this terminal
to ground.
(Some tachometers
must connect from
this terminal to
energizer positive (+).
Some tachometers
may not work at all.
Consult tachometer
manufacturer.)

Connector

Bat. terminal
(connected to
ignition switch)

High energy
ignition distributor

Lead

To
spark
plug

Cap

Vacuum
unit

Latch (4)

Housing

**HIGH ENERGY IGNITION
SYSTEM COMPONENTS
(1975-1977)**

Gear

Electronic Module

Circuits within the electronic module perform 5 functions. These are spark triggering, switching, current limiting, dwell control, and distributor pickup.

Pickup Assembly

The pickup assembly consists of a rotating timer core with external teeth (turned by the distributor shaft), a stationary pole piece with internal teeth, and a pickup coil and magnet located between the pole piece and a bottom plate.

Centrifugal and Vacuum Advance

The centrifugal and vacuum advance mechanisms are basically identical to units used in breaker point ignition systems.

Operation

As the distributor shaft turns the timer core teeth out of alignment with the pole piece teeth, a voltage is created in the magnetic field of the pickup coil. The pickup coil sends this voltage to the electronic module, which determines from the rotational speed of the distributor shaft when to start building current in the ignition coil primary windings. When the timer core teeth are again aligned with the pole piece teeth, the magnetic field is changed, creating a different voltage. This signal is sent to the electronic module by the pickup coil and causes the module to shut off the ignition coil primary circuit. This collapses the coil magnetic field and induces a high secondary voltage to fire one spark plug.

The electronic module limits the 12-volt current to the ignition coil to 5-6 amperes. The module also triggers the opening and closing of the coil primary circuit with zero energy loss. In a conventional breaker point ignition system some energy can be lost due to point arcing and/or capacitor charging-time lag. Although a capacitor is present in the HEI system, it is used only as a radio noise suppressor. The efficiency of the triggering system allows up to approximately 35,000 volts to be delivered through the secondary wiring system to the spark plugs.

The module circuit controlling dwell angle causes the angle to increase as engine speed increases.

Preventive Maintenance

Routine maintenance is not required for the HEI system itself. If parts or components fail, they are not repairable and must be replaced. However, engine timing should be checked and the distributor components visually checked for cracks, wear, dust, moisture, burns, etc., every 18 months or 22,500 miles (36,000 km), whichever comes first. At the same time, the secondary wiring (spark plug wires) should be inspected, checked out with an ohmmeter, and replaced if necessary.

NOTE: *The HEI system has larger (8mm) diameter, silicone-insulated, spark plug wires. While these gray-colored wires are more heat resistant and less vulnerable to deterioration than conventional wires, they should not be mistreated. When removing wires from spark plugs, grasp only on the boots. Twist boot a ½ turn in either direction to break seal, then pull to remove.*

Spark plugs also should be replaced after every 22,500 miles (36,000 km).

The procedure for ignition timing is identical to that given above for conventional ignition systems, except that timing light connections should be made in parallel using an adapter at the No. 1 spark plug wire terminal on the distributor. The ignition coil has a special terminal marked TACH. Connect one lead of the tachometer to this terminal and the other to ground.

NOTE: *Some tachometers must connect from the TACH terminal to the battery positive terminal. Check the manufacturer's instructions before making connections.*

Corrective Maintenance

If a part in the HEI system fails, it must be replaced. See Chapter Three for diagnostic procedures. If the replacement of a part is necessary (other than the ignition coil) it may be necessary or more convenient to remove the distributor from the engine.

Distributor Removal

1. Unplug wiring harness connectors at side of distributor cap.

2. Remove distributor cap and position to one side out of the way.

3. Disconnect hose from vacuum advance mechanism.

4. Note the alignment of the rotor and make marks on the engine and the distributor housing so alignment can be duplicated when distributor is reinstalled.

5. Remove distributor hold-down clamp.

6. Lift distributor straight up and away from engine. Note and mark housing with final position of rotor. Also note position of vacuum advance unit in relation to engine.

Distributor Installation
(Engine Undisturbed)

If engine has not been disturbed since distributor was removed, proceed as follows.

1. Position the rotor to align with the last mark made on distributor body (Step 6 above).

2. Insert the distributor shaft into its hole and push down into position in the engine block. When fully inserted, the rotor should be aligned with the marks made in Step 4 above.

> NOTE: *It may be necessary to turn rotor slightly to mesh distributor gear with camshaft gear. However, rotor should line up with mark when fully inserted. If not, remove and repeat Steps 1 and 2.*

3. Install hold-down clamp and nut. Tighten nut snugly after making certain distributor body and rotor are in same relative position to engine as noted during removal.

4. Reinstall distributor cap with 4 latches after verifying that tab in base of cap is aligned with notch in distributor housing.

5. Connect all external wiring.

6. Time engine in accordance with procedure *Ignition Timing*, given in Chapter Two.

Distributor Installation
(Engine Disturbed)

If the engine has been disturbed, reinstall the distributor as follows.

1. Position the No. 1 piston in firing position by one of the following methods.

> NOTE: *The No. 1 cylinder, piston, or spark plug is the one closest to the front of the vehicle.*

  a. Remove spark plug from No. 1 cylinder and place finger over plug hole. Crank engine until compression is felt. Continue cranking until timing mark on crankshaft pulley lines up with proper timing mark on tab attached to engine front cover.

  b. Remove rocker cover and crank engine until intake valve for No. 1 cylinder closes. Continue cranking until timing marks on pulley and timing tab are aligned.

2. Place the distributor in its hole in the normally installed position, as noted in the removal procedure.

3. While holding the distributor in the position described in Step 2, turn the rotor to point to the front of the engine, then turn rotor about 1/8 turn counterclockwise. Push down on distributor to engage gear with camshaft gear, rotating rotor slightly to assist in engagement, if necessary.

4. Verify that rotor lines up with No. 1 spark plug terminal on distributor cap when cap is in proper position.

5. Install distributor hold-down clamp and nut.

6. Install distributor cap and secure with 4 latches, making certain tab in base of cap is aligned with notch in distributor housing.

7. Connect all external wiring.

8. Time the engine, using the procedure *Ignition Timing*, given in Chapter Two.

Ignition Coil Removal/Installation

Refer to Figure 28.

1. Disconnect ignition switch and distributor lead wires from coil.

2. Remove 4 attaching screws, then remove coil from side of engine.

3. Installation is the reverse of these steps.

INSTRUMENTS

All instruments are removed from the driver side of the instrument panel. All light sockets are removed from the rear by twisting ¼ turn.

The standard instrument cluster and wiring is shown in **Figures 30 and 31**; the GT wiring is shown in **Figures 32 and 33**.

There are 2 separate wiring harnesses; one for the instrument panel wiring, and one for the instrument cluster. They meet at 2 junction blocks bolted together left of the steering column. The instrument panel harness is routed over the brake pedal support bracket and across the car to the heater resistor.

Instrument Removal

1. Remove instrument cluster bezel (standard, 9 screws; GT, 6 screws), clock stem, and lens.

2. GT instruments are now exposed and can be removed as shown in **Figure 34**. The clock and fuel gauge can be removed from the standard cluster only after removing the 2 outer screws at the bottom of the speedometer and lifting it out.

3. After removing the 2 screws from the clock or fuel gauge, insert a small-bladed screwdriver and release the locking tab while rocking and pulling the instrument straight out. Other than removal, servicing of instruments requires delicate equipment and special training. Turn defective components over to dealer.

HORN

If horn sounds weak or out of tune, physically check for interference from adjacent sheet metal or low voltage (horn should have 11 volts across terminal to ground for good operation). If horn

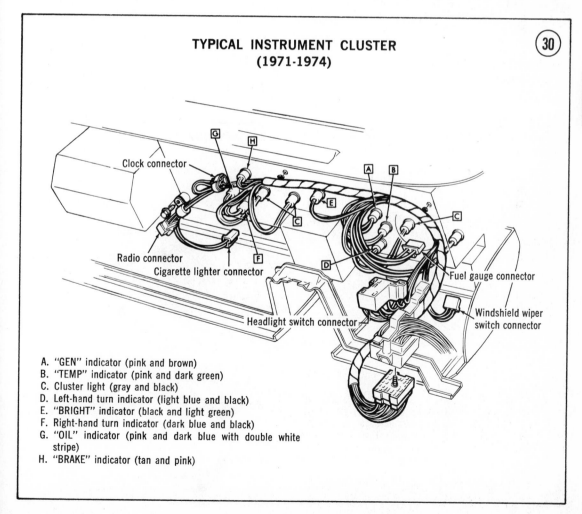

TYPICAL INSTRUMENT CLUSTER
(1971-1974)
30

Clock connector

Radio connector
Cigarette lighter connector

Fuel gauge connector

Headlight switch connector

Windshield wiper switch connector

A. "GEN" indicator (pink and brown)
B. "TEMP" indicator (pink and dark green)
C. Cluster light (gray and black)
D. Left-hand turn indicator (light blue and black)
E. "BRIGHT" indicator (black and light green)
F. Right-hand turn indicator (dark blue and black)
G. "OIL" indicator (pink and dark blue with double white stripe)
H. "BRAKE" indicator (tan and pink)

7

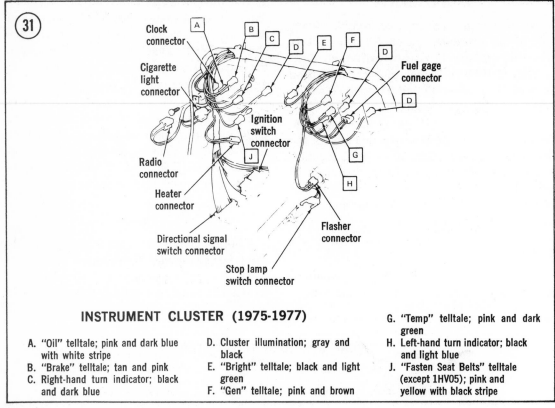

(31)

Clock connector

Cigarette light connector

Radio connector

Heater connector

Ignition switch connector

Fuel gage connector

Directional signal switch connector

Flasher connector

Stop lamp switch connector

INSTRUMENT CLUSTER (1975-1977)

A. "Oil" telltale; pink and dark blue with white stripe

B. "Brake" telltale; tan and pink

C. Right-hand turn indicator; black and dark blue

D. Cluster illumination; gray and black

E. "Bright" telltale; black and light green

F. "Gen" telltale; pink and brown

G. "Temp" telltale; pink and dark green

H. Left-hand turn indicator; black and light blue

J. "Fasten Seat Belts" telltale (except 1HV05); pink and yellow with black stripe

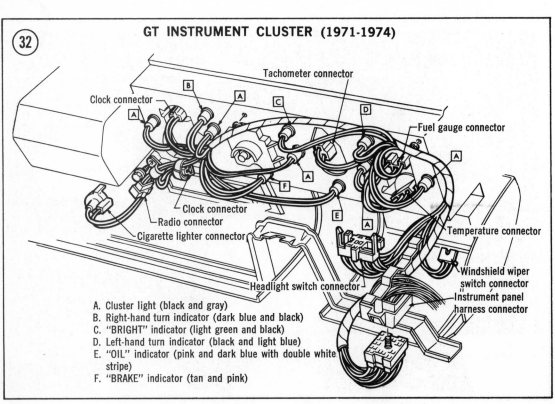

(32)

GT INSTRUMENT CLUSTER (1971-1974)

Tachometer connector

Clock connector

Fuel gauge connector

Clock connector

Radio connector

Cigarette lighter connector

Temperature connector

Windshield wiper switch connector

Instrument panel harness connector

Headlight switch connector

A. Cluster light (black and gray)

B. Right-hand turn indicator (dark blue and black)

C. "BRIGHT" indicator (light green and black)

D. Left-hand turn indicator (black and light blue)

E. "OIL" indicator (pink and dark blue with double white stripe)

F. "BRAKE" indicator (tan and pink)

(33)

Generator connector
Tachometer connector
Fuel gage connector
Clock connector
Radio connector
Cluster
Cigarette light connector
Temperature connector
Ignition switch connector
Heater connector
Directional signal switch connector
Flasher connector
FWD
Stop lamp switch connector

GT INSTRUMENT CLUSTER
(1975-1977)

A. Right-hand turn indicator; dark blue and black
B. Cluster illumination; gray and black
C. "Bright" indicator; light green and black
D. Left-hand turn indicator; light blue and black
E. "Oil" telltale; pink and dark blue with white stripe
F. "Brake" telltale; tan and pink
G. "Fasten Seat Belts" telltale; pink and yellow with black stripe

7

(34)

RPM/100

MPH

PUSH

HI
LO
FAN

OFF
COLD

HEATER

DEICE

HOT

operates continuously, disconnect black lead from horn relay and look for shorts to ground in wire through steering column. Trouble is often found under horn button on steering wheel.

CAUTION
When working around horn relay observe the stud with red lead is always HOT *and protected with a fuse link. If accidently shorted, fuse link may open, disabling vehicle until repaired or jumpered.*

1. To locate an inoperable horn, disconnect green wire at horn and jumper battery positive terminal to horn. Horn should operate or replace horn.

2. Measure resistance to ground at black wire of horn relay. Push horn button. Read short to ground. If horn button operates properly, replace horn relay.

3. If no response to operating horn button, check for loose connection to horn button; usually found at upper steering column. Remove horn actuator shroud on steering wheel. Check for bent contacts or broken or disconnected wire.

IGNITION SWITCH

Steering column must be lowered for access to the ignition switch, which is mounted on the column surrounded by the channel section of the brake pedal support. Refer to procedures under *Steering Column* in Chapter Ten.

1. With the column lowered or removed, put the switch in the LOCK position. If lock cylinder has been removed, pull up on the switch actuating rod then down one detent.

2. Remove the switch by removing the 2 mounting screws.

3. To install, reverse removal procedures. Make sure that the switch is in the LOCK position as shown in **Figure 35**.

DIRECTIONAL SIGNAL SWITCH

1. Remove the steering wheel as described in Chapter Ten.

2. Unscrew the 3 cover screws enough to lift the cover off the shaft (no need to remove them from their plastic retainers).

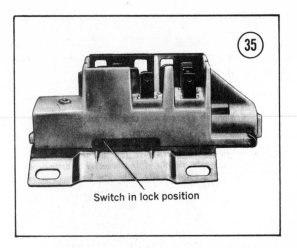
Switch in lock position

3. Compress lock plate as shown in **Figure 36** and remove the snap ring. Use a new snap ring upon reassembly.

CAUTION
Hold the shaft if the column is being disassembled out of the car with the lock plate snap ring and pitman shaft removed, otherwise it might slip out the bottom of the column and become damaged.

IGNITION KEY WARNING SWITCH

1. Remove the steering wheel and directional signal switch as described previously and in Chapter Ten.

2. Hook the clip loop as shown in **Figure 37**. Pull up and out to remove the switch and clip as an assembly. Turn the ignition key to the ON position.

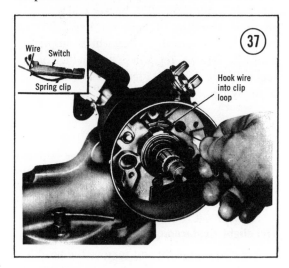

Wire Switch

Spring clip

Hook wire into clip loop

3. To install, depress the buzzer switch actuating button on the lock cylinder, and insert the buzzer switch.

SEAT BELT WARNING AND INTERLOCK SYSTEMS

In 1973 Vegas, a seat belt warning system consisting of a buzzer and dash-mounted warning lamp indicator is activated when either front seat is occupied, emergency brake is released (manual transmission), or transmission was shifted into any forward gear (automatic transmission). A more intricate system was introduced in 1974 models which prevented starting the engine unless all appropriate seat belts were fastened (Starter Interlock System).

Seat Belt Warning System

A normally-closed switch is located in each seat belt retractor mechanism (refer to wiring diagram). In addition, a normally open passenger sensor is located in the right front seat. A wiring circuit from the ignition switch through a diode in the harness between the handbrake switch and left-hand instrument panel support and through the switches operates a relay on the instrument panel support. If the ignition switch is operated and transmission is shifted without the belts being fastened, a buzzer and indicator lamp are activated. The circuit is protected by a 20A fuse in the fuse block.

Seat Belt/Starter Interlock System (1974 and Early 1975)

To start vehicle, all passengers and the driver must buckle seat belt. A mechanic's start is available by reaching in, without sitting down, and turning the ignition switch. If the transmission is shifted into a forward gear after a mechanic's start, the alarm buzzer will operate. To turn buzzer off, pull out a seat belt several inches, then release it. Refer to **Figure 38** for the following troubleshooting procedure.

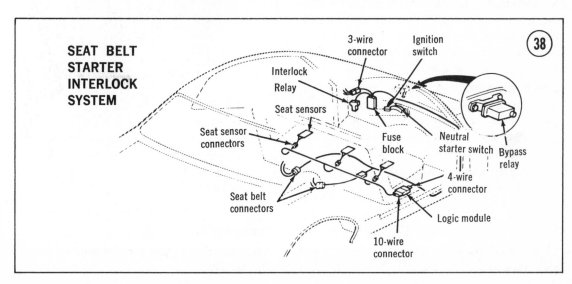

SEAT BELT STARTER INTERLOCK SYSTEM

3-wire connector

Ignition switch

Interlock Relay

Seat sensors

Seat sensor connectors

Fuse block

Neutral starter switch

Bypass relay

Seat belt connectors

4-wire connector

Logic module

10-wire connector

1. *Starter will not operate.*

   a. Depress bypass relay button and try to start engine.

   b. Check battery condition.

   c. Try mechanic's start; if OK, problem is in seat belt section.

   d. Check wiring between electronic module and various switches.

   e. Check neutral start switch. Both left-hand terminals viewed from rear should be "hot."

   f. Replace bypass relay.

   g. If problem persists, remove interlock relay. Apply 12 volts to purple connection. If starter cranks, replace interlock relay.

2. *Seat belt buzzer and light will not operate or remains on at all times.*

   a. Check fuses for taillight and gauges.

   b. Ground yellow lead at 3-wire connector. If buzzer and lamp do not operate, check neutral start switch connections. If buzzer and lamp operate, replace logic module. Otherwise look for broken yellow wire.

   c. If buzzer and lamp remain on when 3-wire connector is disconnected, check yellow/black wire for short to ground. If buzzer and lamp turn off when connection is opened, replace logic module.

3. *Seat belt system diagnosis.*

   a. Turn ignition switch on, leave belts unfastened. Push and release each front seat position in turn. You should hear 2 clicks from the interlock relay at each seat. If one or no click, check connections, replace logic module.

   b. If clicks heard at only one seat position, disconnect seat sensor connection under seat and check for continuity. Replace if necessary; this may involve removing the front seat.

   c. If 2 clicks were heard, the seat belt system is OK.

Seat Belt Warning System (1975-1977)

All Vegas built after early 1975 have a seat belt warning system which is not interlocked with the ignition system. Whenever the ignition switch is turned on, the instrument panel warning light is illuminated, regardless of whether or not the driver's belt is buckled. If the driver's seat belt is not buckled, a buzzer will sound in addition. Duration of both warning light and buzzer is 4-8 seconds, after which they automatically shut off regardless of whether or not seat belts are buckled. **Figure 39** is a schematic of the system.

LIGHTING

This section includes both interior and exterior lighting and associated switches. Bulb specifications are found in **Table 3**.

Headlight Replacement

Refer to **Figure 40** and remove the headlight bezel. Unhook the retaining spring and turn the headlight to release it from the aiming pins. Unplug connector and remove the retaining ring.

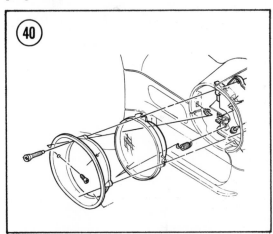

Parking Light

Replace bulb by removing lens and twisting bulb 90° counterclockwise. **Figure 41** shows the parking light assembly, which can be removed as a unit by unscrewing it from the bumper and the valance panel.

Marker Light

Replace bulb by turning socket counterclockwise ¼ turn.

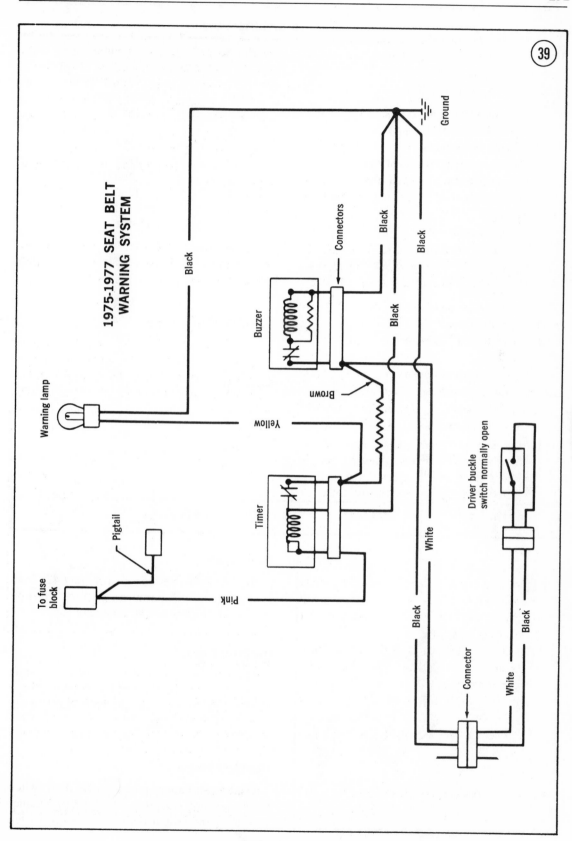

1975-1977 SEAT BELT WARNING SYSTEM

Table 3　BULB SPECIFICATIONS

	Candle Power	Bulb Type
Headlight unit—high beam	60W	6014 (6012)①
—low beam	50W	Sealed beam
Front park and directional signal	32-3	1157③
Front fender side marker light	2	194
Rear side marker light	2	194
Tail, stop, and rear directional signal	32-3	1157
License plate light	4	168 (194)②
Back-up lights	32	1156
Dome light	12	211 or 211-1 (561)②
Instrument panel cluster lights	2	194
Transmission control indicator	2	194
Heater or air conditioner control panel light indirect lighting		(194)①
Indicator lights		
Automatic transmission	2	194
Generator	2	194
High beam headlight	2	194
Oil	2	194
Temperature system	2	194
Brake warning	2	194
Turn signal	2	194
Stop engine	2	194
Radio dial light	3	1816
Rear window defogger	3	168
Seat belt warning light	2	194
Glove compartment	3	1891

① 1976-1977　　　　② 1975-1977　　　　③ 1157NA G.T. equipped

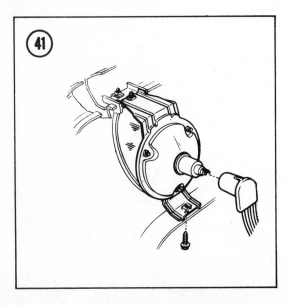

④ 41

Rear Lights

Replace bulbs on the sedan (**Figure 42**) from inside the rear compartment. Replace bulbs on the wagon (**Figure 43**) by removing lens.

Quadrant Light

The bulb is located at the front of the shift quadrant. It can be reached by removing the 4 Phillips head screws from the floor shift console and lifting the console.

Headlight Switch

Disconnect battery ground cable. Pull switch to ON position. Depress switch shaft retainer button on the switch body and remove switch

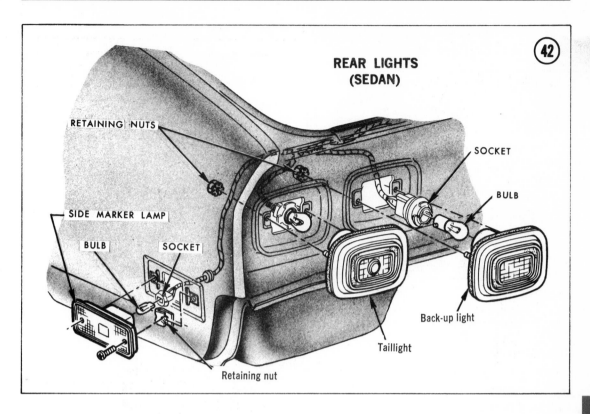

REAR LIGHTS (SEDAN)

RETAINING NUTS

SIDE MARKER LAMP

BULB

SOCKET

SOCKET

BULB

Back-up light

Taillight

Retaining nut

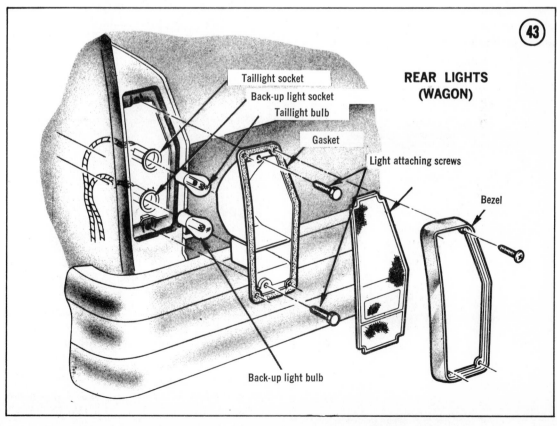

REAR LIGHTS (WAGON)

Taillight socket

Back-up light socket

Taillight bulb

Gasket

Light attaching screws

Bezel

Back-up light bulb

7

control shaft. Remove the switch from the dash panel as shown in **Figure 44**.

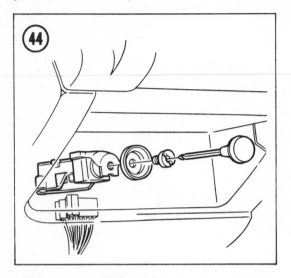

Stoplight Switch

Refer to **Figure 45**. Unplug connector and pull switch from mounting. Install new switch by depressing brake pedal and pushing the switch into the clip. Adjust placement of the switch in the clip so that lights go on when brake is depressed ⅛-⅝ in. (3-15mm).

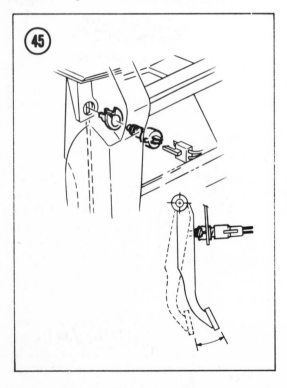

Back-up Light Switch

When car is equipped with automatic transmission, this switch is part of the neutral start switch (see *Starter*). In standard transmission vehicles, the switch is located at the rear of the transmission. It is on the left side of 3-speed transmissions; on right side of 4-speed units.

CAUTION
Use safety stand when working under the car. Do not rely solely on hydraulic or mechanical jacks.

Dome Light

Refer to **Figure 46** for dome light replacement. This light is controlled by a door jamb switch and by the headlight switch, both of which ground to complete the circuit.

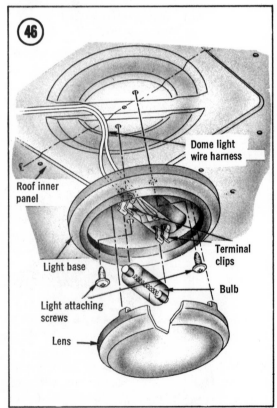

Dome light wire harness

Roof inner panel

Light base

Terminal clips

Bulb

Light attaching screws

Lens

Parking Brake Warning Light Switch

Refer to **Figure 47**. Remove the boot and 2 bolts securing the parking brake lever assembly. Tilt assembly to the right to reveal the switch retaining screw.

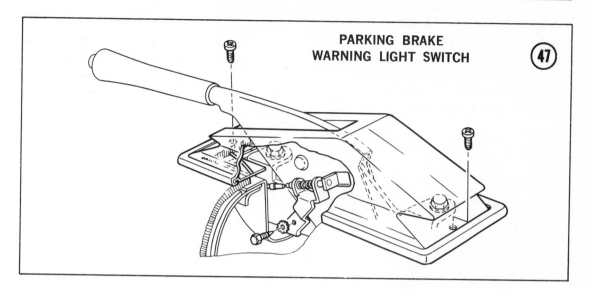

PARKING BRAKE
WARNING LIGHT SWITCH ㊼

Radio Bulb Replacement

For AM models, set dial at 16 and slide dial plate down about ⅛ in. (3mm); tip out and remove. Unclip light mounting tab on left (**Figure 48**).

For AM/FM models, set radio for AM and unlock the third pushbutton from the left by pulling outward. Insert 5/64 in. Allen wrench through square hole in the third pushbutton, loosen set screw, and remove slide bar. Remove the 2 Phillips head screws from the face plate. Set dial to 16 and unclip light mounting tab on left (**Figure 49**).

CAUTION
After reassembling, reset the third pushbutton before changing to FM.

ACCESSORIES

Cigarette Lighter

Disconnect battery ground cable before removing the cigarette lighter. Remove the lighter. Reach behind the instrument panel and hold the lighter housing. Unscrew the element receptacle from the front of the instrument panel with a small screwdriver.

Radio

Figure 50 shows the radio and speaker mounting. The antenna wires are imbedded in the windshield and require a special tool (J-23520) for testing. The antenna lead hookup is shown

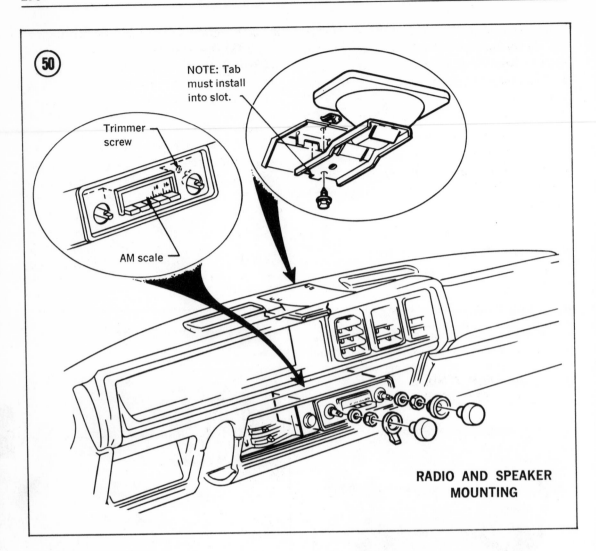

NOTE: Tab must install into slot.

Trimmer screw

AM scale

RADIO AND SPEAKER MOUNTING

in **Figure 51**. See *Lighting* for radio bulb replacement.

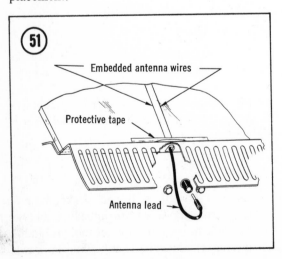

Embedded antenna wires

Protective tape

Antenna lead

Radio Removal

1. Disconnect battery ground cable.

2. Remove knobs and nuts from radio control.

3. Disconnect antenna lead. If antenna lead is to be replaced, remove 2 mounting screws on cowl, reach under cowl grille and unplug antenna from windshield.

4. Disconnect power and speaker leads from the back of the receiver.

5. After removing the 2 screws where the radio mounting bracket is secured to the lower instrument panel, radio can be removed.

Speaker Removal

The speaker is secured with one mounting bolt as shown in Figure 50. Speaker access requires removal of the center bezel (9 screws). The air conditioning outlet for cars so equipped must be removed as follows.

1. Disconnect the battery ground cable and remove bezel.

2. Remove the retainer and 2 screws from the center air conditioning duct.

3. Remove radio and cigarette lighter.

4. Push the air conditioning duct back, down, and rotate to the left. Speaker can now be removed.

Rear Window Defogger

This optional device consists of a switch and control system on the dash and a series of ceramic silver element lines backed on the rear window. The 2 are connected by the engine wiring harness which contains fusible links for protection. The defogger can be turned on and off by the instrument panel switch. It will automatically turn off after 10 minutes operation, or if the engine stalls, or if the ignition switch is turned off. The elements can be repaired, but this is best left to the dealer.

Refer to **Figure 52** for removal of the switch and controls. Remove the switch by unplugging the 3-lead connector, twisting the light socket ¼ turn and removing the 2 retaining nuts. Before removing the control, disconnect the battery ground cable. Open the driver's door, and remove the 3 control mounting screws from the left end of the instrument panel. Lower the control, and remove the ground wire from the control base and the lower instrument panel reinforcement. Unplug the electrical connector by first lifting the plastic strip lock.

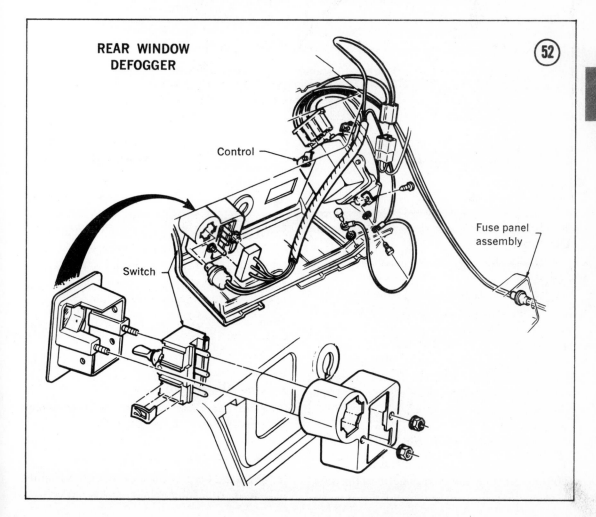

REAR WINDOW DEFOGGER   ⑤²

Control

Switch

Fuse panel assembly

WINDSHIELD WIPER SYSTEM

Windshield Washer/Wiper Switch

The windshield washer switch and washer pump are integrally mounted. The washer pump is hand operated.

To remove the wiper and washer controls (**Figure 53**), unplug the headlight switch for access to the mounting screws.

> NOTE: *Do not remove washer pump hoses without protecting floor mat if washer fluid is used. The washer pump can be repaired by replacing the piston, valves, and O-rings.*

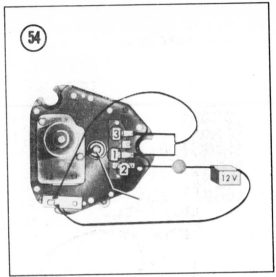

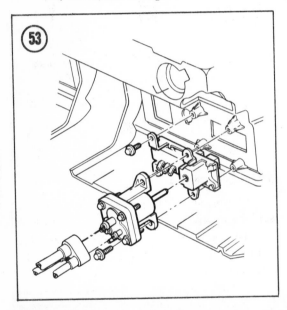

Diagnosis

Wiper motor and switch must be securely mounted for proper operation to ensure ground.

If wiper still fails to operate, disconnect wiring harness and test as shown in **Figure 54**. If wiper now operates correctly, check for broken or shorted wires in the harness, or replace the switch. If wiper fails to operate, disconnect linkage. If wiper now operates, trouble has been isolated; if not, wiper must be removed from the car.

Wiper Motor Assembly Removal

1. From the engine compartment, loosen the 2 nuts attaching the motor crank arm to the transmission drive link, and remove the link.

2. Disconnect wiring, remove the 3 mounting screws and remove the motor.

Wiper Motor Assembly Checks

If the assembly will not operate when tested according to Figure 48, there is a possibility of a broken or damaged gear train. Other possibilities include open armature circuit, binding brushes, or poor connections at the terminal board or brush plate. These conditions may permit intermittent operation. If wiper will not shut off, but has normal high and low speeds, check for defective part switch or grounded red lead wire. If wiper will not shut off and has low speed only, check for a grounded shunt field coil or a grounded black wire. If wiper will not shut off and has high speed only, check for an open shunt field coil circuit or an open circuit in the black lead wire. If wiper will not park, check for dirty contacts or a defective park switch. A defective resistor will cause the motor to operate in high speed only.

Gearbox Disassembly

1. *Hold crank arm* and remove retaining nut (**Figure 55**).

2. Using a 9/32 in. drill bit, drill out staking securing cover, as shown in **Figure 56**.

3. Remove output gear and shaft assembly, intermediate gear and pinion, in that order.

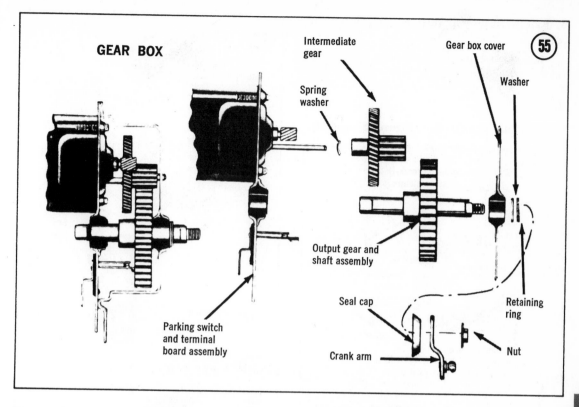

GEAR BOX

Intermediate gear

Gear box cover

Washer

Spring washer

Output gear and shaft assembly

Seal cap

Retaining ring

Nut

Crank arm

Parking switch and terminal board assembly

⑤⑤

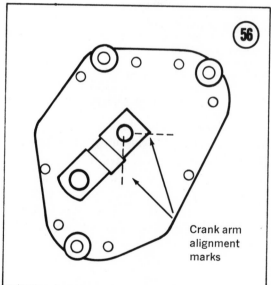

⑤⑥

Crank arm alignment marks

4. Terminal board and park switch assembly can be removed by drilling out rivets with a 7/64 in. drill bit and unsoldering terminals.

> NOTE: *Cover and switch hardware are available from the dealer to replace stakes and rivets.*

Motor Disassembly

1. If frame or field needs to be replaced, unsolder terminal connections and motor leads.

2. Remove motor through bolts (**Figure 57**), holding end cap against frame. Separate motor and gearbox.

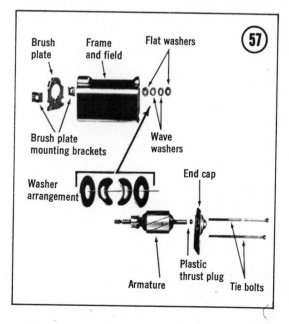

⑤⑦

Brush plate

Frame and field

Flat washers

Brush plate mounting brackets

Wave washers

Washer arrangement

End cap

Armature

Plastic thrust plug

Tie bolts

3. Release brush springs, move brushes off commutator.

4. Remove armature and end caps, being careful not to lose thrust plug.

Tests

Test motor components (**Figures 58 and 59**).

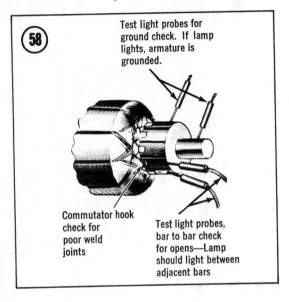

Test light probes for ground check. If lamp lights, armature is grounded.

58

Commutator hook check for poor weld joints

Test light probes, bar to bar check for opens—Lamp should light between adjacent bars

Gearbox Reassembly

Reverse disassembly procedures observing the following: output gear and shaft assembly should be installed with cam at least 90° from the parking switch; output gear shaft end play should not exceed 0.005 in. (0.13mm); install crank arm with wiper in park position and index marks on crank arm and gearbox aligned.

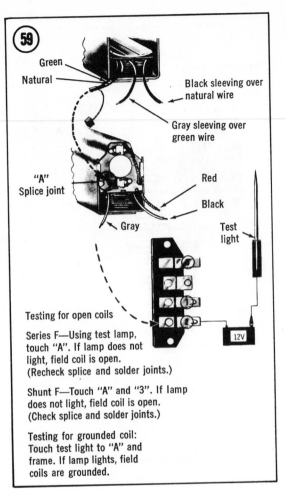

59

Green

Natural

Black sleeving over natural wire

Gray sleeving over green wire

"A" Splice joint

Red

Black

Gray

Test light

12V

Testing for open coils

Series F—Using test lamp, touch "A". If lamp does not light, field coil is open. (Recheck splice and solder joints.)

Shunt F—Touch "A" and "3". If lamp does not light, field coil is open. (Check splice and solder joints.)

Testing for grounded coil: Touch test light to "A" and frame. If lamp lights, field coils are grounded.

SPECIFICATIONS

Specifications and tightening torques for the various electrical systems are given in **Tables 4 through 6**.

Table 4   ELECTRICAL SPECIFICATIONS (1971-1976)

Generator model:	110545 110549 1100559	1102856 1102858	1100546 1100560 1102500	1102891 1102851 1102846
Field current, amps (80°F)	4-4.5	4-4.5	4-4.5	4-4.5
Output, amps (5,000 rpm)	31-32	33-37	50-55	51-55
Distributor Model:	1110435①	1110492①	1110496②	1112862 (HEI) ③
Dwell, degrees	31-34	31-34	31-34	
Centrifugal advance, Degrees/rpm	0/945, 2/1455 22/4,000	0/1185, 2/1615 24/4,000	0/1600, 5/2000 22/4,800	0/1620, 5/2000 22/4,800
Vacuum advance, Degrees/in. Hg.	0/7 24/15	0/7 24/15	0/7 24/15	0/5 24/12
Coil:		115430	HEI	
Primary resistance, ohms		1.41-1.63	Less than 1	
Secondary resistance, ohms		3,000-20,000	6,000-30,000	
Ignition resistor, ohms		1.8		
Starter (all):				
Free speed, rpm	6,500-10,000			
Volts	9			
Amps	50-75 (includes solenoid)			

① 1971-1972 models
② 1973-1974 models.
③ 1975-1976 models.

Table 5   ELECTRICAL SPECIFICATIONS (1977)

Generator model:	1102893
Field current, amps (80°F)	4-4.5
Output, amps (5,000 rpm)	60-37
Distributor model:	1110538 (HEI)
Centrifugal advance, Degrees/rpm	0/850, 8/1200 17/2000
Vacuum advance, Degrees/in. Hg.	0/5 24/10

Table 6   TORQUE SPECIFICATIONS

Battery cable	80 in.-lb.
Battery hold down	70 in.-lb.
Generator brace adjustment	120 in.-lb.
Generator pulley	50 ft.-lb.
Starter mount	30 ft.-lb.
Starter brace	18 ft.-lb.

CHAPTER EIGHT

CLUTCH AND TRANSMISSION

Chevrolet has offered a large number of manual and automatic transmission options on the Vega. The 3-speed Opel transmission, which was standard on 1971-1972 models, was replaced in 1973 with the 3-speed Saginaw transmission. This unit continued as standard equipment through 1977. The 4-speed Opel transmission was optional in 1971-1972. The 4-speed Saginaw was offered in 1973 through 1975, and the 70mm Brazil 4-speed transmission became optional equipment in 1976-1977 models. A 5-speed Borg Warner transmission also was optional in 1976.

Automatic transmission options offered include the 2-speed Powerglide (1971-1973) and the semi-automatic Torque Drive (a non-automatic-shifting Powerglide, 1971-1972), the Turbo-Hydramatic 350 (1972-1973), and the Turbo-Hydramatic 250 (1973-1977). The Turbo-Hydramatic 250 is similar to the 350, except that the former has an externally adjustable intermediate band. Both have 3 forward speeds.

Repairs requiring disassembly are not recommended for home mechanics or garage mechanics without special skills and a large assortment of special tools. In fact, the cost of the necessary tools far exceeds the price of a professionally rebuilt transmission.

Considerable money can be saved by removing the old transmission and installing a new or rebuilt one yourself. See Chapter Three for fault isolation procedures.

The Vega clutch for manual 3- and 4-speed transmissions is a conventional, single plate, dry friction type. The clutch release mechanism consists of a ball thrust (throwout) bearing and cable linkage to control release. The clutch plate is held against the flywheel by a diaphragm-spring pressure plate and clutch cover assembly.

Torque specifications are included in **Tables 1 through 6** at the end of this chapter.

CLUTCH

Clutch Adjustments

Two adjustments are provided: the clutch fork ball stud and the clutch cable pin. Adjustment for wear should be made with the ball stud; however, a special gauge is required (tool J-23644, as shown in **Figure 1**) for initial adjustment after clutch or cable replacement.

1. Before attaching cable, locate gauge with flat end against the clutch housing face and the other end hooked around the fork-to-cable attachment as shown in Figure 1.

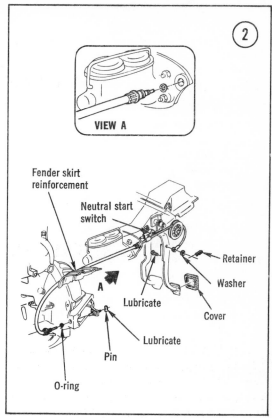

VIEW A

Fender skirt
reinforcement

Neutral start
switch

A

Lubricate

Retainer

Washer

Cover

Lubricate

Pin

O-ring

2. Adjust the ball stud until the throwout bearing contacts the clutch spring, and tighten the locknut to 25 ft.-lb. (3.45 mkg).

3. Remove gauge and connect cable.

4. Pull cable so that clutch pedal is firmly against rubber stop, and push clutch fork forward, until the throwout bearing reaches the clutch spring.

5. Screw the pin onto the cable until it contacts fork, then drop it into fork groove by turning an additional ¼ turn clockwise. Attach the return spring. The clutch pedal lash should now be 0.90 ± 0.25 in. (22.8 ± 6.4mm).

Cable Replacement

1. Remove cover from left side of housing and disconnect cable and return spring.

2. Disconnect cable from pedal and disconnect bolt holding cable to body reinforcement.

3. Pull each end of cable assembly into engine compartment and release the cable from the fender skirt clip (**Figure 2**).

4. Install new cable, and lubricate connection at pedal arm with graphite grease.

Clutch Replacement

1. Remove engine as outlined in Chapter Four, or transmission as outlined in this chapter.

2. Remove plate on left side of clutch housing. Disconnect clutch cable and return spring.

3. Remove clutch housing if transmission has been removed. Scribe the pressure plate location on the flywheel to ensure correct balance on reassembling.

4. Remove 6 bolts securing pressure plate to flywheel. Loosen each bolt a little at a time to avoid distorting clutch assembly.

5. Inspect flywheel and pressure plate surfaces for scoring.

6. Examine clutch plate surfaces for oil, loose rivets, and wear. Check for loose or broken springs.

7. Check the pilot bushing in the flywheel for wear. Inspect for oil leaks at rear main bearing, transmission input shaft seal, throwout bearing, support gasket, etc.

8. Make certain clutch plate slides easily on transmission input shaft spline.

9. Check throwout bearing for wear and its fit on the support sleeve.

10. Inspect clutch fork at all wear points.

11. Check input shaft oil seal and throwout bearing support gasket.

12. Reassemble as described under *Engine Installation* in Chapter Four and adjust as described previously.

8

MANUAL TRANSMISSIONS
(1971-1972)

Both the 3- and 4-speed transmissions are controlled by floor-mounted shift levers. See **Figure 3**. They are fully synchronized in all forward speeds.

> NOTE: *Both transmissions use metric threads throughout. Spiral pins, holding shiftforks, and levers, are also metric and cannot be replaced with standard roll pins.*

The front and rear main shaft bearings are interchangeable. The 3-speed extension is used also on the 4-speed transmission by plugging the back-up switch hole. The extension cannot be removed without first removing countershaft.

> NOTE: *The manual transmission lubricant includes an orange dye to detect any leaks.*

Cross sections of the 3- and 4-speed transmissions are shown in **Figures 4 and 5**, respectively.

Gearshift Lever Replacement

1. With lever in NEUTRAL position, remove bezel retaining screws (**Figure 6**).

2. Lift rubber boot, unhook anti-rattle spring, and remove retainer pin and spring washer.

3. To replace the control wire on 4-speed lever, pull off gearshift knob. Loosen set screw and drive out spiral pins (**Figure 7**). Shift finger can now be removed, and Bowden control wire can be pulled out of lever.

4. Feed new control wire through lever, and install stop sleeve with cutout facing left. Insert long spiral pin so that it is flush on both sides.

5. Tighten set screw so that reverse lockout knob has approximately 1/16 in. (1.5mm) free travel.

6. Attach shift finger with short spiral pin.

7. Install gearshift lever knob. Clearance between shift knob and reverse lockout knob should be 0.30 in. (7.6mm) as shown in **Figure 8** (page 148).

8. Refer to exploded view of transmission. Adjust reverse gearshift blocker by engaging the reverse locknut and adjusting the selector shaft

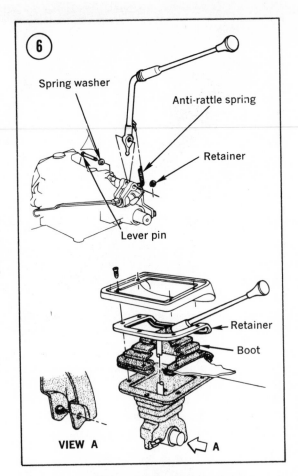

6

Spring washer

Anti-rattle spring

Retainer

Lever pin

Retainer

Boot

VIEW A   A

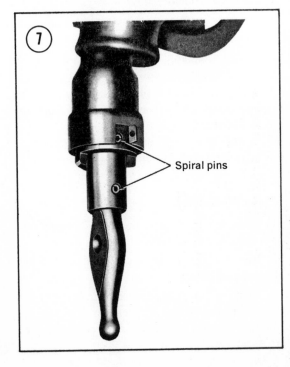

7

Spiral pins

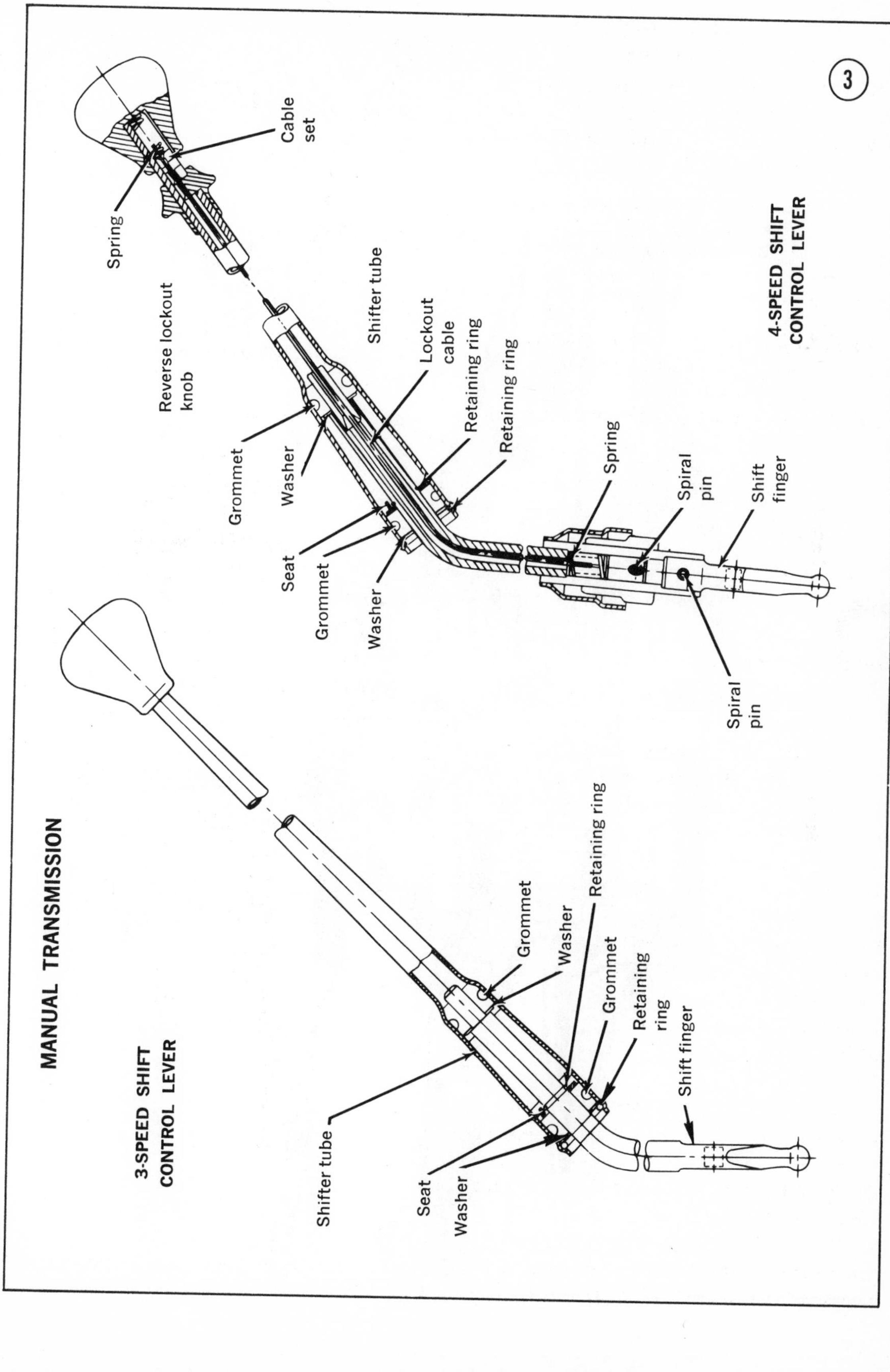

3

Cable set

Spring

Reverse lockout knob

Shifter tube

Lockout cable

Retaining ring

Retaining ring

Spring

Grommet

Washer

Seat

Grommet

Washer

Spiral pin

Shift finger

Spiral pin

4-SPEED SHIFT CONTROL LEVER

MANUAL TRANSMISSION

3-SPEED SHIFT CONTROL LEVER

Grommet

Washer

Retaining ring

Grommet

Retaining ring

Shift finger

Shifter tube

Seat

Washer

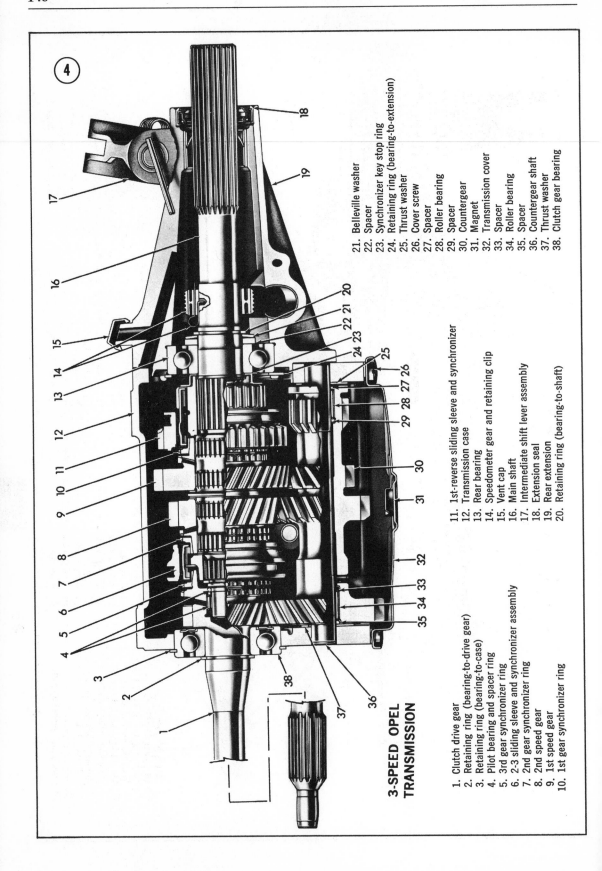

3-SPEED OPEL TRANSMISSION

1. Clutch drive gear
2. Retaining ring (bearing-to-drive gear)
3. Retaining ring (bearing-to-case)
4. Pilot bearing and spacer ring
5. 3rd gear synchronizer ring
6. 2-3 sliding sleeve and synchronizer assembly
7. 2nd gear synchronizer ring
8. 2nd speed gear
9. 1st speed gear
10. 1st gear synchronizer ring
11. 1st-reverse sliding sleeve and synchronizer
12. Transmission case
13. Rear bearing
14. Speedometer gear and retaining clip
15. Vent cap
16. Main shaft
17. Intermediate shift lever assembly
18. Extension seal
19. Rear extension
20. Retaining ring (bearing-to-shaft)
21. Belleville washer
22. Spacer
23. Synchronizer key stop ring
24. Retaining ring (bearing-to-extension)
25. Thrust washer
26. Cover screw
27. Spacer
28. Roller bearing
29. Spacer
30. Countergear
31. Magnet
32. Transmission cover
33. Spacer
34. Roller bearing
35. Spacer
36. Countergear shaft
37. Thrust washer
38. Clutch gear bearing

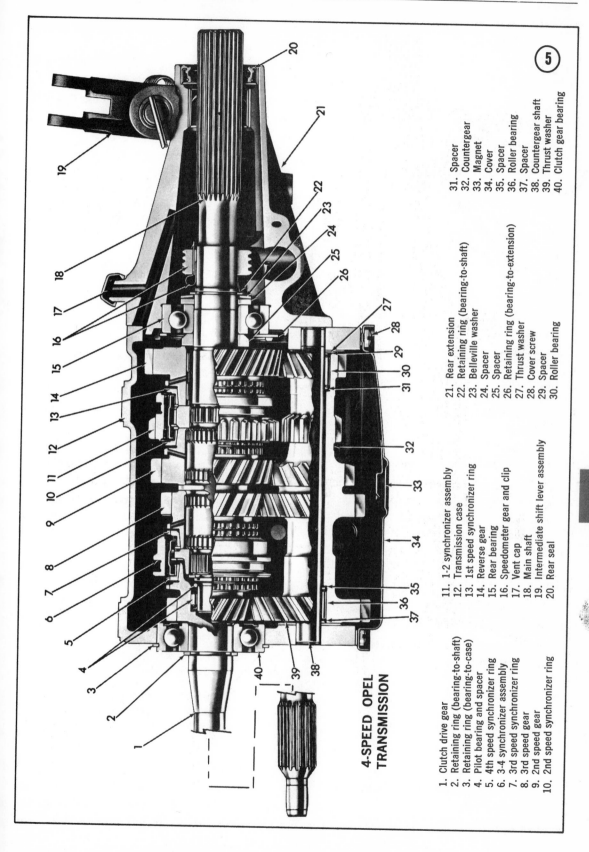

4-SPEED OPEL TRANSMISSION

1. Clutch drive gear
2. Retaining ring (bearing-to-shaft)
3. Retaining ring (bearing-to-case)
4. Pilot bearing and spacer
5. 4th speed synchronizer ring
6. 3-4 synchronizer assembly
7. 3rd speed synchronizer ring
8. 3rd speed gear
9. 2nd speed gear
10. 2nd speed synchronizer ring
11. 1-2 synchronizer assembly
12. Transmission case
13. 1st speed synchronizer ring
14. Reverse gear
15. Rear bearing
16. Speedometer gear and clip
17. Vent cap
18. Main shaft
19. Intermediate shift lever assembly
20. Rear seal
21. Rear extension
22. Retaining ring (bearing-to-shaft)
23. Belleville washer
24. Spacer
25. Spacer
26. Retaining ring (bearing-to-extension)
27. Thrust washer
28. Cover screw
29. Spacer
30. Roller bearing
31. Spacer
32. Countergear
33. Magnet
34. Cover
35. Spacer
36. Roller bearing
37. Spacer
38. Countergear shaft
39. Thrust washer
40. Clutch gear bearing

8

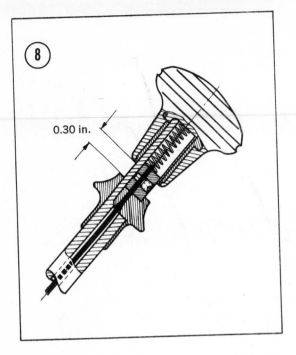

⑧

0.30 in.

adjusting ring so that the shift finger ball is equidistant from both sides of the hole in the idler lever. Now back off selector ring ¼ turn and tighten lock.

Speedometer Gear Replacement

Disconnect speedometer cable, and remove lock plate. Pry gear and shaft assembly from transmission extension. To reinstall, coat new O-ring and gear shaft with transmission lubricant, then install the assembly so that the slot will mate with the lock plate boss. Insert lock plate in groove and install attaching bolt.

Intermediate Lever Bushing

Remove snap ring. Drive out bushing, with a brass drift, from snap ring side. Install new bushing from the opposite direction, with the bushing cutout facing up. Install snap ring.

Extension Oil Seal Replacement

1. Remove trunnion bearing U-bolt from rear universal joint.

> NOTE: *Tape bearing cups so they do not drop off.*

2. Pull shaft from transmission.

3. Pry seal out of extension. Clean and inspect seal counterbore.

4. Lubricate new seal, and coat the outside circumference with a suitable sealant.

5. Tap seal into counterbore, leading edge first, until it is flush.

6. Reinstall drive shaft.

MANUAL TRANSMISSION REMOVAL/INSTALLATION (3- AND 4-SPEED, 1971-1977)

Removal

1. Remove shift levers as previously described.

2. Drain transmission.

> ### CAUTION
> *Use safety stand when working under the car. Do not rely solely on hydraulic or mechanical jacks.*

3. Carefully mark the relationship of the drive shaft to companion flange for reference during installation.

4. Disconnect rear universal joint by removing U-bolts from trunnion bearings. Tape bearing cups to prevent loss of bearing rollers.

5. Move shaft rearward to withdraw front yoke from transmission. Pass shaft under rear axle housing. Check for oil leakage at transmission output shaft housing.

6. Disconnect back-up light switch, throttle control switch, and speedometer cable.

7. Support engine and remove crossmember-to-transmission bolts and crossmember-to-frame bolts. Remove crossmember.

8. Remove transmission-to-clutch housing bolts and remove transmission.

> NOTE: *Remove the 2 top bolts first, and replace with studs to facilitate transmission removal and installation.*

Installation

1. Raise transmission into position and, using the studs installed during removal as guides, slide forward to clutch housing. Make sure

clutch drive gear splines mesh properly into clutch pilot bearing.

2. Install transmission-to-clutch housing retaining bolts. On 1971-1972 models, torque to 24 ft.-lb. (3.3 mkg), or 55 ft.-lb. (7.6 mkg) on 1973-1977 models.

3. Position crossmember to frame and install retaining bolts. Do not tighten at this time. Install crossmember-to-transmission bolts. Now torque crossmember-to-frame bolts to 28 ft.-lb. (3.9 mkg) and crossmember-to-transmission bolts to 26 ft.-lb. (3.6 mkg).

4. Remove engine support and check position of engine in front mounts. Realign engine, if necessary.

5. Connect throttle control switch, back-up light switch, and speedometer cable.

6. Insert front yoke of the drive shaft into the transmission extension. Make sure splines of output shaft mate properly with splines of drive shaft front yoke.

7. Align drive shaft with companion flange, using marks made during removal procedure as a reference. Remove tape from trunnion bearing caps and connect caps to companion.

8. Fill transmission with lubricant (80W or 90W gear lubricant). Lower vehicle and remove from hoist.

9. Lubricate shift finger bolt and spherical shaft end. Install shift lever in housing, install bolt, and secure with retaining clip.

10. Install shift lever spring, shift lever boot, and bezel.

11. Check transmission for proper shifting operating.

MANUAL TRANSMISSIONS (3- AND 4-SPEED SAGINAW)

The procedures contained in this section pertain to 1973-1977 3-speed and 1973-1975 4-speed Saginaw transmissions. See **Figures 9** (3-speed) **and 10** (4-speed).

Removal/Installation

The procedures for removing and installing 3- and 4-speed Saginaw transmissions are given earlier in this chapter.

Checking Transmission Mounts

1. Raise car on hoist and push up and pull down on transmission tailshaft. If transmission mount rubber separates from metal plate, or if tailshaft moves up but not down, replace the mount.

2. Check for movement between the mount metal plate and its attaching point. If movement is present, tighten the attaching screws or nuts.

Linkage Adjustment

Refer to **Figure 11** for this procedure.

1. Be sure ignition switch is off, then raise car on a hoist.

2. Loosen locknuts on shift rod swivels so that rods pass freely through swivels.

3. Place shift levers in NEUTRAL, then place shift control lever in NEUTRAL. Align control levers and install a gage pin into bracket and levers.

4. Tighten first/reverse (3-speed) or first/second (4-speed) shift rod nut against swivel to 120 in.-lb. (1.38 mkg).

5. Tighten second/third (3-speed) or third/fourth (4-speed) shift rod nut against swivel to 120 in.-lb.

6. Tighten the reverse (4-speed) shift control rod nut to 120 in.-lb.

7. Remove gage pin and check operation of shift control lever. Readjust if necessary.

Shift Control Assembly Replacement

Refer to **Figure 12** for this procedure.

1. Remove control lever knob and locknut (3-speed) or T-handle and spring (4-speed).

2. Remove boot retainer, boot, and insulator, then turn back edge of carpet and remove attaching bolts from control assembly.

3. Raise vehicle and remove retaining pins and disconnect control rods from shift control levers. Remove second/third (3-speed) or third/fourth (4-speed) swivel from lever.

4. Disconnect back-up light switch and speedometer cable from transmission.

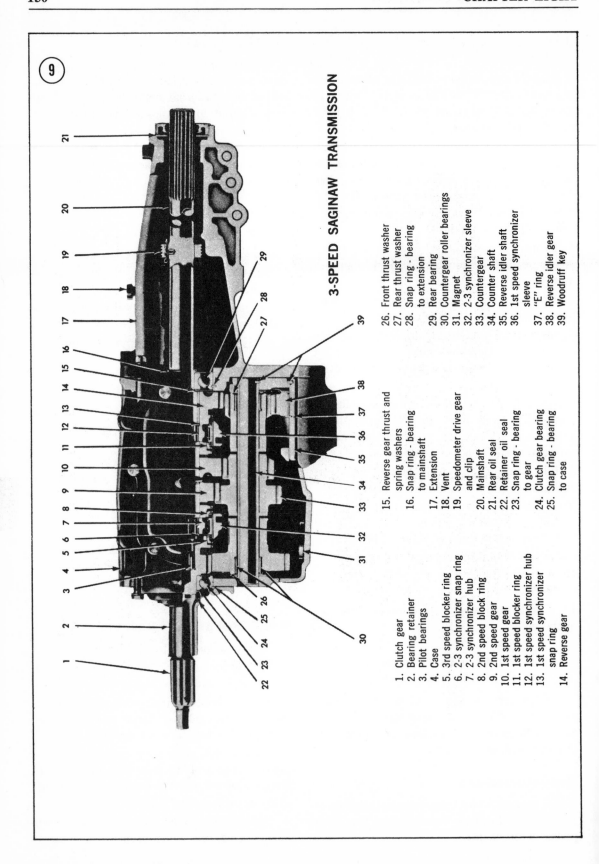

3-SPEED SAGINAW TRANSMISSION

1. Clutch gear
2. Bearing retainer
3. Pilot bearings
4. Case
5. 3rd speed blocker ring
6. 2-3 synchronizer snap ring
7. 2-3 synchronizer hub
8. 2nd speed block ring
9. 2nd speed gear
10. 1st speed gear
11. 1st speed blocker ring
12. 1st speed synchronizer hub
13. 1st speed synchronizer snap ring
14. Reverse gear
15. Reverse gear thrust and spring washers
16. Snap ring - bearing to mainshaft
17. Extension
18. Vent
19. Speedometer drive gear and clip
20. Mainshaft
21. Rear oil seal
22. Retainer oil seal
23. Snap ring - bearing to gear
24. Clutch gear bearing
25. Snap ring - bearing to case
26. Front thrust washer
27. Rear thrust washer
28. Snap ring - bearing to extension
29. Rear bearing
30. Countergear roller bearings
31. Magnet
32. 2-3 synchronizer sleeve
33. Countergear
34. Counter shaft
35. Reverse idler shaft
36. 1st speed synchronizer sleeve
37. "E" ring
38. Reverse idler gear
39. Woodruff key

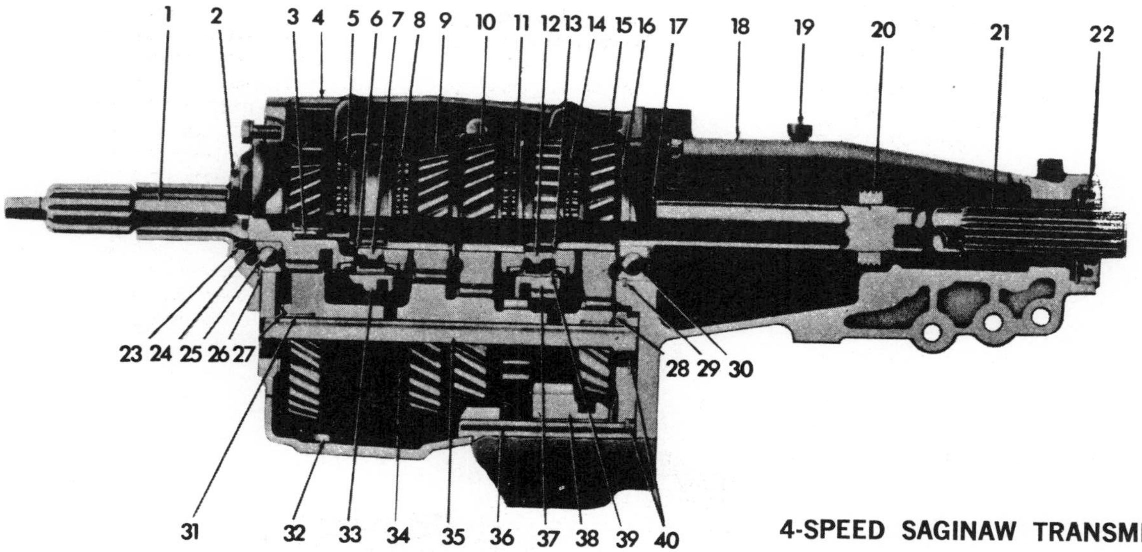

4-SPEED SAGINAW TRANSMISSION

1. Clutch gear
2. Bearing retainer
3. Pilot bearings
4. Case
5. 4th speed blocker ring
6. 4-3 synchronizer snap ring
7. 4-3 synchronizer hub
8. 3rd speed blocker ring
9. 3rd speed gear
10. 2nd speed gear
11. 2nd speed blocker ring
12. 1-2 speed synchronizer hub
13. 1-2 speed synchronizer snap ring
14. 1st speed blocker ring
15. First gear
16. Reverse gear thrust and spring washers
17. Snap ring - bearing to mainshaft
18. Extension
19. Vent
20. Speedometer drive gear and clip
21. Mainshaft
22. Rear oil seal
23. Retainer oil seal
24. Snap ring - bearing to gear
25. Clutch gear bearing
26. Snap ring - bearing to case
27. Front thrust washer
28. Rear thrust washer
29. Snap ring - bearing to extension
30. Rear bearing
31. Countergear roller bearings
32. Magnet
33. 4-3 Synchronizer sleeve
34. Countergear assembly
35. Counter shaft
36. Reverse idler shaft
37. 1-2 speed synchronizer sleeve and reverse gear
38. Reverse idler gear (sliding)
39. Clutch key
40. Woodruff key

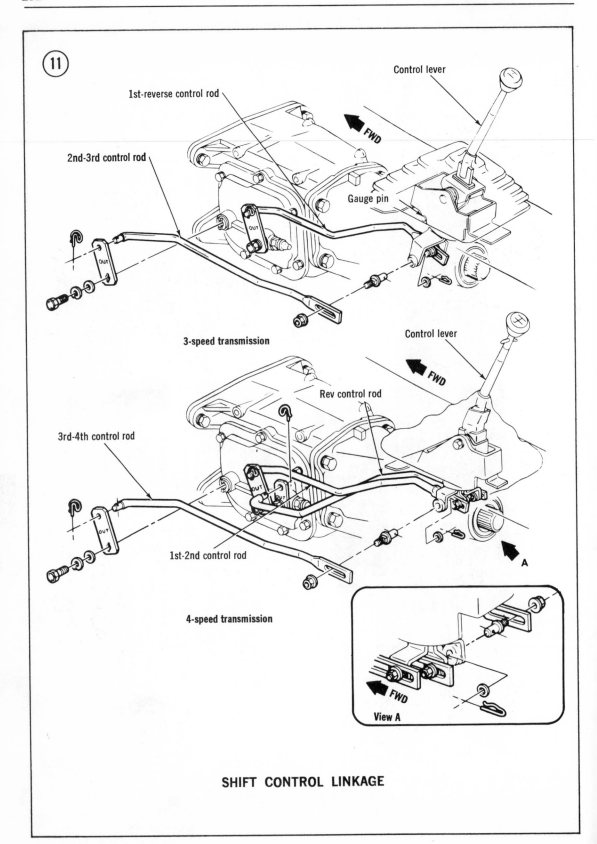

⑪

Control lever

1st-reverse control rod

FWD

2nd-3rd control rod

Gauge pin

3-speed transmission

Control lever

FWD

Rev control rod

3rd-4th control rod

1st-2nd control rod

A

4-speed transmission

FWD

View A

SHIFT CONTROL LINKAGE

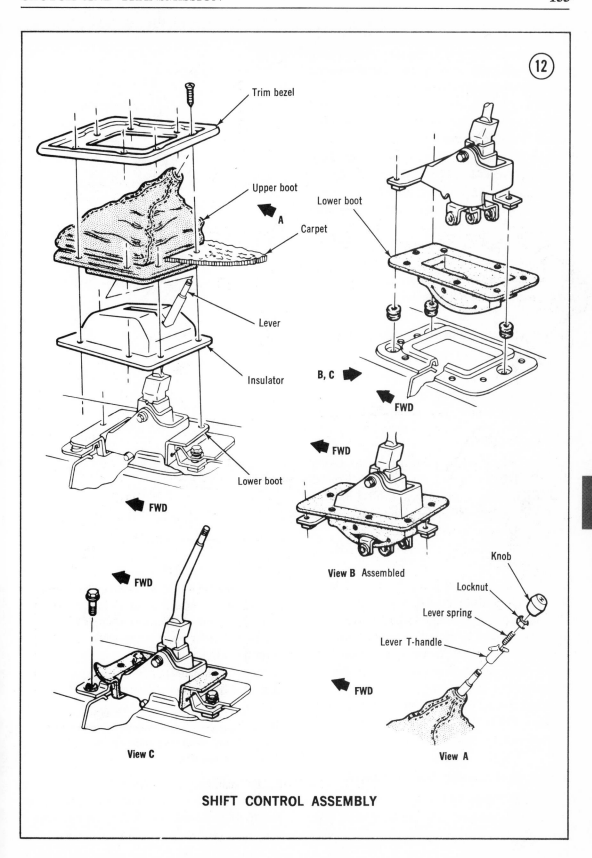

Trim bezel

Upper boot

A

Lower boot

Carpet

Lever

Insulator

B, C

FWD

Lower boot

FWD

FWD

View B Assembled

Knob

Locknut

Lever spring

Lever T-handle

FWD

View C

FWD

View A

SHIFT CONTROL ASSEMBLY

5. Push other control rods up to floor pan. Move control assembly to the rear and left until it clears extension, then tip the rear downward and remove shift control lever.

6. To install, place control lever and lower seal in opening in floor pan and install bolts. Then install insulator, upper seal, and retainer.

7. Install locknut and lever knob (3-speed) or T-handle (4-speed).

8. Install second/third (3-speed) or third/fourth (4-speed) swivel and control rod to shift control lever.

9. Connect back-up light switch and speedometer cable to transmission.

10. Check shift lever operation and adjust linkage if required. Lower vehicle.

Shift Control Assembly Repair (3-speed)

Refer to **Figure 13** for this procedure.

1. Remove retainer, then remove control lever pivot pin from control assembly.

2. Compress control lever spring by depressing control lever, then remove control lever assembly from control housing.

3. After noting relation of spacers to levers, remove shift levers and spacers from control housing. Remove isolator from control lever.

4. Clean and inspect all parts and replace those that appear to be worn or broken.

5. Lubricate levers and spacers with a water-repellant lubricant, such as Lubriplate.

6. Install a new isolator on the control lever, then install shift levers and spacers in control housing in the order noted in Step 3.

7. Insert control lever into housing assembly. Compress control lever spring and push lever into housing. Make sure control lever engages shift levers.

8. Insert control lever pivot pin and secure with retainer. Verify that the flat on the pivot pin is aligned with flat in the housing.

Shift Control Assembly Repair (4-speed)

Refer to **Figure 14** for this procedure.

1. Remove retainer, then remove shift lever pivot pin. Remove shift control lever assembly.

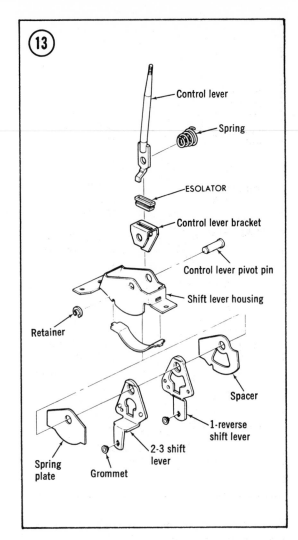

(13)

Control lever
Spring
ESOLATOR
Control lever bracket
Control lever pivot pin
Shift lever housing
Retainer
Spacer
1-reverse shift lever
2-3 shift lever
Spring plate
Grommet

2. After noting the relation of spacers to levers, remove spacers and levers from control housing.

3. Remove reverse lockout spring and retainer from shift control lever assembly. Then remove the control lever pivot pin retainer, pin, and the lever from the housing.

4. Clean and inspect all parts and replace those that appear to be worn or broken.

> NOTE: *If the reverse lever adjusting screw must be removed, grind or chisel off the weld and then remove screw from housing.*

5. To reassemble, position control lever in housing. Install control lever pivot pin and retainer. If removed, install (but do not weld at this time) reverse lever adjusting screw.

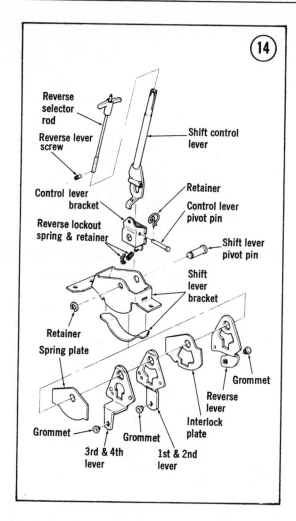

(14)

Reverse selector rod

Reverse lever screw

Shift control lever

Control lever bracket

Retainer

Control lever pivot pin

Reverse lockout spring & retainer

Shift lever pivot pin

Shift lever bracket

Retainer

Spring plate

Grommet

Grommet

Grommet

Reverse lever

Interlock plate

3rd & 4th lever

1st & 2nd lever

6. Lubricate levers and spacers with a water-repellant lubricant, such as Lubriplate.

7. Install levers and spacers in housing in the order noted in Step 2.

8. Install reverse lockout spring and retainer in housing.

9. Install shift lever pivot pin and retainer. Make sure control lever engages shift levers.

10. If reverse lever adjusting screw was removed, adjust as follows:

  a. Place control lever in first/second shifter lever and touching the interlock plate between the first/second and reverse levers.

  b. Hold reverse selector rod against the screw and tighten screw to eliminate any contact of the control finger as it travels across neutral gate of spacer plate.

  c. Weld screw in this position.

Speedometer Gear Replacement

1. Raise vehicle and disconnect speedometer cable.

2. Remove bolt and lockwasher, then remove lock plate from extension.

3. Remove gear from fitting in lock plate slot by prying out with screwdriver. Remove O-ring from groove in fitting.

4. To reassemble, lubricate new O-ring with transmission lubricant and install in groove. Lubricate driven gear shaft with transmission lubricant and insert shaft.

5. Hold assembly so fitting slot is toward lock plate boss on extension. Install assembly in extension, then insert lock plate in groove.

6. Install and tighten bolt and lockwasher, then reconnect speedometer cable. Lower vehicle.

MANUAL TRANSMISSIONS
(1976-1977)

The standard 3-speed Saginaw transmission offered in 1976 is described earlier in this chapter. A new 4-speed 70mm and a 5-speed Borg Warner are the manual transmission options offered in 1976 and 1977. **Figure 15** shows a cross section of the 4-speed 70mm transmission and **Figure 16** shows the 5-speed Borg Warner transmission.

Removal/Installation (3- and 4-speed)

The procedures for removing and installing the 3-speed Saginaw and the 4-speed 70mm transmissions are given earlier in this chapter.

Removal/Installation of Shift Control Lever (3-speed)

The procedure for shift control lever removal and installation is identical to that given for 3- and 4-speed Saginaw transmissions. Refer, however, to **Figure 17** rather than Figure 12.

Removal/Installation of Shift Control Lever (4-speed 70mm)

Refer to **Figure 18** for this procedure.

1. Loosen locknut, then remove knob, locknut, and spring.

4-SPEED 70mm TRANSMISSION

1. Drive gear
2. Bearing retainer
3. Pilot bearings
4. Case
5. Bellhousing
6. 3-4 synchronizer assembly
7. 3-4 shifter fork
8. Third speed gear
9. Detent bushing
10. Second speed gear
11. 1-2 shifter fork
12. 1-2 synchronizer assembly
13. First speed gear
14. Shifter shaft
15. Extension
16. Speedometer drive gear and clip
17. Mainshaft
18. Rear oil seal
19. Retainer oil seal
20. Snap ring—bearing to gear
21. Drive gear bearing
22. Snap ring —bearing to case
23. Countergear roller bearings
24. Countergear assembly
25. Counter reverse gear
26. Reverse idler gear
27. Reverse gear
28. Snap ring—bearing to extension
29. Rear bearing

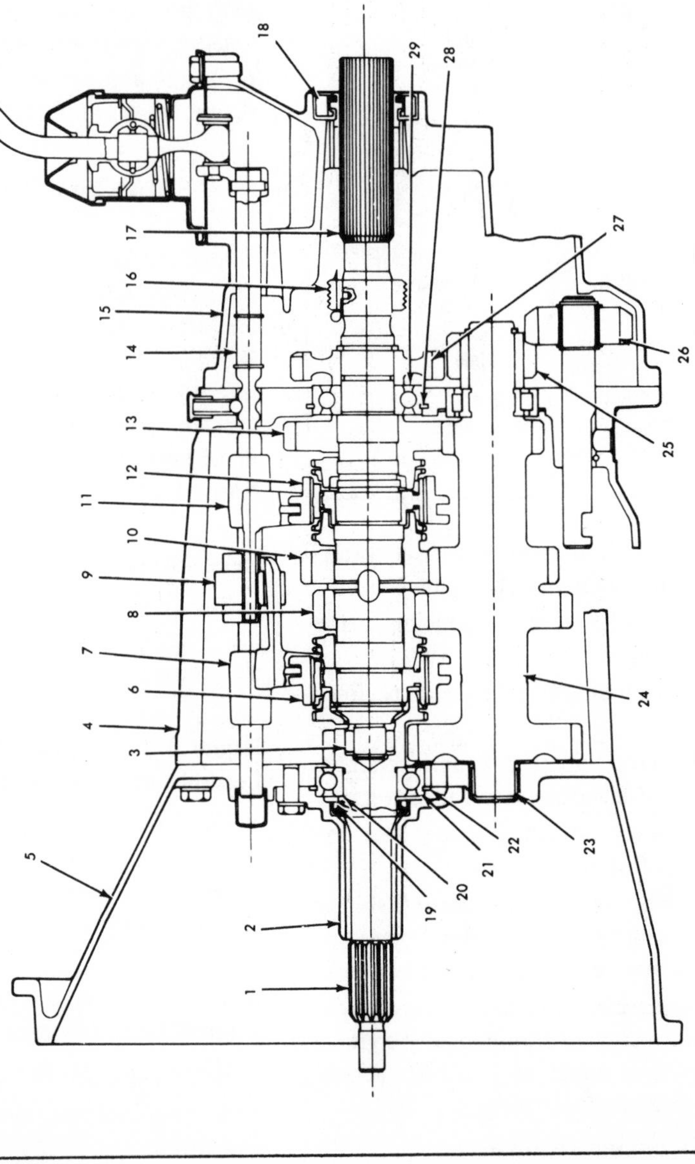

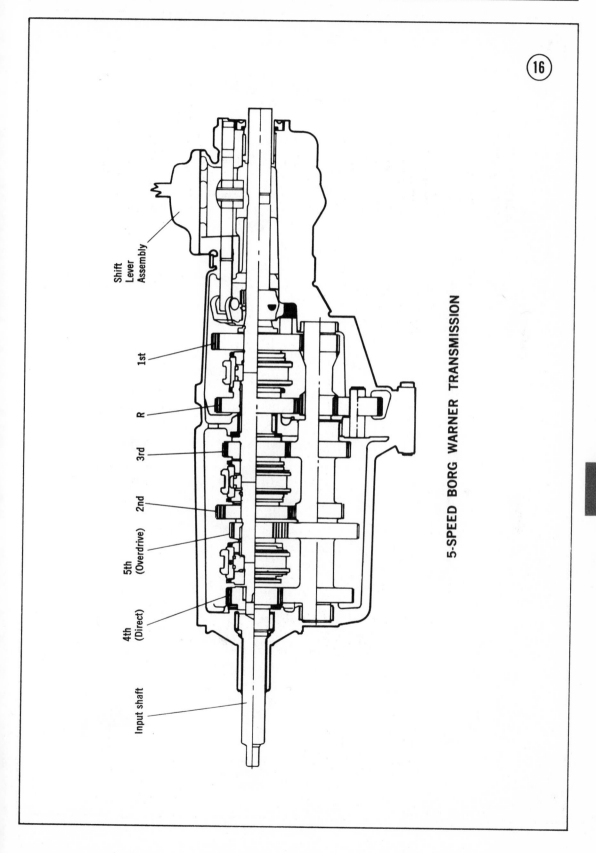

Shift Lever Assembly

1st

R

3rd

2nd

5th (Overdrive)

4th (Direct)

Input shaft

5-SPEED BORG WARNER TRANSMISSION

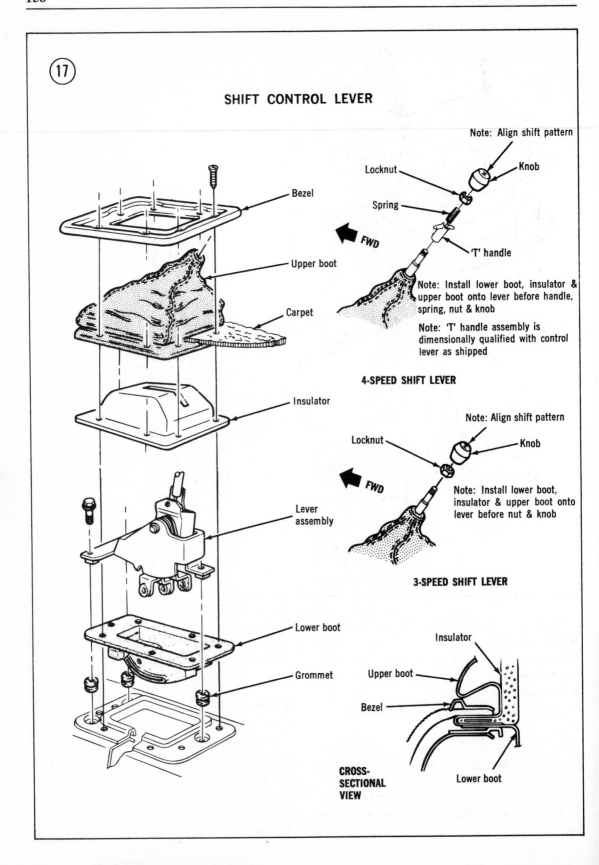

⑰

SHIFT CONTROL LEVER

Bezel

Upper boot

Carpet

Insulator

Lever assembly

Lower boot

Grommet

FWD

Note: Align shift pattern

Locknut

Knob

Spring

'T' handle

Note: Install lower boot, insulator & upper boot onto lever before handle, spring, nut & knob

Note: 'T' handle assembly is dimensionally qualified with control lever as shipped

4-SPEED SHIFT LEVER

Note: Align shift pattern

Locknut

Knob

FWD

Note: Install lower boot, insulator & upper boot onto lever before nut & knob

3-SPEED SHIFT LEVER

Insulator

Upper boot

Bezel

Lower boot

CROSS-SECTIONAL VIEW

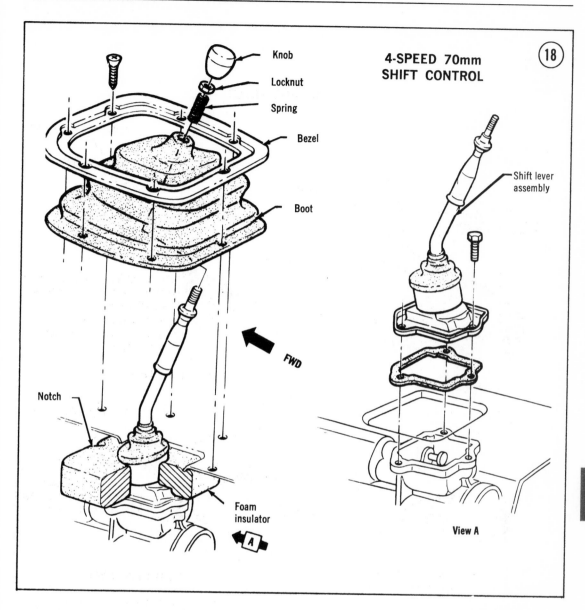

Knob

Locknut

Spring

Bezel

Boot

4-SPEED 70mm
SHIFT CONTROL

(18)

Shift lever
assembly

FWD

Notch

Foam
insulator

A

View A

2. Remove retaining screws, then remove boot retaining bezel. Remove boot.

3. Remove foam insulator, then remove shifter control assembly attaching bolts. Lift out shift lever assembly.

4. Cover opening in transmission to keep out contamination.

5. To reinstall, insert shift lever assembly into transmission and make sure fork at lower end engages head on shift rail. Install attaching bolts and torque to 35 in.-lb. (0.40 mkg).

6. Install foam insulator, making sure notch is toward front of car.

7. Install boot and retaining bezel. Then install spring, locknut, and knob. Align knob as desired and tighten locknut.

Removal/Installation of Shift Control Lever (5-speed)

Refer to **Figure 19** for this procedure.

1. Remove boot retainer bezel and slide boot up on shift control lever.

2. Remove foam insulator, if present, and remove 4 retaining bolts from shift lever assembly. Remove assembly with knob and boot attached.

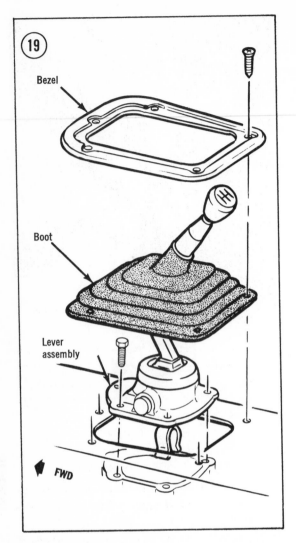

(19)

Bezel

Boot

Lever assembly

FWD

3. Remove the damper assembly, converter bracket, then disconnect the back-up light switch and speedometer cable.

4. Use a suitable transmission sack to support transmission, then remove transmission support.

5. Remove the bolts attaching the transmission to the clutch housing and slide the exhaust bracket forward.

6. Slide the transmission to the rear and remove from vehicle.

Transmission Installation (5-speed)

1. Lift the transmission with a suitable transmission jack and position it behind the clutch housing. Slide the transmission forward, making sure splines on the clutch gear mesh with those in pilot bearing. Make sure main drive gear splines are clean and dry.

2. Slide exhaust bracket into position, then install transmission-to-clutch housing attaching bolts. Torque to 55 ft.-lb. (7.6 mkg).

3. Install rear transmission mount and support. Torque bolts to 32 ft.-lb. (4.4 mkg). Remove jack.

4. Install converter bracket, damper, and torque arm. Install drive shaft as described earlier in this chapter under *Manual Transmission Removal/Installation*.

5. Connect back-up light switch and speedometer cable. Fill transmission to proper level with 80W or 90W SAE gear lubricant.

6. Lower vehicle and install shift control lever assembly as described above.

3. Cover hole in transmission to keep out contamination.

4. To reinstall, insert shift control lever assembly into transmission, making sure fork on control lever engages with head on shift rail.

5. Install retaining bolts and torque to 35 in.-lb. (0.40 mkg). Install insulator over bolts.

6. Slide boot down into place and install retaining bezel.

Transmission Removal (5-speed)

1. Remove shift control lever assembly as described above.

2. Raise vehicle and remove drive shaft as described in this chapter under *Manual Transmission Removal/Installation*.

POWERGLIDE AND TORQUE DRIVE TRANSMISSIONS

NOTE: *Automatic transmissions are complex, delicate, and expensive devices. Disassembly and repair should not be undertaken by the average home mechanic. Unless you are experienced and have a full bench of specialized tools, turn over any transmission problems to your dealer. Think twice before risking a costly blunder!*

The case and converter housing for both transmissions are single aluminum castings.

The Powerglide case is modified for the Torque Drive transmission. The vacuum modulator can-tap hole, governor feed passage, and governor support machining has been omitted. The transmission case is adapted to the extension with a pilot ring. The throttle valve lever hole has been omitted on the parklock and range selector lever, and the valve body contains only the pressure regulator, hydraulic modulator, and manual shift valves. The valve body is identified by the letters TD on the casting, and is accessible through removal of the oil pan.

Because of similarities in these 2 transmissions, the following Powerglide procedures can be used for the Torque Drive where applicable.

Low Band Adjustment (Powerglide)

1. A torque wrench is required for this operation. All adjustments must be precise.

2. On the left side of the transmission case, loosen the low servo adjusting screw lock pin, tighten adjusting screw to 70 in.-lb. (0.80 mkg) (simultaneously rotate the input and output shaft to center the low band on the clutch drum). Back off the 70 in.-lb. torque exactly 4 complete turns (exactly 3 complete turns for a band with less than 6,000 miles use), and tighten the locknut to 15 ft.-lb. (2.1 mkg) torque.

Throttle Valve Pressure Adjustment (Powerglide)

1. There is no tap to check throttle valve pressure. Use care, therefore, in adjustment of the throttle valve adjustment nut (**Figure 20**). Adjustment is made with the *nut*. One complete turn will change throttle valve pressure 3 psi. Tighten the nut to decrease; back off to increase. A 3 psi (0.21 kg/cm^2) change in throttle valve pressure changes wide-open throttle upshift point by 2-3 mph.

Throttle Valve Linkage Adjustment (Powerglide)

1. Referring to **Figure 21**, remove retainer (E). Fully depress the accelerator pedal and make certain that bellcrank (A) is in wide-open throttle position and transmission lever (B) is against internal stop.

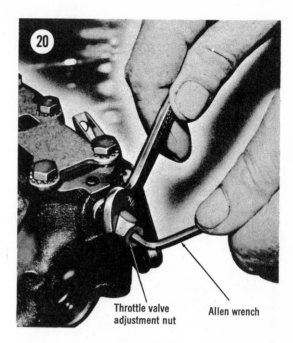

Throttle valve adjustment nut   Allen wrench

2. Disconnect rod (F) from lever (G) and, with throttle valve control rod (D) pulled rearward against bellcrank lever stud (A), adjust rod (F) to align with lever hole, plus or minus one turn.

3. Install clip and retainer.

Shift Lever Replacement and Linkage Adjustment (Powerglide)

1. Refer to **Figure 22** and the procedure for removal of the neutral safety switch as described in Chapter Seven.

2. Remove 2 pivot bolts (Figure 22) and insert drift punch into shaft hole.

3. Remove cable drive lever and spread handle to remove lever strap and button.

4. Remove pawl by spreading the control lever strap, and disassemble button mechanism. Remove screws and disassemble handle from lever.

Transmission Removal (Powerglide)

1. Drain oil and disconnect vacuum modulator (Powerglide), speedometer drive cable, manual (Powerglide throttle valve) control lever, and drive shaft.

2. Support the engine at oil pan and the transmission at pan.

3. Disconnect transmission mount and crossmember at frame. Remove crossmember.

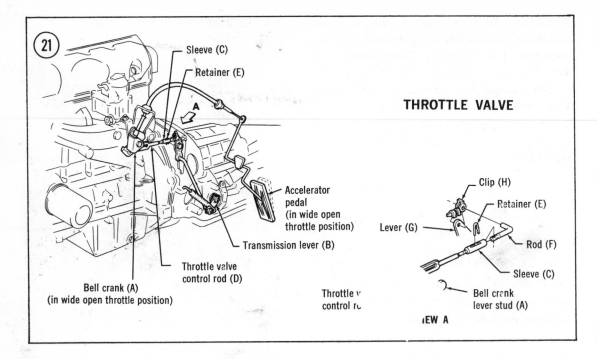

② Sleeve (C)

Retainer (E)

A

THROTTLE VALVE

Accelerator pedal
(in wide open throttle position)

Transmission lever (B)

Throttle valve control rod (D)

Bell crank (A)
(in wide open throttle position)

Clip (H)

Retainer (E)

Lever (G)

Rod (F)

Sleeve (C)

Bell crank lever stud (A)

Throttle v
control r.

EW A

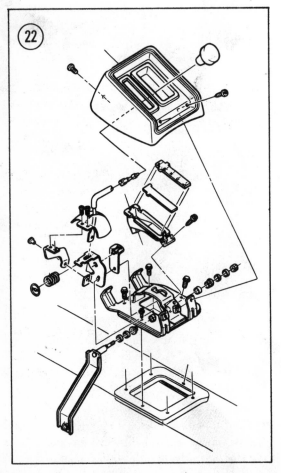

②

4. Remove the converter pan, mark flywheel-to-converter relationship, and remove flywheel-to-converter attaching bolt.

5. Lower transmission slightly to gain access to the transmission housing-to-engine bolts. Remove the bolts.

6. Remove transmission, making sure that converter comes with it and does not stick to flywheel. Hold front of transmission higher than back so that converter will not slide off shaft. Retain converter on shaft with a piece of safety wire through the transmission housing and converter-to-flywheel mounting bolt holes.

Transmission Installation (Powerglide)

1. Position transmission in place (remove temporary means of securing the converter), and install mounting bolts. Torque bolts to 35 ft.-lb. (9.9 kgm).

2. Match converter-to-flywheel scribe marks and install attaching bolts, torquing to specification. Install converter underpan.

3. Raise transmission high enough to install rear mount and crossmember. Torque all bolts to specifications.

4. Install drive shaft.

5. Connect the manual and throttle valve control lever rods, vacuum modulator line, and speedometer drive cable. Connect oil cooler lines if used.

6. Fill transmission as described in Chapter Two. Start engine, and check for leaks.

7. Check for main line pressure and shift points according to the specifications at the end of this chapter.

TURBO-HYDRAMATIC 250/350 TRANSMISSIONS

In the Turbo-Hydramatic 250, a 3-element torque converter driving 2 planetary gear sets provides a smooth 3-speed automatic transmission with more flexibility than the earlier Powerglide. The torque converter is a welded unit and serviced as an assembly. A vacuum modulator senses changes in engine load and signals a pressure regulator which controls transmission shifting. Transmission fluid level (Chapter Two) should be checked before proceeding with any further tests or disassembly.

The Turbo-Hydramatic 350 is similar, but has no provision for externally adjusting the intermediate band.

Intermediate Band Adjustment (Turbo-Hydramatic 250)

An intermediate band that is too tight sometimes results in a transmission starting up in second range instead of low.

> NOTE: *A special tool, Chevrolet J-24367, facilitates making this adjustment but is not mandatory. A torque wrench is required.*

1. Place shift lever in NEUTRAL; raise vehicle. Locate intermediate band adjustment on right side of transmission and loosen locknut ¼ turn (½ turn on 1975-1977 cars).

2. Tighten adjusting screw to 30 in.-lb. (0.35 mkg), then back off 3 complete turns. Tighten the locknut to 15 ft.-lb. (2.07 mkg).

Shift Linkage Adjustment (1973-1974)

> CAUTION
> *This adjustment must be precise or premature failure can occur even though the transmission appears to operate properly.*

1. Loosen nut (E) on end of transmission lever (F). Refer to **Figure 23**. Move transmission lever (F) fully counterclockwise to L1 range detent than clockwise 3 detent positions to NEUTRAL.

2. Move shift lever, control rod (J) to NEUTRAL. Adjust position of swivel (D) so flat surface fits into slot in rod (A). Tighten nut (E) to 120 in.-lb. (1.38 mkg).

3. This may require readjustment of neutral start switch. Refer to Chapter Seven.

Shift Linkage Adjustment (1975)

> CAUTION
> *This adjustment must be precise, or premature failure of the transmission will result.*

1. Refer to **Figure 24**. Loosely assemble nut (E) and swivel (D) on rod (A) and actuating lever.

2. Place transmission lever (F) in NEUTRAL by moving first to PARK position, then back 2 detent positions to NEUTRAL.

3. Place control rod (J) in neutral notch of detent (G). See View B of Figure 24.

4. Insert flats of swivel (D) into slot in rod (A) and attach washer and retainer. Tighten nut (E) to 120 in.-lb. (1.38 mkg).

5. If necessary, adjust neutral start switch to correct relationship with transmission detent positions.

Shift Cable Linkage Adjustment (1976-1977)

> CAUTION
> *This adjustment must be precise, or premature failure of the transmission will result.*

1. Install transmission control cable through transmission control bracket and attach to shifter assembly. See **Figure 25**.

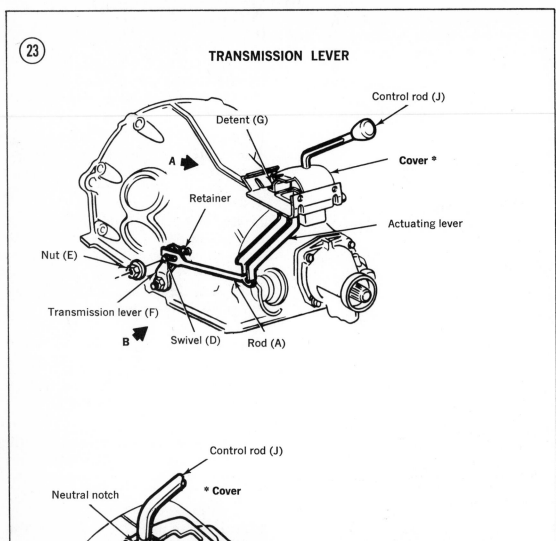

TRANSMISSION LEVER

Control rod (J)

Detent (G)

Cover *

A ▶

Retainer

Actuating lever

Nut (E)

Transmission lever (F)

B ◤

Swivel (D)   Rod (A)

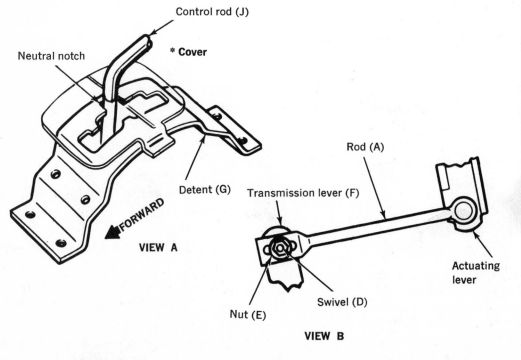

Control rod (J)

Neutral notch

* Cover

Detent (G)

Rod (A)

Transmission lever (F)

◀ FORWARD

VIEW A

Nut (E)

Swivel (D)

Actuating lever

VIEW B

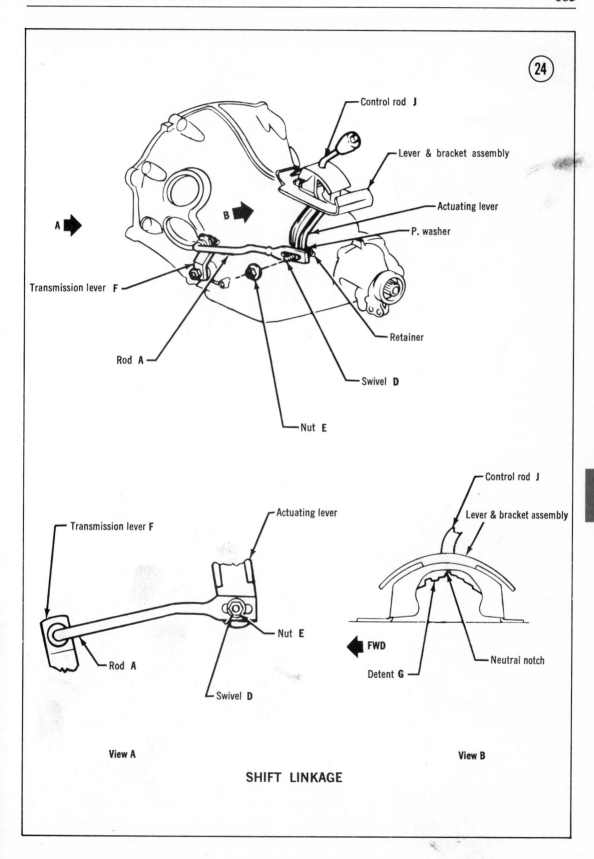

SHIFT LINKAGE

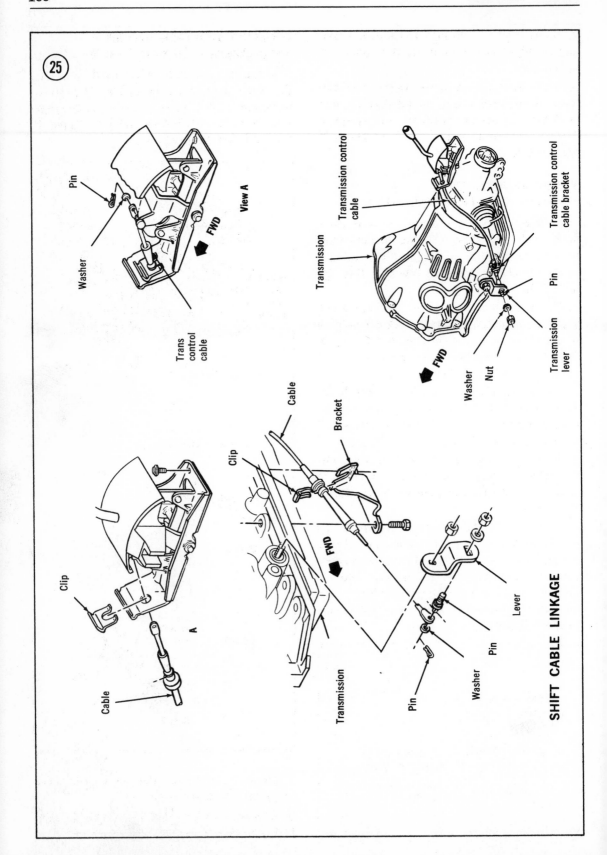

(25)

Pin

Washer

Trans
control
cable

View A

FWD

Transmission control
cable

Transmission

Transmission control
cable bracket

Pin

Transmission
lever

Washer

Nut

FWD

Cable

Bracket

Clip

Clip

Cable

A

Transmission

FWD

Lever

Pin

Washer

Pin

SHIFT CABLE LINKAGE

2. Insert lever pin through transmission lever and install washer and nut. Do not tighten nut at this time.

3. Place transmission in NEUTRAL by moving lever counterclockwise to the L1 position, then clockwise 4 detent positions to NEUTRAL. Tighten nut installed in Step 2 to 20 ft.-lb. (2.76 mkg).

Vacuum Modulator Check and Replacement (Turbo-Hydramatic)

A defective vacuum modulator can cause harsh or delayed shifts, slipping in gear, transmission overheating, or engine burning transmission fluid (evidenced by low fluid level but no leaks).

1. Insert a pipe cleaner as far as possible into vacuum connector pipe and check for fluid on pipe cleaner. If any transmission fluid is observed (not gasoline or water which may settle in pipe), replace vacuum modulator.

2. Check seam around modulator for leaks. Apply soapy water and blow on vacuum connection wtih lung power (not compressed air). If any leaks, replace modulator.

3. Roll modulator main body along a flat surface while observing concentricity of sleeve to cam. If out-of-round or plunger sticks, replace the modulator.

4. Make a tool as indicated in **Figure 26** and compare spring pressure with known good unit. Fit modulators on each end of gauge and slowly move them together. If gap between units is greater than 1/16 in. (1.6mm) when one or the other modulator reaches center line, replace the used modulator.

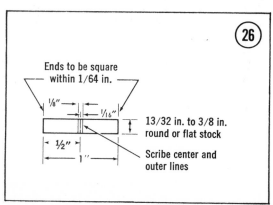

Ends to be square within 1/64 in.

1/8" 1/16"

13/32 in. to 3/8 in. round or flat stock

1/2" 1"

Scribe center and outer lines

Detent Downshift Cable Adjustment and Replacement (Turbo-Hydramatic)

If transmission fails to downshift properly, the detent cable could be sticking, broken, or misadjusted. This cable connects the transmission to the throttle linkage; refer to **Figure 27** for the following procedure.

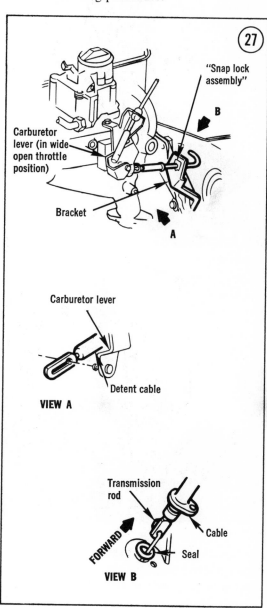

"Snap lock assembly"

B

Carburetor lever (in wide open throttle position)

Bracket

A

Carburetor lever

Detent cable

VIEW A

Transmission rod

Cable

FORWARD

Seal

VIEW B

1. Remove air cleaner. Push up on snap lock and release lock and cable.

2. Compress locking tabs and disengage snap lock assembly from cable bracket.

3. To adjust, operate throttle to wide open position and push down on snap lock to reseat.

4. To replace cable, remove clamp around filler tube; remove the screw attaching the cable to the transmission.

Transmission Fluid Change and Screen Cleaning (Turbo-Hydramatic)

This procedure can be performed with transmission in place and can sometimes eliminate rough or noisy shifting.

CAUTION
Transmission fluid can reach 350°F (175°C) during operation. Either do this operation with transmission cold or be careful not to let fluid splatter.

1. Drain transmission oil with transmission warm. Remove oil pan and discard gasket.

2. Remove 2 screen-to-valve body attaching screws as in **Figure 28**. Remove oil pump suction screen and gasket from valve body.

Oil pump suction screen

3. Clean and inspect screen and replace. Using new gaskets, replace oil pan and refill transmission with new fluid to ADD mark on dipstick. Drive 1-2 miles, recheck level, add fluid to bring to FULL mark. *Do not overfill.*

Transmission Fluid Leak

To locate a transmission fluid leak, first degrease and clean underside of transmission. Operate vehicle for several miles to get transmission up to operating temperature. If a leak is bad, it may be necessary to clean transmission case again. Visually check for leak both with engine running and shut off. Compare fluid leaked with dipstick to confirm leak is transmission fluid and not engine oil that has blown back from oil pan or rear main bearing. Some common leak areas are:

a. Transmission oil pan
b. Extension housing
c. Case leak
d. Front pump seal
e. Converter in weld area
f. Vent or filler pipe

If fluid is expelled from vent, check for too high fluid level or water in fluid. Case porosity can cause leaks and can be alleviated by cleaning the area and sealing exterior of case with epoxy cement.

Transmission Replacement (Turbo-Hydramatic)

In many cases, it is more expeditious to merely replace old, worn transmissions with new or rebuilt units rather than to attempt to fix a single fault when there may be other worn parts.

1. Disconnect battery, detent downshift cable, speedometer cable, modulator vacuum line, and shift linkage. Drain fluid.

2. Release the parking brake and remove the drive shaft.

3. Support transmission with hydraulic jack or other suitable support.

4. Disconnect transmission rear mount from frame crossmember.

5. Remove 2 bolts at end of crossmember and remove crossmember.

6. Remove converter under pan. Remove the converter-to-flywheel bolts and lower the transmission slightly.

7. Remove the transmission-to-engine mounting bolts and remove the oil filler tube at the transmission.

8. Raise transmission back to normal position. Support engine with another jack or suitable

blocks. Slide transmission to rear and lower it away from frame.

CAUTION
Use suitable support for convertor to keep rear of transmission lower than front to prevent losing convertor.

9. Installation is the reverse of removal.

10. Fill transmission and check for main line, clutch, and intermediate pressure points and shift points according to procedure and specifications in Chapter Three, *Turbo-Hydramatic Basic Pressure Check.*

Table 1   CLUTCH AND MANUAL TRANSMISSION TORQUE SPECIFICATIONS (1971-1972)

	Torque		Torque
Clutch fork cover bolts	80 in.-lb.	Transmission mount-to-rear extension bolts	30 ft.-lb.
Transmission to clutch housing bolts	24 ft.-lb.	Clutch cover to pressure plate attaching bolts	18 ft.-lb.
Transmission fill plug	18 ft.-lb.	Clutch fork ball stud lock nut	25 ft.-lb.
Clutch housing lower cover bolts	80 in.-lb.	Rear extension to case bolts	31 ft.-lb.
Clutch housing to engine attaching bolts	25 ft.-lb.	Filler plug	30 ft.-lb.
Clutch fork ball stud locknut	25 ft.-lb.	Transmission cover screws	48 in.-lb.
Crossmember-to-frame bolts	28 ft.-lb.	Speedometer driven gear retainer bolt	48 in.-lb.
Crossmember-to-mount bolts	26 ft.-lb.		

Table 3   CLUTCH AND MANUAL TRANSMISSION TORQUE SPECIFICATIONS (1975-1977)

	Torque		Torque
Clutch fork cover bolts	81 in.-lb.	TCS switch	25 ft.-lb.
Transmission to clutch housing bolts	52.5 ft.-lb.	Speedometer driver gear retainer bolt	42 in-lb.
Transmission filler plug	22 ft.-lb.	Transmission control lever bolts	30 in.-lb.
Clutch cover and pressure plate bolts	18 ft.-lb.	Transmission control rod to swivel locknut	120 in.-lb.
Clutch housing lower cover bolts	82 in.-lb.	Shift control lever retaining bolts	120 in.-lb.
Clutch housing to engine bolts	25 ft.-lb.	Shift control trim plate screws	28 in.-lb.
Clutch fork ball stud locknut	25 ft.-lb.	Shift knob locknut	60 in.-lb.
Crossmember to frame bolt and nut	28 ft.-lb.	Transmission cover attaching bolts	22 ft.-lb.
Crossmember to rear mount bolts	26 ft.-lb.	Transmission rear extension bolts	45 ft.-lb.
Rear mount to transmission bolts	26 ft.-lb.	Clutch gear bearing retainer bolts	15 ft.-lb.
Damper attaching nuts	30 ft.-lb.		

Table 2   CLUTCH AND MANUAL TRANSMISSION TORQUE SPECIFICATIONS (1973-1974)

	Torque		Torque
Clutch fork cover bolts	80 in.-lb.	TCS switch	115 in.-lb.
Transmission-to-clutch housing bolts	40 ft.-lb.	Speedometer drive gear retainer bolt	42 in.-lb.
Transmission filler plug	18 ft.-lb.	Transmission control lever bolts	30 in.-lb.
Clutch cover and pressure plate bolts	18 ft.-lb.	Transmission control rod-to-swivel locknut	120 in.-lb.
Clutch housing lower cover bolts	82 in.-lb.	Shift control lever retaining bolts	120 in.-lb.
Clutch housing-to-engine bolts	25 ft.-lb.	Shift control trim plate screws	28 in.-lb.
Clutch fork ball stud locknut	25 ft.-lb.	Shift knob locknut	60 in.-lb.
Crossmember-to-frame bolt and nut	28 ft.-lb.	Transmission cover attaching bolts	22 ft.-lb.
Crossmember-to-rear mount bolts	26 ft.-lb.	Transmission rear extension bolts	45 ft.-lb.
Rear mount-to-transmission bolts	26 ft.-lb.	Clutch gear bearing retainer bolts	16 ft.-lb.
Damper attaching nuts	30 ft.-lb.		

Table 4   FOUR-SPEED 70MM TRANSMISSION TORQUE SPECIFICATIONS (1976-1977)

	Torque		Torque
Bellhousing to engine bolts	25 ft.-lb.	Bellhousing to case bolts	26 ft.-lb.
Crossmember to transmission		Bearing retainer to bellhousing bolts	105 in.-lb.
Center nut	33 ft.-lb.	Speedometer driven gear retaining bolts	44 in. lb.
End nut	21 ft.-lb.	Clutch fork ball stud locknut	24 ft.-lb.
Crossmember to frame bolts	40 ft.-lb.	Clutch cable locknut	53 in.-lb.
Shift control lever retaining bolts	35 in.-lb.	Bellhousing lower cover bolts	90 in.-lb.
Transmission filler plug	25 ft.-lb.	Rear support to transmission bolts	32 ft.-lb.
Clutch cover to flywheel bolts	18 ft.-lb.	Converter bracket to rear support nuts	150 in.-lb.
Extension housing to case bolts	26 ft.-lb.	Back-up lamp switch	25 ft.-lb.

Table 5   POWERGLIDE TORQUE SPECIFICATIONS

Transmission case-to-engine	35 ft.-lb.	Lower-to-upper valve body attaching bolts	15 ft.-lb.
Transmission oil pan-to-case	8 ft.-lb.	Inner control lever Allen head screw	2½ ft.-lb.
Transmission extension-to-case	25 ft.-lb.	Parking lock pawl reaction bracket	
Speedometer driven gear fitting retainer	4 ft.-lb.	attaching bolts	10 ft.-lb.
Servo cover-to-transmission case bolts	20 ft.-lb.	Pressure test point plugs	5 ft.-lb.
Front pump-to-transmission case bolts	15 ft.-lb.	Low band adjustment locknut	15 ft.-lb.
Front pump cover-to-body attaching bolts	20 ft.-lb.	Converter-to-engine bolts	35 ft.-lb.
Pinion shaft lock plate attaching screws	2½ ft.-lb.	Under pan-to-transmission case	7½ ft.-lb.
Governor body-to-hub attaching bolts	7 ft.-lb.	Vacuum modulator-to-transmission case	15 ft.-lb.
Governor hub drive screw	8 ft.-lb.	Parking brake lock and range selector	
Governor support-to-transmission case bolts	10 ft.-lb.	inner lever Allen head screw	2½ ft.-lb.
Valve body-to-transmission case bolts	15 ft.-lb.	Control lever	25 in.-lb.
Valve body suction screen attaching screws	2½ ft.-lb.	Manual shaft-to-lever	20 ft.-lb.
Upper valve body plate bolts	5 ft.-lb.	Control rod-to-swivel	120 in.-lb.

Table 6   TURBO-HYDRAMATIC 250-350 TORQUE SPECIFICATIONS

Inner selector lever-to-shaft	25 ft.-lb.	Pump cover-to-pump body	17 ft.-lb.
Detent valve actuating bracket	52 in.-lb.	Pump assembly-to-case	18½ ft.-lb.
Converter-to-flywheel bolts	35 ft.-lb.	Valve body and support plate	130 in.-lb.
Under pan-to-transmission case	110 in.-lb.	Parking lock bracket	29 ft.-lb.
Transmission case-to-engine	35 ft.-lb.	Oil suction screen	40 in.-lb.
Control lever	25 in.-lb.	Oil pan-to-case	130 in.-lb.
Manual shaft-to-lever	20 ft.-lb.	Extension-to-case	25 ft.-lb.
Control rod-to-swivel	120 in.-lb.	Modulator retainer-to-case	130 in.-lb.
Intermediate band adjustment	15 ft.-lb.		

CHAPTER NINE

BRAKES

Front wheel brake design includes a 10 in. diameter by ½ in. thick disc and a single piston sliding caliper as shown in **Figure 1**. No brake adjustment is required.

Rear brakes used on 1971-1975 models are self-adjusting drum brakes, 9 in. by 1¼ in. (**Figure 2**). In 1976, a self-adjusting drum brake, 9½ in. by 2 in. was introduced (**Figure 3**). Both also serve as parking brakes. The 1971-1975 brake is automatically adjusted whenever the parking brake is applied. The 1976-1977 brake is adjusted whenever the service brake is applied while the car is in reverse gear.

STRUT AND ROD ASSEMBLY

PULL-BACK SPRING

TRAILING SHOE

HOLD-DOWN CLIP

PARKING BRAKE LEVER

LEADING SHOE

LOWER PIVOT

RETAINER SPRING

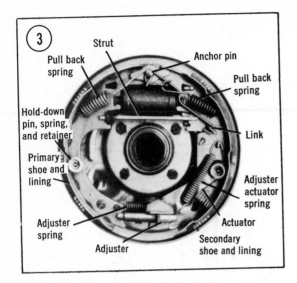

③

Strut
Pull back spring
Anchor pin
Pull back spring
Hold-down pin, spring, and retainer
Link
Primary shoe and lining
Adjuster actuator spring
Adjuster spring
Actuator
Adjuster
Secondary shoe and lining

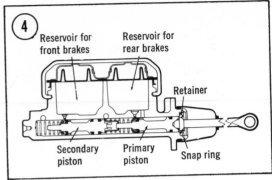

④

Reservoir for front brakes
Reservoir for rear brakes
Retainer
Secondary piston
Primary piston
Snap ring

The dual reservoir, dual piston master cylinder actuates the front wheel brakes and the rear wheel brakes independently (**Figure 4**). When a failure occurs, or when there is air in the front or rear system, either pair of brakes alone is adequate to stop the car. The pressure loss is detected by the distribution switch assembly which illuminates the brake alarm indicator light on the instrument panel.

Brake line routing and connections are shown in **Figures 5 and 6** (1971-1975) or **Figures 7 and 8** (1976-1977), for the front and rear brakes, respectively. Brake lines are constructed of a special high-strength, double layer steel tubing; copper tubing should never be used as a replacement.

No special tools are required for brake work, but brake lines must be double-lap flared. The tool for this operation is not too expensive; however, most replacement lines are already flared with new fittings installed.

Tables 1, 2, and 3 at the end of this chapter provide specifications and tightening torques.

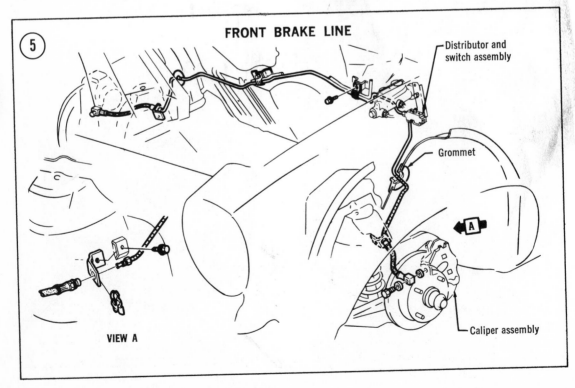

FRONT BRAKE LINE

⑤

Distributor and switch assembly

Grommet

A

Caliper assembly

VIEW A

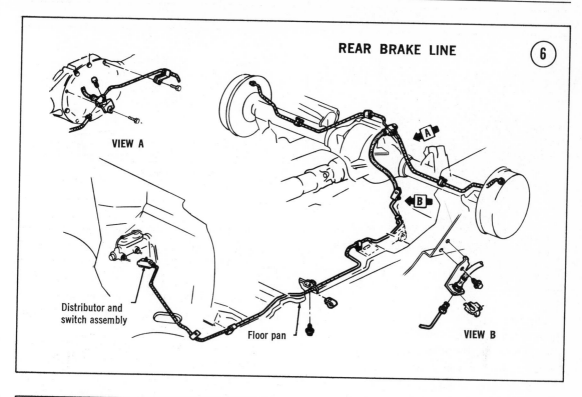

REAR BRAKE LINE

VIEW A

Distributor and
switch assembly

Floor pan

VIEW B

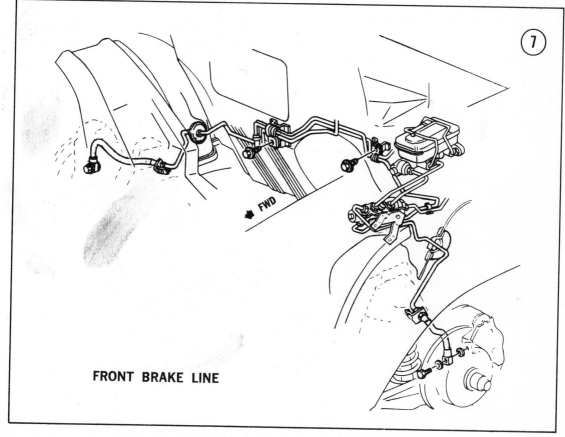

FWD

FRONT BRAKE LINE

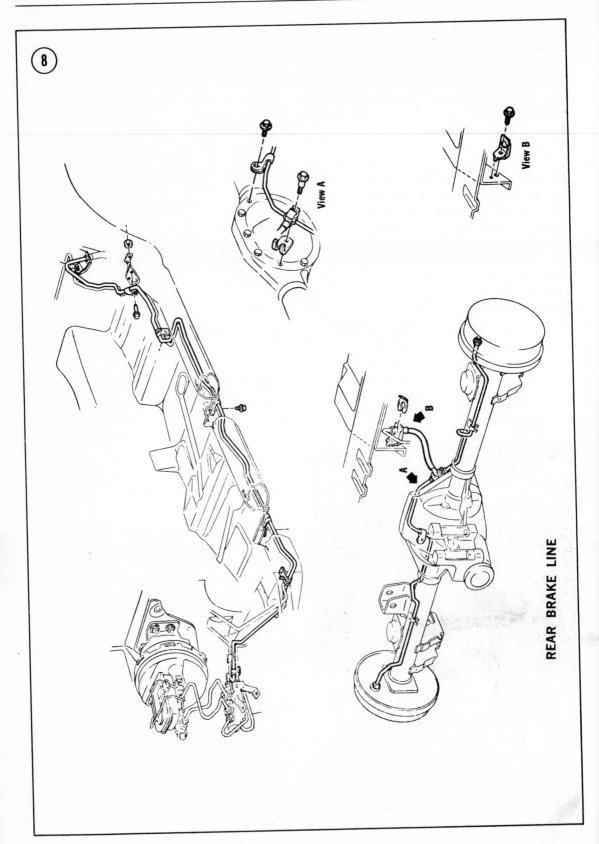

8

View A

View B

REAR BRAKE LINE

BRAKE BLEEDING

The brake hydraulic system will require bleeding following overhaul. If the brake fluid level in the master cylinder reservoir gets too low, or if any repair requires opening the hydraulic lines, the brakes will also have to be bled. There are bleeder valves at each of the 4 wheels.

A soft brake pedal is one indication that air has entered the system. The Vega has a characteristically soft brake pedal when standing; however, the pedal should be firm when the brakes are applied while the car is in motion.

Equipment is available that will put the system under pressure and maintain fluid level while the brakes are being bled, but it is expensive. With an assistant, the brakes can be bled manually.

NOTE: *On 1976-1977 models the combination valve must be held open during the bleeding operation. A special tool (J-23709) or its equivalent (*Figure 9*) can be used to hold the valve open. Make sure mounting bolt is retightened after tool is removed.*

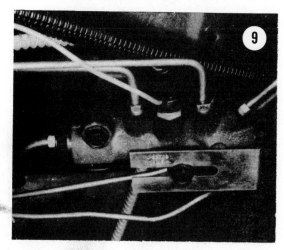

1. Fill the master cylinder with fluid.

2. Starting at the right-hand side of the car (front or back), connect one end of a bleeder hose to the bleeder valve, and submerge the other end into a small amount of brake fluid in the bottom of a clean jar.

3. Have an assistant maintain pressure on the brake pedal, then open the bleeder valve ¼

turn, and close it when the brake pedal reaches the floor; release brake pedal pressure, and repeat until air stops escaping from the hose in the jar.

4. Repeat for the remaining wheel on the right-hand side of the car, then perform the same operations on the left side.

5. If all wheels have been bled, but there is still evidence of air in the system, repeat the entire bleeding process.

NOTE: *Check the fluid level in the master cylinder frequently while bleeding the brakes. If the fluid is depleted anytime during the bleeding process, more air will be fed into the system.*

BRAKE ADJUSTMENT

Front disc brakes cannot be adjusted. Rear brakes are automatically adjusted whenever the parking brake is applied (1971-1975), or when the service brake is applied while in reverse gear (1976-1977). Rear brakes do require initial adjustment, however, after linings have been replaced.

Rear Service Brake Adjustment

1. Turn star wheel until a slight drag is felt when wheel is turned.

2. Back star wheel off 1¼ turns to retract the shoes.

3. Make final adjustment by applying parking brake several times (1971-1975 models) or by making a number of forward and reverse stops.

4. If unable to obtain a firm brake pedal, bleed the system as described above under *Brake Bleeding.*

Parking Brake Adjustment

To adjust parking brake, pull up one notch from the fully released position, and adjust the equalizer (where the 2 brake cables meet) until the rear wheels drag slightly. Tighten the locknut, set the parking brake at the fully released position, and turn the rear wheels; there should be no drag.

9

BRAKE PEDAL

Refer to **Figure 10**. Note that the brake pedal and clutch pedal are hinged on the same bolt. Parts are identical for cars equipped with automatic transmissions, except that a short bolt is used. The brake pedal can be removed by disconnecting the pushrod, removing the pivot bolt nut, and sliding the bolt out to release the clutch pedal. When reinstalling, apply a small amount of chassis lubricant to the bushing.

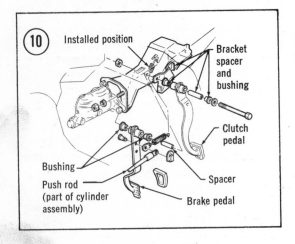

FRONT BRAKES

Removal/Disassembly

1. Remove the caliper by prying off the speed nuts (**Figure 11**), removing the pins (**Figure 12**), and lifting the caliper assembly from the disc.

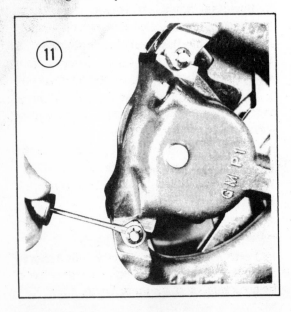

2. Place the caliper on the frame so there is no strain on the flexible hose.

3. If disc requires refinishing, remove the hub.

4. Remove the brake shoes by sliding them to the mounting sleeves opening as shown in **Figure 13**.

Cleaning and Inspection

Inspect the caliper for fluid leakage. If there are no leaks, wipe the caliper with a rag; do not use compressed air, it might unseat the dust boot.

Examine the disc for scoring, scratches, and porosity.

Caliper Overhaul

1. Disconnect the hose from the brake line; plug the brake line, and remove the hose-fitting retainer. The caliper and hose can now be removed as an assembly.

2. Using only denatured alcohol or brake fluid, clean the exterior of the caliper.

3. Remove the brake hose. A new copper gasket should be used on reassembly.

4. Drain the brake fluid and remove the piston by applying air pressure at the fluid inlet fitting.

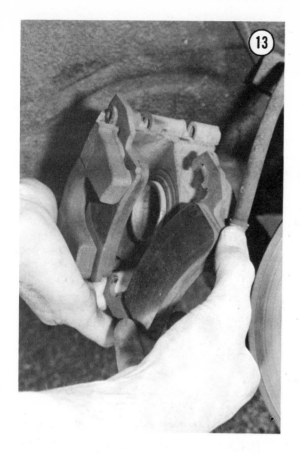

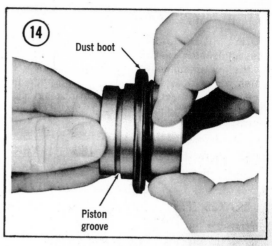

Dust boot

Piston groove

10. Install the piston. Between 50 and 100 lb. (22-45 kg) force is required to seat the piston in the bottom of the bore.

11. Install the dust boot and tap into place, making sure that it is seated straight in the bore.

12. Install brake hose with new copper gasket.

Disc Refinishing

A damaged or worn brake disc can be refinished, provided that the finished thickness is at least 0.470 in. (11.90mm). A disc should be discarded if the thickness measures 0.440 in. (11.2mm) or less. Precision refinishing is required to the following accuracy.

1. Both disc surfaces must be flat within a reading of 0.002 in. (0.05mm).

2. The 2 disc surfaces must be radially parallel within 0.003 in. (0.07mm) of each other.

3. Circumferential thickness at any radius must not vary more than 0.0005 in. (0.018mm).

4. Lateral runout must not exceed 0.005 in. (0.18mm) with the maximum rate of change no greater than 0.001 in. (0.03mm) in 30°.

5. Both surfaces must be perpendicular to the spindle center line within 0.003 in.

6. A non-directional, 20-60 micro inch finish is required.

Installation

1. Install the mounting sleeves and bushings in the caliper grooves with the shoulders away from each other as shown in Figure 13.

CAUTION
Pad the surface with shop towels; do not attempt to catch the piston. Apply no more air pressure than is needed.

5. Remove the dust seal by prying with a screwdriver. Be careful not to scratch the piston bore.

6. Remove the piston seal from the piston bore with a wooden or plastic stick. Do not use a metal object.

7. Remove the bleeder valve, and examine the piston and bore surfaces for damage. Any damage to the bore that cannot be repaired with crocus cloth requires replacement of the caliper and piston. Do not use emery cloth, or any other abrasive. The piston itself is plated; *do not use any abrasive—not even crocus cloth.*

8. Generously lubricate all parts with brake fluid for reassembly.

9. Install a new piston and seal in the bore, and assemble the piston and dust boot as shown in **Figure 14**.

9

2. Install the shoes; inner first, then outer.

3. If new shoes are being used, it may be necessary to remove ½ the master cylinder fluid before installing the caliper.

4. Hold the caliper in place and install the mounting pins with the heads to the outside.

5. Install new speed nuts, using a small socket with an outside diameter equal to the speed nut outside diameter.

6. Bleed the system as previously described. Check master cylinder fluid level before operating vehicle.

REAR BRAKES (1971-1975)

Removal/Disassembly

> NOTE: *Rear brake drums may be worn sufficiently to require release of the brake adjuster before removal. If the drum does not slide off readily, knock out the adjuster access plug (*Figure 15*), and release the rod assembly by pushing in on the rod as shown. This will permit the return spring to pull the shoes together and the drum to be removed. Install a replacement plug upon assembly.*

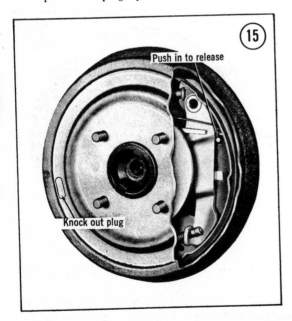

1. Back off on the parking brake equalizer to loosen the cable, then unhook the cable from the parking brake lever on the rear shoe.

2. Remove the return spring and the shoes. The hold-down clips need not be removed unless they are broken or worn.

3. With tool J-23730, or a pair of pliers and suitable shim, compress adjuster locks and work rod assembly free.

4. If wheel cylinder is leaking, disconnect brake line, remove mounting screws and cylinder. Rebuild or replace the cylinder (**Figure 16**).

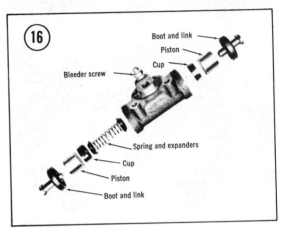

Cleaning and Inspection

1. Disassemble cylinder and clean only with alcohol or brake fluid. Check for corroded or otherwise damaged cylinder bore and condition of rubber parts.

2. Inspect the drums for heat cracks, scoring, and proper roundness. Drum must measure at least 0.030 in. (0.76mm) after refinishing.

3. If drums are replaced, new drums should be cleaned thoroughly to remove rust proofing. Use a greaseless solvent such as alcohol; *do not use gasoline or kerosene.*

Assembly/Installation

1. Assemble the adjuster by positioning the lock mechanism as shown in **Figure 17**, then sliding the assembly together (**Figure 18**) until it reaches the position shown in **Figure 19**.

> NOTE: *The 2 adjuster spring tabs may have been bent down during disassembly so that they do not engage the serrated surface. Bend the tabs up again with needle-nose pliers so that the lock mechanism works.*

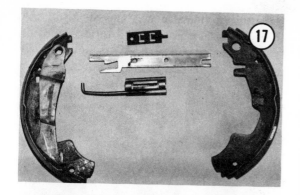

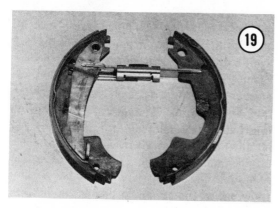

9

2. Assemble the brake lever to the trailing shoe (it has a hole in the web for the parking brake lever and an oblong hole for the adjuster rod), and lubricate the backing plate-to-brake shoe contact surfaces as shown in **Figure 20**.

3. Assemble the brake shoe by installing the lower pivot, retaining spring, parking brake strut, and adjuster assembly. Then install the assembled brake shoes to the backing plate, engaging the hold-down clips and aligning the shoe web with the cylinder links.

4. Install return spring as shown in **Figure 21**.

Connect the parking brake cable; install brake drums and wheels, and adjust the parking brake as described previously.

5. Pull the parking brake handle 2 or 3 times to adjust the rear brakes.

REAR BRAKES (1976-1977)

Removal/Disassembly

> NOTE: *It may be necessary to retract the adjusting screw if brake drums are severely worn. Knock out the lanced area in the drum with a chisel to gain access to the star wheel adjusting screw. Use a wire hook or similar device to hold the adjusting lever and back off the star wheel with a screwdriver (*Figure 22*). After drum is removed, be sure to remove the metal knocked out of the lanced area.*

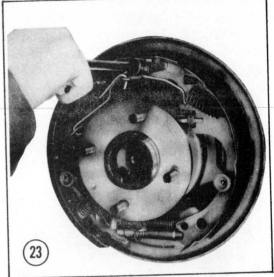

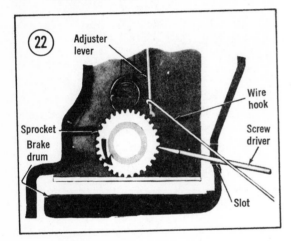

1. Raise vehicle and loosen parking brake equalizer nut enough to remove all tension from brake cable.

2. Remove brake drums.

CAUTION
> *Do not depress brake pedal while drums are removed. To do so could result in damage to wheel cylinders.*

3. Remove brake shoe pull-back springs from anchor pin and link end. A special tool is available that will greatly simplify this job (**Figure 23**). See Figure 3 for parts locations.

4. Remove actuator return spring and link.

5. Remove hold-down pins, retainers, and springs (**Figure 24**).

6. Remove actuator assembly. Do not disassemble actuator assembly unless a part is broken.

7. Remove adjusting screw and spring and separate and remove brake shoes. Mark position of shoes if they are to be reinstalled.

8. Remove parking brake lever from secondary shoe.

Cleaning and Inspection

1. Remove all dirt from drum and inspect for roughness, scoring, or out-of-round condition. Replace or recondition drum as required.

> NOTE: *Drum original inside diameter is 9.500 in. Maximum refinish diameter is 9.560 in. Discard the drum if the diameter exceeds 9.590 in.*

2. Inspect wheel bearing oil seal for evidence of leakage. If leakage is present, replace seals and other parts as required.

3. Carefully lift part of boot far enough out of wheel cylinder to inspect for leakage. If excessive brake fluid can be seen (a small amount is normal), replace or recondition the cylinder.

4. Check all attaching bolts on the flange for tightness and clean all rust and dirt from flange contact surfaces (**Figure 25**) with fine emery cloth.

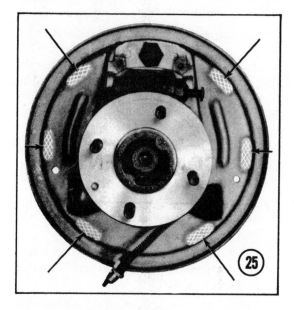

Assembly/Installation

CAUTION
If original shoes and linings are to be reinstalled, they must be installed in original positions.

NOTE: *Use a brake lubricant, such as as Delco Brake Lube No. 5450032, wherever lubrication is called for in the following procedure.*

1. Inspect contact surfaces of new linings for cleanliness, nicks, and burrs. Also inspect contact surfaces on brake flange. Remove any rough spots.

2. Lubricate parking brake cable.

3. Lubricate fulcrum end and attach parking brake lever to secondary shoe. Be sure lever moves freely.

4. Lightly lubricate flange contact surfaces and threads of adjusting screw. Make sure the adjusting screw is thoroughly clean before applying lubricant.

5. Connect primary and secondary shoes with adjusting screw spring, then install adjusting screw, socket, and nut.

CAUTION
Adjusting screws are marked "L" and "R" for left and right. Be sure to install the screw marked "L" on the left side brake. Also make certain that the screw is installed with the star wheel closest to the secondary brake shoe, and that the spring does not interfere with the operation of the screw. Star wheel must also line up with the adjusting hole in the flange plate.

6. Connect cable to parking brake lever.

7. Install the primary shoe (shorter lining) on forward hold-down pin and spring and install retainer.

8. Install secondary shoe and actuator assembly on rear hold-down pin and spring and install retainer. Position parking brake strut and spring.

9. Install guide plate over anchor pin.

10. Fasten wire link to actuator assembly, and attach other end to anchor pin by hand while holding the adjuster assembly in the fully down position. Do not use a spring hook tool.

11. Install actuator return spring.

CAUTION
Use the end of a screwdriver or other suitable flat tool to ease actuator return spring into place. Do not pry on actuator lever.

12. Install brake pull-back springs. Install spring from primary shoe first.

NOTE: *If old springs are nicked, rusted, or otherwise in damaged or doubtful condition, replace them with new ones. After springs are installed, make sure actuator lever operates easily by operating the self-adjusting feature (**Figure 26**).*

13. Install drum, wheel, and tire. Adjust service and parking brakes as described under *Brake Adjustment* in this chapter. Lower vehicle.

9

5. Apply slight air pressure to front outlet to remove secondary piston.

Cleaning and Inspection

Clean all parts only with alcohol or clean brake fluid. Blow out all passages and inspect bore for damage or wear.

Assembly and Installation

1. If a replacement secondary piston is being used, its identification mark should match that on the original piston. Lubricate the piston seals, and install them on the secondary piston. (The loop of the front seal and the second seal should face the front of the cylinder. The loop of the third seal should face the rear of cylinder.)

2. Lubricate all parts with clean brake fluid and install spring seat and spring on secondary piston. Then slip the assembly into the cylinder bore.

3. Install the primary piston, followed by the pushrod, and retain with the snap ring.

4. Install the rubber boot; fill the cylinder with fluid, operating the pushrod several times to bleed the cylinder.

5. Mount the cylinder, reversing disassembly procedures, and bleed the system. If the seats require replacement, remove by drilling the insert with a 13/64 in. bit and tapping the hole for a ¼ in. x 20 bolt that is ½ in. to ¾ in. long.

MASTER CYLINDER

Removal and Disassembly

1. Disconnect pushrod from brake pedal as described previously.

2. Disconnect the 2 brake lines (**Figure 27**). Remove mounting nuts and cylinder.

3. Remove cover, drain fluid from reservoir, and pump fluid from body.

4. Remove boot, snap ring, pushrod, and primary piston. Primary piston is replaced as assembly, so there is no need to disassemble it.

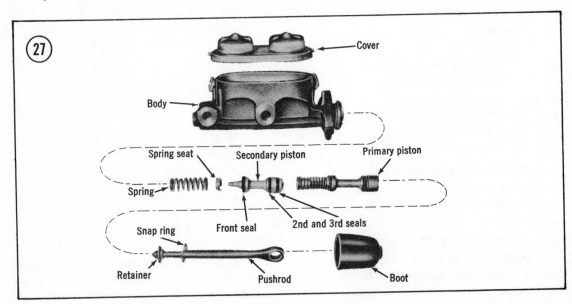

Install a washer on the bolt, and thread the bolt into the seat. Tighten until seat is removed. Put a new brass seat in place and press into position with a spare brake line fitting.

BRAKE SWITCH AND DISTRIBUTION ASSEMBLY

The switch and distribution assembly (combination valve and switch on 1976-1977 models) shown in **Figure 28** is located near the master cylinder. The switch can be checked by removing and grounding the electrical connection with the ignition key on. If warning lamp does not light, replace the bulb or repair the electrical circuit.

If the warning lamp lights, turn off the ignition, and replace the connection. Check further by bleeding one of the front wheels and one of

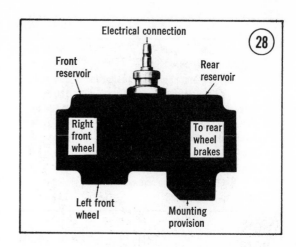

the back wheels, with the ignition ON, while an assistant observes the warning light. If the light fails to go on during either of these operations, the switch is defective and should be replaced.

Table 1   BRAKE SPECIFICATIONS

	1971-1975	1976-1977
Front (discs)		
Diameter	10 in.	10 in.
Thickness new	0.500 in.	0.500 in.
Thickness, after turning	0.455 in.	0.455 in.
Thickness, minimum	0.440 in.	0.440 in.
Flatness	0.002 in.	0.002 in.
Runout	0.005 in.	0.005 in.
Pads, minimum visible	0.03 in. ($\frac{1}{32}$ in.)	0.03 in. ($\frac{1}{32}$ in.)
Rear (drums)		
Diameter, new	9 in.	9.5 in.
Diameter, maximum	9.03 in.	9.56 in.
Width	1.25 in.	2.0 in.
Lining, minimum	0.03 in. ($\frac{1}{32}$ in.)	0.03 in. ($\frac{1}{32}$ in.)
Pedal		
Free height, cold, minimum	2.25 in.	2.25 in.

9

Table 2   TIGHTENING TORQUES (1971-1975)

Master cylinder-to-dash	25 ft.-lb.	Front flex hose bolt-to-caliper	22 ft.-lb.
Brake pedal mounting bolt nut	30 ft.-lb.	Front flex hose bracket-to-body	100 in.-lb.
Front and rear brake pipe nut-to-cylinder	150 in.-lb.	Rear pipe-to-flex hose	150 in.-lb.
Brake pipe nuts-to-switch	150 in.-lb.	Rear pipe-to-connector block	
Brake pipe nut from switch	150 in.-lb.	and wheel cylinders	150 in.-lb.
Differential switch-to-bracket	150 in.-lb.	Rear pipe bracket-to-body	100 in.-lb.
Front brake pipe retainer screw	100 in.-lb.	Parking brake cover-to-floor pan screw	30 in.-lb.
Rear brake pipe clip-to-body screws	100 in.-lb.	Parking brake lever-to-floor pan bolt	85 in.-lb.
Rear brake pipe block and pipe		Parking brake equalizer jam nut	85 in.-lb.
clip-to-axle housing screws	20 ft.-lb.	Parking brake cable rear hanger-to-	
Front flex hose-to-pipe	150 in.-lb.	frame bolt	150 in.-lb.

Table 3   BRAKE TORQUE SPECIFICATIONS (1976-1977)

	Torque		Torque
Master cylinder to dash or power cylinder	25 ft.-lb.	Front flex hose bolt to caliper	22 ft.-lb.
Power cylinder to dash	25 ft.-lb.	Front flex hose bracket to body	100 in.-lb.
Power cylinder to skirt brace	25 ft.-lb.	Rear line bracket to body screw	
Splash shield to steering knuckle	65 in.-lb.	(at rear hose)	100 in.-lb.
Brake pedal bracket to steering column		Floor console to bracket screws—front	25 in.-lb.
bracket (Monza)	24 ft.-lb.	Floor console to bracket screws—rear	18 in.-lb.
Brake pedal mounting bolt-nut	30 ft.-lb.	Console trim plate screws	18 in.-lb.
Brake line nuts to master cylinder, combination		Parking brake cover to floor pan screw	30 in.-lb.
valve, wheel cylinders & flex hose	150 in.-lb.	Parking brake lever to floor pan screw	85 in.-lb.
Combination valve to bracket screw	150 in.-lb.	Parking brake equalizer jam nut	85 in.-lb.
Combination valve bracket to skirt screw	100 in.-lb.	Parking brake cable rear hanger to	
Front brake line retainer screw	100 in.-lb.	frame bolt	80 in.-lb.
Rear brake line clip to body screws	100 in.-lb.	Bleeder valves	*
Rear brake hose block bracket and line clip		* Note: Torque to seal or 100 in-lb. (max.).	
to axle housing screws	20 ft.-lb.	Replace if it will not seal at 100 in.-lb.	

CHAPTER TEN

FRONT SUSPENSION AND STEERING

The Vega is equipped with either manual or power steering. Both systems use energy absorbing steering columns that collapse under a predetermined load. The steering column incorporates the ignition switch and an anti-theft device which locks the steering when the key is in the LOCK position.

The front suspension incorporates A-frame control arms, coil springs, and ball-joint steering knuckles. Camber and caster adjustment is achieved through the lower control arm eccentric bolts (**Figure 1**).

WHEEL ALIGNMENT

Correct front end alignment is extremely important to road handling stability, steering ease, and tire wear. Before performing front wheel alignment adjustments, check for loose or improperly adjusted steering gear, loose steering gear mounting, worn ball-joints, loose or worn ball stud connections, improper front spring heights, unbalanced or underinflated tires, loose wheel bearings, and worn shock absorbers. Correct torque specifications are very important and can be found, along with general specifications, in **Tables 1, 2, and 3** at the end of this chapter.

Front wheel alignment involves camber, caster, and toe-in and toe-out. Camber and caster cannot be adjusted by the home mechanic. Toe,

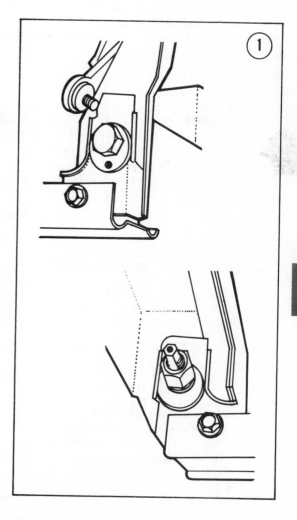

however, is easily measured and adjusted. If abnormal tire wear (not resulting from incorrect inflation) is indicated, have the dealer or front-end specialist align caster, camber, and toe-in.

Front Suspension Geometry

Refer to **Figure 2**. Camber is the relative position of the top to the bottom of the wheel when viewed from the front of the car. It is *positive* when the top of the wheel is farther *out* from the car than the bottom; and *negative* when the top is farther *in* than the bottom. Caster is the angle of the turning axis with respect to the vertical axis when viewing the wheel from the side of the car. It is *positive* when the turning axis is tipped *backward* from the vertical; and *negative* when tipped *forward*. Toe-in is the difference in measurement between the front and back tread centers of the front wheels.

Camber, caster, and toe-in should be adjusted in that order. Toe-in must be adjusted whenever camber or caster is adjusted.

Camber is adjusted by the front lower control arm pivot which moves the lower control arm in or out. Caster is adjusted by the rear lower control arm pivot which moves the lower control arm forward or backward. Figure 1 gives front and rear views of the lower control arm pivot bolt and cam assembly. Toe is adjusted by turning the tie rod sleeves on each side of the vehicle an equal amount to retain correct steering wheel alignment and bringing the front tread center measurement into the specified relationship with the rear tread center measurement (Table 1). Steering wheel alignment helps determine whether the steering gear is at its high point when the wheels are pointing straight ahead. Refer to *Steering* later in this chapter for steering wheel adjustment.

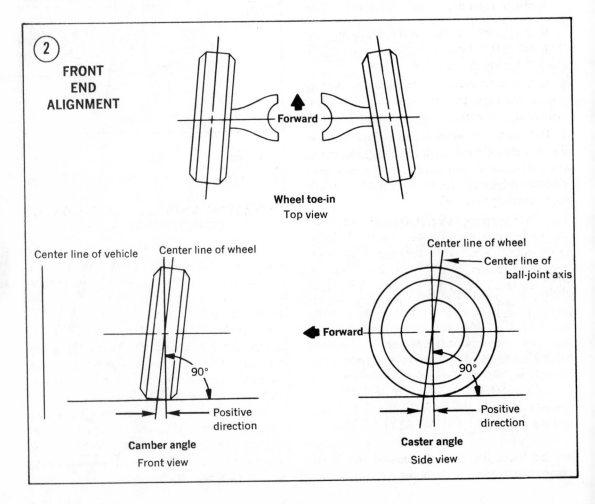

② **FRONT END ALIGNMENT**

Wheel toe-in
Top view

Camber angle
Front view

Caster angle
Side view

FRONT WHEEL BEARINGS

1. Raise vehicle and remove wheels.

2. Remove the brake caliper as described in Chapter Nine.

3. Pry grease cup from hub, remove cotter pins, spindle nut, and washer. Remove the hub.

4. Lift outer bearing from hub, and tap the inner bearing and grease seal out with a hammer handle.

5. Wash all parts in solvent.

CAUTION
If an air hose is used after cleaning bearings with solvent, do not direct airstream to cause bearings to spin.

6. Inspect bearing for cracked cages, and pitted or scored races or rollers.

> NOTE: *If either bearing needs replacement, the associated bearing race must also be replaced.*

7. If outer bearing races need replacing, tap them out with a brass drift at the notches provided in the hub for removal.

8. Install new races by continually tapping around the perimeter of the race with a brass drift until it is seated.

9. Pack inner or outer bearings (see Chapter Two for correct packing procedures), and install inner bearing followed by a new grease seal. Grease seal should be flush with edge of hub when properly installed.

10. Place hub on spindle, and install outer bearing washer and nut. Tighten nut to 12 ft.-lb. (1.67 mkg) torque while rotating wheel, then back off to nearest cotter pin hole (but at least ⅙ turn) and install cotter pin. Bearings should now have no preload and 0.001-0.005 in. (0.03-0.13mm) end play.

CAUTION
Vega front wheel bearings are tapered roller bearings and have a slightly loose feel when properly adjusted. Do not preload bearings in an attempt to correct this loose feel as damage to bearings can result.

11. Be sure disc is clean. Install the brake caliper and wheel.

SHOCK ABSORBERS

Shock absorber life varies according to road conditions. Generally speaking, a shock absorber is sufficiently worn after 10,000-15,000 miles of service to require replacement.

Shock absorber replacement is a simple operation. **Figure 3** shows the front shock absorber mounting and a rubber plug for access to the top mount. Rear shock absorbers are similarly mounted, except that the stud mount is on the lower end rather than the top.

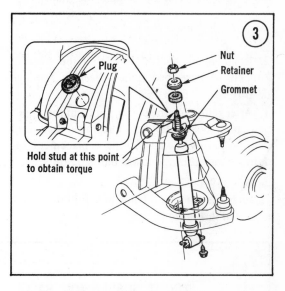

Stud nuts should be torqued to 10 ft.-lb. (1.38 mkg). Torque bolts to 20 ft.-lb. (2.76mkg).

STEERING KNUCKLE, BALL-JOINTS, AND CONTROL ARMS

A number of special tools are required for front suspension work. Because of the configuration of front end parts, disassembly and replacement of parts is nearly impossible without the use of most of these tools, or similar ones.

Generally, front suspension repair is best accomplished by completely disassembling and removing the front suspension. Most home mechanics may wish to leave such repairs to the dealer or a front end specialist.

The following procedures cover complete front suspension disassembly. However, the steering knuckle and ball-joints can be serviced without removal of the shock absorber, spring, or control arm.

NOTE: *A wear indicator is built into lower ball-joints on 1975-1977 Vegas. See* **Figure 4** *for details.*

1. With vehicle on a hoist and front wheels removed, support the lower control arm with a floor jack. Use a block of wood between the jack and arm for a secure grip. Remove disc brake caliper, wheel hub, and splash shield.

NOTE: *If the coil springs are to be removed, install a safety chain through the spring coil and around the frame or crossmember so that the spring will not fly loose if the jack slips.*

2. Remove the tie rod end from the steering knuckle as described under *Steering Linkage* **(Figure 5)**.

3. After removing the cotter pin from the upper ball stud, loosen the nut. The lower ball stud may be removed first. Spring replacement requires removal of the lower ball stud only.

4. Remove shock absorber.

5. Install a wheel stud nut and tool J-8806-1 as shown in **Figure 6**.

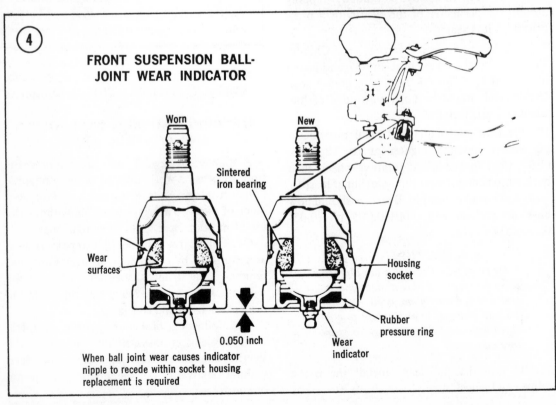

FRONT SUSPENSION BALL-JOINT WEAR INDICATOR

Worn

New

Sintered iron bearing

Wear surfaces

Housing socket

0.050 inch

Rubber pressure ring

Wear indicator

When ball joint wear causes indicator nipple to recede within socket housing replacement is required

WHEEL STUD NUT

BUMPER
REMOVED FOR
CLARITY

J—8806-1

6. After breaking the joint loose, remove the tool and wheel stud nut. Repeat for the lower ball stud.

7. Steering knuckle can now be removed by slowly releasing jack until sufficient clearance is established. If spring is to be removed, make sure safety chain is connected, then lower the control arm until spring tension is released.

8. Check ball-joints for wear by installing stud nut and checking torque required to turn the joint in its socket. A new ball-joint should register 2-4 ft.-lb. (0.26-0.55 mkg) torque. Both joints should register some torque. If torque is too high, even though ball-joints are adequately

lubricated, replace ball-joint. See NOTE preceding Step 1 for 1975-1977 models.

9. If ball-joint requires replacement, grind off the ball-joint rivets, and install new joint with retaining bolts and nuts supplied. Install a new lube fitting in the ball-joint. Position the new ball-joint so that the grease bleed vent in the rubber boot is facing toward the engine.

10. If control arms are to be removed, mark the position of the lower pivot bolt heads to facilitate reinstallation. Bushing wear can best be checked while control arms are still installed. If excessive play is observed, replace the bushings.

11. When reinstalling control arm, bolt heads should be toward the front on the front bushing and toward the rear on the rear bushing.

12. Reverse the removal procedures to install, torquing all bolts to specifications.

STEERING

Vega uses recirculating ball type steering. Rotational forces from the steering wheel are translated to the steering linkage by ball bearings acting in a spiral groove on the lower end of the steering column at the steering gear. **Figure 7** illustrates the internal cross section of the steering gear. The normal manual steering gear ratio is 22.5:1. A quick-steer option is available with a 16.6:1 ratio. Variable ratio power steering is

10

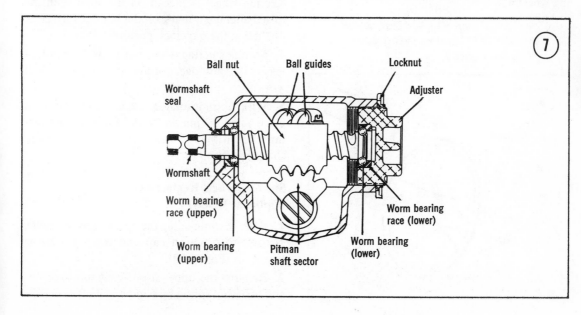

Ball nut

Ball guides

Locknut

Wormshaft
seal

Adjuster

Wormshaft

Worm bearing
race (upper)

Worm bearing
race (lower)

Worm bearing
(upper)

Pitman
shaft sector

Worm bearing
(lower)

available with a 16.0:1 straight-line to 13.1:1 ratio with the steering wheel fully turned.

Steering Wheel Adjustment

The following procedure for steering wheel alignment (and correct high point adjustment) should be performed following camber, caster, and toe-in adjustment.

1. With the front wheels pointing straight ahead, check to see that flat surface on the worm shaft stub is at the 12 o'clock position. The flat designates the steering gear high point. If the steering wheel is properly installed on the shaft, the spokes will be horizontal within ½ in. when the gear is at high point.

2. If the worm shaft stub flat is at the 12 o'clock position and the wheels are straight ahead, but the steering wheel spokes are not horizontal, remove the steering wheel and reinstall as described under *Steering Wheel*.

If the wheels are straight ahead, but the worm shaft stub flat is not at the 12 o'clock position, turn the tie rod sleeves an equal amount in the same direction to bring the gear to its high point.

Steering Wheel Replacement (Production Wheel)

1. After disconnecting the battery ground cable, remove the 2 screws retaining the steering wheel shroud as shown in **Figure 8**. Remove the steering wheel nut.

> NOTE: *A snap ring has been added to 1975-1977 steering wheel assemblies. See* **Figure 9**.

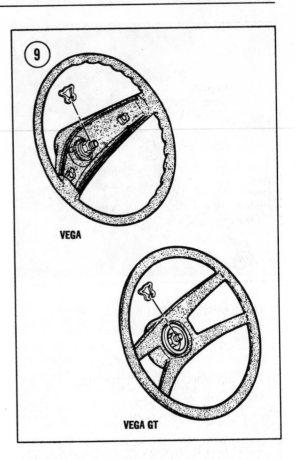

VEGA

VEGA GT

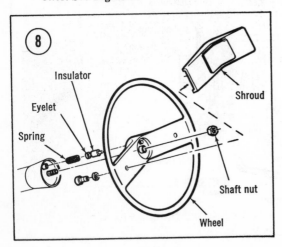

Insulator

Eyelet

Spring

Shroud

Shaft nut

Wheel

2. Remove steering wheel with a suitable puller.

3. When reinstalling, the turn signal mechanism should be in neutral position. Make certain the wheels are positioned straight ahead and that the steering wheel is placed on the shaft with the raised alignment mark on the bottom surface of the hub at the 6 o'clock position.

4. Torque steering wheel nut to 30 ft.-lb. (4.14 mkg). Do not over-torque, or steering wheel will rub.

5. With horn insulator, eyelet, and spring in place, align the pin on the right side of the steering wheel with the hole in the shroud, and install shroud screws.

Steering Wheel Replacement (Optional Wheel)

1. After disconnecting the battery ground cable, pry off horn button cap and remove steering wheel nut (**Figure 10**).

2. Remove the upper horn insulator, receiver, and belleville spring by removing 3 screws.

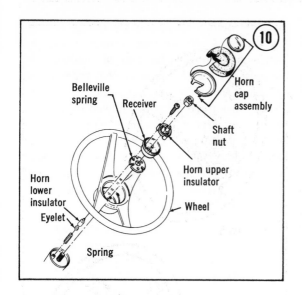

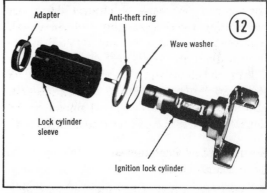

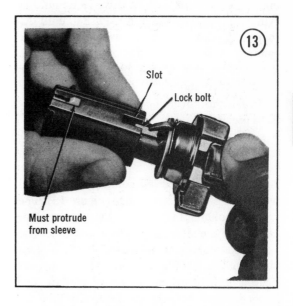

3. Using suitable puller, remove steering wheel.

4. When reinstalling, turn signal lever should be in neutral position. Place wheel onto shaft with front wheels positioned straight ahead and the steering wheel spokes horizontally aligned.

5. Install nut, and torque to 30 ft.-lb. (4.14 mkg). Do not over-torque, or steering wheel will rub.

6. With lower horn insulator, eyelet, and spring in place, secure the belleville spring, receiver, and upper insulator. Use the 3 screws, then install horn cap assembly.

Lock Cylinder

The lock cylinder cannot be overhauled. Replace with a new cylinder coded to the old key.

1. Remove the steering wheel and directional signal as outlined previously.

2. Referring to **Figure 11**, insert a small screwdriver where indicated to break loose the housing flash, and depress the spring latch. Now remove the lock cylinder.

3. To reassemble, place the key part of the way into the lock cylinder assembly and install the wave washer and anti-theft ring as shown in **Figure 12**.

4. With the plastic keeper in the sleeve assembly protruding, align the anti-theft ring and lock bolt with the slot in the cylinder. Push the sleeve onto the lock cylinder assembly. See **Figure 13**. Push the key in and turn the lock cylinder clockwise; now turn it in the oppostie direction to the lock position.

5. Install adaptor ring as shown in **Figure 14**. Before staking, make sure the key can be rotated at least 120°. Stake with a ⅛ in. diameter flat punch.

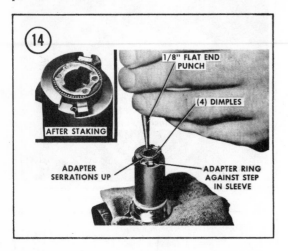

6. To install the lock into the steering column, pull the lock cylinder sleeve and rotate the knob counterclockwise against the stop. Insert the cylinder into the housing bore, with the key on the cylinder sleeve aligned with the keyway in the cylinder housing. Push the cylinder into abutment of cylinder and sector. Hold an 0.070 in. drill between the lock bezel and the housing. Rotate the cylinder counterclockwise, maintaining a light pressure until the drive section of the cylinder mates with the sector. Push in until the snap ring pops into the grooves and the lock cylinder is secured in the housing. Remove the 0.070 in. drill. Check the lock cylinder for freedom of rotation.

7. Install the directional signal switch as outlined previously.

STEERING COLUMN

The standard steering columns for manual and power steering are similar (**Figure 15**). The manual column incorporates a 2-piece shaft coupled to the steering gear by a pot joint. The power steering column incorporates a 3-piece shaft with a flexible coupling and a support bearing at the lower end of the upper shaft. The lower shaft on both designs has a slip joint secured with plastic pins that sheer at a predetermined load. Use care when working on the

steering column. Because of the energy absorbing design of the steering column, it can be damaged if roughly handled or inadequately supported. If damage is suspected, examine the column support bracket mounting capsule to see whether the bracket has moved toward the engine compartment. Examine the jacket section of the column for looseness and the steering shaft to determine whether the plastic pins have been sheared. If the pins are sheared, shaft will be loose and some play will be felt in the steering wheel.

> NOTE: *Special spacers are required for reassembly of manual steering column. See Step 7 under* Column Installation.

A tilt steering column is offered as optional equipment on 1975-1977 models. See **Figure 16**.

Column Removal

1. Disconnect the battery ground cable, and remove steering wheel as described previously.

2. Remove the pot joint coupling clamp bolt next to the gear housing on manual steering columns or the flexible coupling pinch bolt at the top end of the intermediate shaft on power steering.

3. Remove the 3 floor pan bracket screws and the 2 instrument panel bracket nuts. Lower the column and disconnect the wiring harnesses for the directional signal and ignition switch.

4. Remove the column. Lightly tap the pot joint or flexible coupling if difficulty is encountered in pulling the column rearward.

Standard Column Disassembly

1. Remove the dash panel bracket-to-column mounting screws and remove the bracket.

2. Hold the column in a vise by clamping one of the 2 sets of welded nuts. Do not clamp one welded nut only.

3. Remove the directional signal switch, lock cylinder, ignition key warning switch, and ignition switch as previously discussed.

4. From the lower end of the column, remove the steering shaft, and on power steering columns, remove the lower bearing.

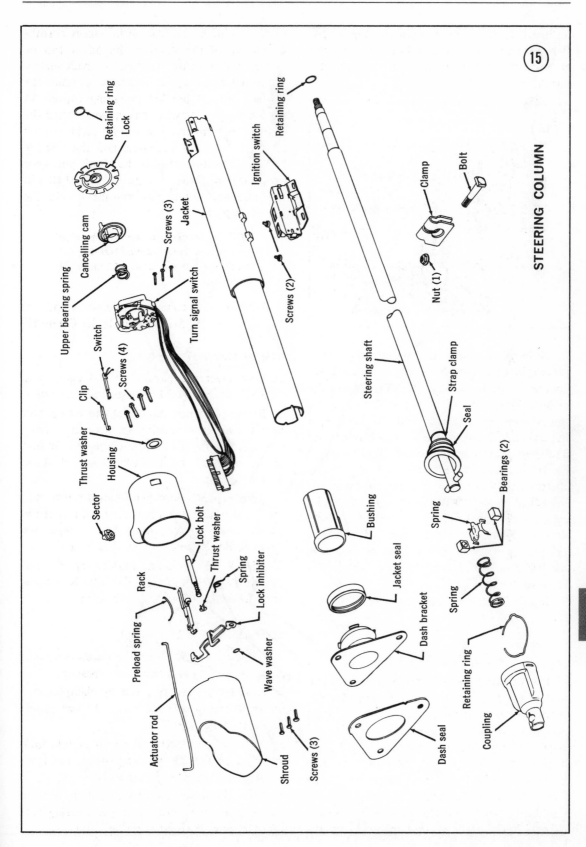

STEERING COLUMN

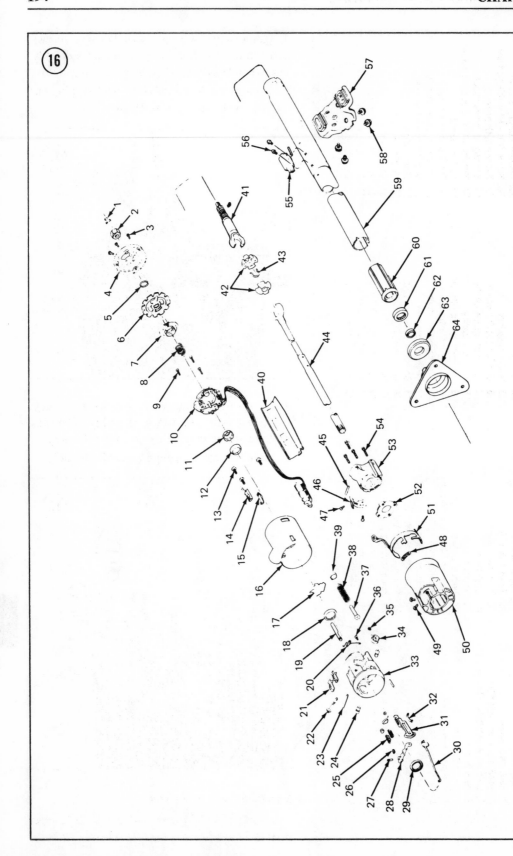

⑯

TILT STEERING COLUMN

1. Nut retainer
2. Shaft nut
3. Lock cover screws
4. Shaft lock cover assembly
5. Lock plate retaining ring
6. Lock plate
7. Cancelling cam
8. Bearing preload spring
9. Turn signal screws
10. Turn signal switch
11. Upper bearing seat
12. Upper bearing race
13. Turn signal housing screws
14. Key warning switch
15. Switch clip
16. Turn signal housing
17. Tilt lever opening shield
18. Upper bearing
19. Shaft lock bolt
20. Lock bolt spring
21. Lock shoes
22. Sector shaft
23. Lock shoe pin
24. Bearing housing pivot pins
25. Shoe release springs
26. Release lever spring
27. Shoe release lever pin
28. Shoe release lever
29. Lower bearing
30. Ignition switch rod
31. Ignition switch rack
32. Ignition switch rack spring
33. Bearing housing
34. Sector
35. Sector snap ring
36. Lock bolt spring screw
37. Tilt lever spring guide
38. Tilt lever spring
39. Tilt lever spring retainer
40. Wiring protector cover
41. Upper steering shaft
42. Centering spheres
43. Centering sphere spring
44. Lower steering shaft
45. Pin
46. Lock inhibitor retaining plate
47. Retaining plate screws
48. Inhibitor return spring
49. Housing shroud screws
50. Column housing shroud
51. Key lock inhibitor release lever
52. Support lock plate
53. Bearing housing support
54. Bearing housing support screws
55. Ignition switch
56. Ignition switch screws
57. Column support bracket
58. Support bracket screws
59. Mast jacket
60. Bearing adapter
61. Lower bearing
62. Steering shaft spacer
63. Dash bracket seal
64. Dash bracket

5. Remove the 4 turn signal housing screws, and remove the housing and shroud assembly. Disassemble by removing the 3 retaining screws.

6. Remove the lock inhibitor lever, cupping one hand over the spring wire (**Figure 17**).

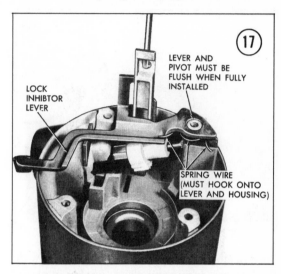

LEVER AND PIVOT MUST BE FLUSH WHEN FULLY INSTALLED

LOCK INHIBTOR LEVER

SPRING WIRE (MUST HOOK ONTO LEVER AND HOUSING)

7. Referring to **Figure 18**, remove rod, rack, shaft lock bolt, and spring assembly. The rack preload spring may be removed if necessary.

8. Remove sector through lock cylinder hole.

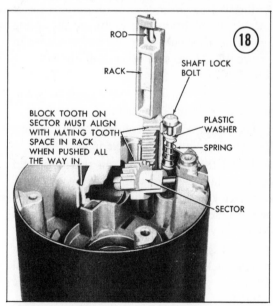

ROD

RACK

SHAFT LOCK BOLT

PLASTIC WASHER

SPRING

BLOCK TOOTH ON SECTOR MUST ALIGN WITH MATING TOOTH SPACE IN RACK WHEN PUSHED ALL THE WAY IN.

SECTOR

10

Standard Column Assembly

Lubricate all friction surfaces with a light coat of lithium soap grease on reassembly.

1. Install sector through the lock cylinder bolt. Tang end should be facing the lock cylinder hole when installed.

2. Install the rack preload spring as shown in **Figure 19**.

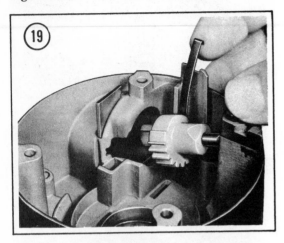

3. Assemble the shaft lock bolt to the rack with the lock bolt spring and plastic washer in place.

4. Install the rack and lock bolt assembly, aligning the first tooth on the sector with the first tooth on the rack. Lock teeth should line up when rack assembly is pushed all the way down.

5. Install lock inner lever with spring. Lever tang should be behind the rack, and the spring anchor hooks should be positioned as shown in Figure 12. Make sure lever is flush with the top of its pivot.

6. Install the turn signal housing assembly and torque to 60 in.-lb. (6.9 kgcm).

7. On power steering columns, press a new lower bearing into the plastic adapter.

8. Install the steering shaft on the lower end of the column. There will be about 3/16 in. clearance (on the manual steering columns), between the clamp on the shaft and the column; do not move the clamp.

9. Install ignition switch, ignition key warning switch, lock cylinder, and directional signal switch as previously described. Remove the column from the vise.

10. Install the dash panel bracket, with the slotted opening for the mounting capsules facing the upper end of the steering column. Torque the 4 mounting screws to 15 ft.-lb. (2.07 mkg).

Tilt Column Disassembly

NOTE: *Due to the complexity of the tilt-type steering column (Figure 16), and the special tools and skills involved in assembly/disassembly, complete disassembly is not recommended. The procedure given here is limited to replacement for the turn direction light switch and the lock cylinder. See procedure above for lock cylinder replacement.*

Turn Direction Switch Replacement

1. Remove steering wheel, described earlier in this chapter under *Steering Wheel Replacement*.

2. Loosen 3 captive screws and remove cover from shaft.

3. Remove screw, then remove directional signal lever.

4. Push in on the hazard warning switch knob and unscrew the knob.

5. Remove shaft lock plate retaining ring as shown in **Figure 20**. If special tool is not available, depress lock plate with fingers and pry out the retaining ring with a screwdriver.

J-23653

6. Remove directional signal cancelling cam and upper bearing preload spring from end of shaft.

7. Remove bolts from mounting bracket and gently lower steering column.

8. Remove signal switch wire protector, then remove wires from protector, taking care not to damage wires (**Figure 21**).

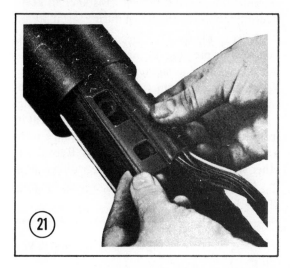

9. Disconnect switch connector from bracket (**Figure 22**), then tape wires as shown in **Figure 23** to prevent snagging when removing switch.

10. Remove mounting screws, then pull switch straight up, guiding wiring harness through column housing (**Figure 24**).

CAUTION
Use only the screws and bolts that were removed during disassembly and use them only in the places from which

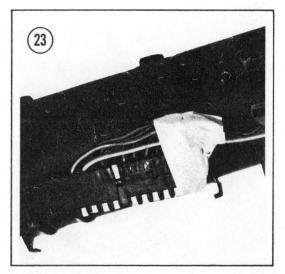

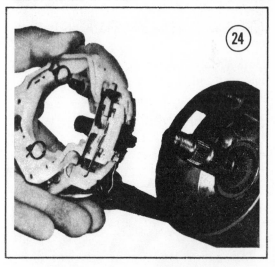

they were removed. Use of over-length fasteners could prevent complete operation of the column collapsing feature under impact.

11. Tape the new wiring harness as shown in Figure 23 and feed harness down through column housing and bowl. Push in on hazard warning switch if necessary to aid in assembly.

12. Insert wires in signal switch wire protector and reinstall protector. Install column bracket and torque to specifications (Table 3).

13. Install mounting screws and clip connector to bracket on jacket (**Figure 25**).

14. Install directional signal lever and hazard warning switch knob. Verify that directional

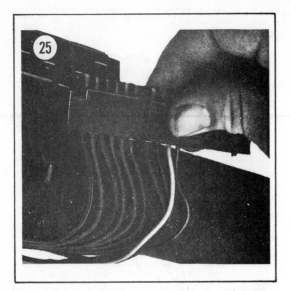

signal lever is in neutral and knob is in the out position.

15. Slide preload spring and cancelling cam onto shaft and place lock plate over end of shaft.

16. Install new snap ring. Depress lock plate as far as it will go and slide snap ring into shaft groove. If special tool is available (**Figure 26**), this operation will be greatly simplified.

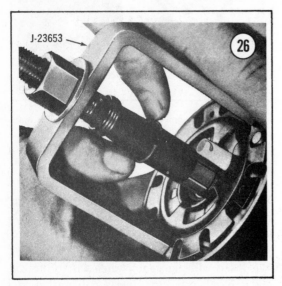

17. Place cover on end of shaft and install retaining screws.

18. Reinstall steering wheel, using the procedure given earlier in this chapter under *Steering Wheel Replacement*.

Column Installation

The sequence of this installation procedure is extremely important. Obtain assistance to keep steering column in alignment during installation.

1. Refer to **Figure 27**. If necessary, replace pot joint seal by pressing the pin out of the shaft (do not remove with a hammer) and removing seal. When reinstalling pin, it must be centered to within 0.012 in. Check by installing a bearing with just enough ⅜ in. flat washers to prevent it from bottoming, and measure the distance with a micrometer as shown in **Figure 28**. Repeat for other side. Measurements must be within 0.012 in. (0.30mm). Lubricate with wheel bearing grease upon reassembly.

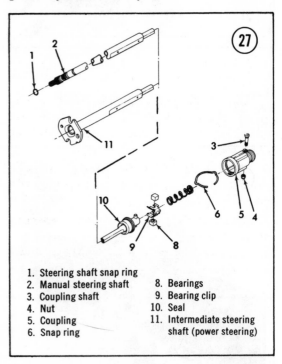

1. Steering shaft snap ring
2. Manual steering shaft
3. Coupling shaft
4. Nut
5. Coupling
6. Snap ring
8. Bearings
9. Bearing clip
10. Seal
11. Intermediate steering shaft (power steering)

2. Referring to **Figure 29**, slip pot joint clamp (H) over the end of the pot joint (J). Align the flat on the stub shaft (K) with the flat on the pot joint; install the shaft and flexible coupling. On power steering models, the flexible coupling flat should be aligned with the steering shaft flat, and the shaft should bottom against the coupling reinforcement before installing bolt (G) and torquing to 30 ft.-lb. (4.15 mkg).

3. Plug in the directional signal and ignition switch connections.

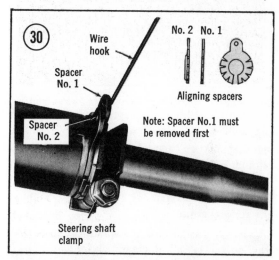

(28)

strument panel stud nuts (E) to 19 ft.-lb. (2.63 mkg).

> NOTE: *Manual steering models require the use of special alignment spacers as shown in* **Figure 30**. *These spacers provide a minimum clearance of 0.180 in. between the steering shaft outside diameter and the column jacket lower plastic bushing inside diameter.*

8. Install steering wheel as described previously.

(30) Wire hook — No. 2 — No. 1

Spacer No. 1

Spacer No. 2

Aligning spacers

Note: Spacer No.1 must be removed first

Steering shaft clamp

4. Install the steering column panel bracket, finger-tight.

5. Align the pot joint clamp (H) and the groove at end of pot joint (J), and install clamp bolt through the shaft undercut. Torque to 55 ft.-lb. (7.60 mkg).

6. With car resting on all 4 wheels, torque instrument panel stud nuts (E) to 19 ft.-lb. (2.63 mkg).

7. Slide toe plate (P) to toe pan—engaging flange (R) in toe pan on power steering models—and install attaching screws (Q). Allow no side load on manual steering models when installing

STEERING LINKAGE

Refer to **Figure 31**. All steering linkage ball studs are secured with castellated nuts and cotter pins. Ball stud threads, stud taper, and tapered holes must be perfectly clean before

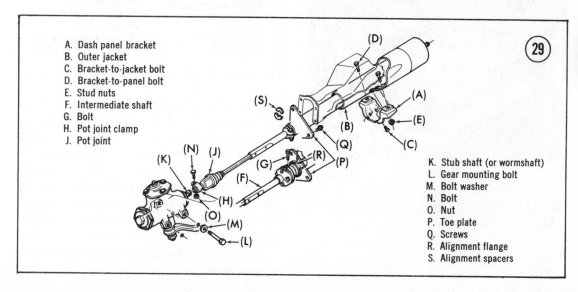

A. Dash panel bracket
B. Outer jacket
C. Bracket-to-jacket bolt
D. Bracket-to-panel bolt
E. Stud nuts
F. Intermediate shaft
G. Bolt
H. Pot joint clamp
J. Pot joint

K. Stub shaft (or wormshaft)
L. Gear mounting bolt
M. Bolt washer
N. Bolt
O. Nut
P. Toe plate
Q. Screws
R. Alignment flange
S. Alignment spacers

(29)

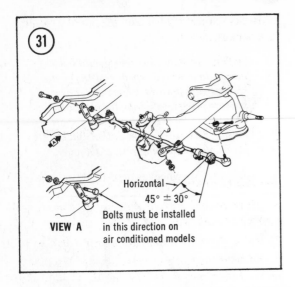

Horizontal
45° ± 30°

Bolts must be installed
in this direction on
air conditioned models

VIEW A

reinstalling. With the exception of the pitman arm, which is removed with a suitable puller, steering linkage tapered ball stud connections should be released by tapping as shown in **Figure 32**. When removing the pitman arm from the shaft, a reference mark should be made for reinstallation.

It is important that all steering linkage bolts be torqued to specifications given at the end of this chapter.

When reassembling the tie rod, make sure both ends are threaded equally into the sleeve. The clamps must be located between the dimples at each end of the sleeve and positioned so that the clamp opening either straddles the sleeve slot or is located away from the slot. After assembly is complete, ball-joints must be aligned so that they can rotate through their complete travel.

MANUAL STEERING

Pitman Shaft Seal Replacement

1. Remove pitman arm as described previously. The gear should be at its high point position. Determine high point by counting the number of turns of the steering wheel from stop-to-stop. Then turn the steering wheel from the stop ½ that number of turns, and check to see that the flat on worm shaft is at the 12 o'clock position.

2. Remove the 3 bolts securing the housing side cover (**Figure 33**) and remove the pitman shaft and side cover assembly.

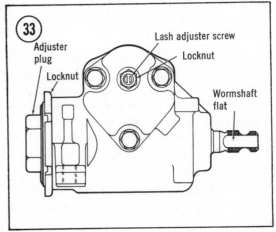

Adjuster
plug

Locknut

Lash adjuster screw

Locknut

Wormshaft
flat

3. Inspect gear lubricant for contamination. If it is contaminated, gear must be removed and overhauled.

4. Pry the old seal from the gear housing. Coat the lips of the new seal with steering gear lubricant and tap it into the housing using a socket of suitable size.

5. Remove the pitman shaft adjuster locknut; turn the adjuster screw clockwise until it is released from the cover.

6. Insert the pitman shaft into the steering gear so that the center tooth of the sector engages the center tooth space of the ball nut.

7. Add steering gear lubricant to the housing if necessary.

8. Holding the side cover and new gasket in place, thread the adjusting screw all the way into the cover by reaching through the threaded hole with a small screwdriver. Install side cover bolts and torque to 18 ft.-lb. (2.49 mkg).

9. Refer to *Steering Gear Adjustment* for setting steering lash (pitman shaft).

Steering Gear Adjustment

There are 2 adjustments for the steering gear. One is worm shaft bearing preload and the other is pitman shaft sector-to-ball nut lash. Adjustment should be performed in that order. See the following.

1. Mark the pitman arm-to-shaft relationship, and remove the pitman arm.

2. Disconnect the battery ground cable and remove the horn button cap or shroud.

3. Loosen the adjuster plug locknut, and back off the adjuster plug ¼ turn.

4. Gently turn the steering wheel to one stop and back ½ turn.

5. With an in.-lb. torque wrench on the steering wheel nut, rotate ¼ turn and note reading. Adjust the bearing preload to 5-8 in.-lb. over the noted reading by turning the adjuster plug. Tighten the plug locknut to 75 ft.-lb. and recheck preload.

6. Turn the wheel to center (high point) position and loosen the pitman shaft adjuster screw locknut.

7. Turn the pitman shaft adjusting screw to remove all lash between the ball nut and pitman shaft sector teeth, and tighten the locknut to 15 ft.-lb. (2.07 mkg).

8. The highest torque reading should now be 4-10 in.-lb. (4.6-11.4 kgcm) *greater* than the thrust bearing preload torque when the steering wheel is turned through its center position.

9. Repeat adjustment if necessary until torque falls within specifications.

> NOTE: *If adjusting screw has been turned too far (torque reading too high), back off on adjusting screw, then retighten to a looser adjustment.*

10. Install the pitman arm, tightening the nut to 93 ft.-lb. (12.86 mkg).

Steering Gear Overhaul

1. Mark pitman arm-to-shaft relationship and remove pitman arm.

2. Remove pot joint coupling clamp bolt.

3. Remove the steering gear-to-frame mounting bolts, and remove gear assembly. Clamp the steering gear in a vise by one of the mounting tabs so that the worm shaft is horizontal.

4. Set gear at high point by rotating the worm shaft from stop-to-stop, counting the number of turns, then turning back half way so that the worm shaft is at the 12 o'clock position.

5. Remove the side cover and pitman shaft assembly from the housing.

6. Remove the adjuster plug, and withdraw worm shaft and ball nut assembly.

> CAUTION
> *If ball nut is allowed to run down to either end of the worm, the ends of the ball guides will be damaged.*

7. Remove the upper bearing from the worm shaft, and pry the lower bearing retainer from the adjuster plug housing.

8. Separate the pitman shaft from the cover by removing the adjuster screw locknut and screwing the adjuster screw clockwise through the housing. The pitman shaft adjusting screw cannot be removed from the shaft. Damage to either requires replacement as an assembly.

9. Pry out pitman shaft and worm shaft seals.

10. Wash all parts and inspect bearings, bearing races, and worm shaft.

11. If side cover needle bearings are worn or damaged, the entire side cover and needle bearing assembly must be replaced.

12. If pitman shaft needle bearings need replacement, remove by pressing out from inside

housing and install as shown in **Figure 34**. If tool J-23645 is not available, measure the location of bearing in bore before removing. New bearings should be inserted so that manufacturer's identification is toward the outside of the housing.

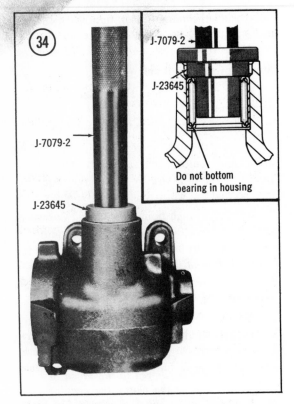

13. Only the worm shaft bearing housing race can be replaced; the adjuster plug race must be replaced as a unit with the adjuster plug. Using a drift or punch, drive the old bearing race out of the housing, and tap a new one into place. Be careful not to damage the race when installing.

14. Install new pitman shaft and worm shaft seals. Be certain they are not installed in a cocked position.

15. If the worm and ball nut assembly show signs of wear or damage, remove the clamp retaining screws and the ball guides from the nut. Turn the nut upside down and remove the balls by rotating the worm shaft.

16. To reassemble the ball nut and worm shaft, slip the nut over the shaft and align it with grooves in the worm. Assemble the ball guides, and install 24 balls into each guide. Rotate the

shaft slightly as the balls are inserted to help feed them into place.

17. Install ball guide clamp, then check the assembly to see that it moves freely.

18. Slide the upper ball bearing over the worm shaft, and insert the worm shaft and nut assembly into the housing.

19. Install the ball bearing in the adjuster plug. Secure with the stamped retainer.

20. Guiding the end of the worm shaft, install the adjuster plug bearing and locknut assembly. Tighten the adjuster plug until end play is nearly removed.

21. Fill the steering gear with 9 ounces of steering gear lubricant and rotate the worm shaft (not hard against the stop) until it is thoroughly lubricated.

22. With the ball nut at the center of its travel, insert the pitman shaft into the housing so that the center tooth enters the center tooth space in the ball nut.

23. Holding the side cover and gasket in place, insert a small screwdriver through the threaded hole in the side cover and thread the pitman shaft adjusting screw all the way into the side cover. Install the side cover bolts and torque to 18 ft.-lb. (2.49 mkg).

24. Take all end play out of the worm shaft by tightening adjuster nut, then backing off ¼ turn.

25. Turn the worm shaft all the way to one stop then back ½ turn. Using an in.-lb. torque wrench fitted with a 12 point 11/16 in. socket, turn the worm shaft while tightening the adjuster plug until a 7 in.-lb. thrust bearing preload registers on the torque wrench.

26. Hold the adjuster plug, and tighten the locknut to 75 ft.-lb. Recheck thrust bearing preload.

27. Turn the worm shaft to the center (high point) position, and then turn the pitman shaft adjusting screw until all lash has been removed between the ball nut and sector teeth. Tighten the locknut.

28. Using a torque wrench, determine highest reading when turning the worm shaft through its center (high point) position. Reading should be 21 in.-lb. (which includes 7 in.-lb. thrust bearing preload). Readjust pitman shaft adjusting screw if necessary to meet this specification, and

tighten the adjusting screw locknut to 15 ft.-lb. (2.07 mkg).

POWER STEERING

Hydraulic System Checks

The following procedure will determine whether hydraulic parts are faulty and, if so, what parts. A high pressure gauge is required (1,500 psi). Engine must be at normal operating temperature, with tire inflation and engine idle at specifications.

1. With engine off, insert gauge into line. Gauge shutoff valve should be open.

2. With correct fluid level in pump reservoir, start engine, hold steering wheel against stop, and check gauge connections for leakage.

3. If necessary, *bleed the hydraulic system:*

   a. Bring fluid to correct level and wait for 2 minutes.

   b. Run engine for about 2 seconds.

   c. Check fluid level, and add if necessary.

   d. Repeat above until oil level remains constant.

   e. Raise front wheels off the ground.

   f. Increase engine speed to 1,500 rpm.

   g. Lightly turn the wheels against the right and left stops.

   h. Check fluid level, and add if necessary.

   i. Lower the car and turn the wheels against both stops.

   j. Check fluid level. If fluid is foamy, shut off engine and wait for 2 minutes, then repeat above procedure.

4. Insert thermometer in hydraulic reservoir and move steering wheel from stop-to-stop until fluid reaches 150-170°F (65-78°C).

5. Read pressure gauge with steering wheel against stop. If maximum pressure is 900-1,000 psi, the hydraulic system is functioning properly. If the pressure is below 900 psi, proceed with the following step to determine whether pump is at fault.

6. With engine idling, slowly close gauge shutoff valve and read pressure, then quickly reopen the valve to avoid pump damage. If pressure is less than 900 psi, pump is at fault.

NOTE: *Repeat this test after rebuilding the pump to determine whether another part of the system may also be faulty.*

Pump Overhaul

1. Disconnect hoses at pump. Cover the connections, and secure the hoses in a raised position to prevent oil loss. On 1975-1977 models, remove radiator and fan shroud.

2. Remove pump belt and pump-to-mount attaching screws. Remove pump.

3. With a suitable puller, remove drive pulley.

4. Referring to **Figure 35**, remove the pump outlet union and O-ring assembly.

5. Remove the pump reservoir mounting studs, and tap the reservoir from the pump with a soft hammer. Discard the pump O-ring seal.

6. Discard the mounting stud and flow control valve square ring seals.

7. Insert a small punch in the ⅛ in. diameter hole in the pump housing, and remove the end plate retaining ring.

8. Remove the end plate and spring.

9. Remove the shaft Woodruff key and gently tap shaft to remove together with the pressure plate, pump ring, rotor assembly, and thrust plate.

10. Separate these parts, and remove the shaft from the rotor—if it is defective—by removing the retainer snap ring. Discard the end plate and pressure plate O-rings.

11. Remove the 2 dowel pins.

12. Remove flow control valve spring assembly.

13. Remove the shaft seal from the pump housing and discard.

14. Wash all metal parts. Check flow control valve for freedom in bore. Make sure the cap screw on the end of the flow control valve is tight. Examine pressure plate and pump plate surfaces for scoring or excessive wear. Check for freedom of pump veins in rotor slots (they should be installed with the round end toward the pump ring). Check all other parts for breaks, scoring, galling, and other signs of damage or wear.

15. All parts should be absolutely clean and

10

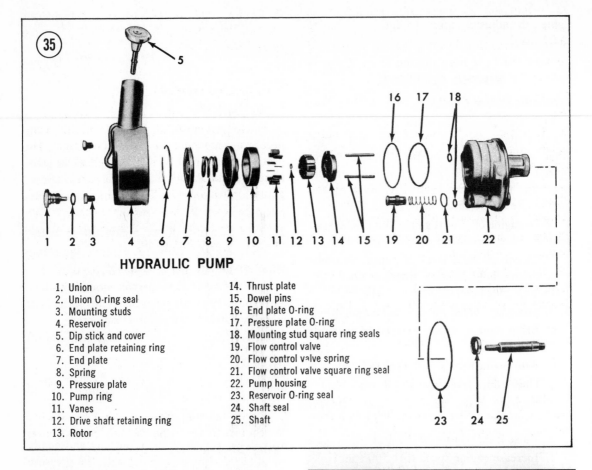

HYDRAULIC PUMP

1. Union
2. Union O-ring seal
3. Mounting studs
4. Reservoir
5. Dip stick and cover
6. End plate retaining ring
7. End plate
8. Spring
9. Pressure plate
10. Pump ring
11. Vanes
12. Drive shaft retaining ring
13. Rotor
14. Thrust plate
15. Dowel pins
16. End plate O-ring
17. Pressure plate O-ring
18. Mounting stud square ring seals
19. Flow control valve
20. Flow control valve spring
21. Flow control valve square ring seal
22. Pump housing
23. Reservoir O-ring seal
24. Shaft seal
25. Shaft

generously lubricated with power steering or automatic transmission fluid during reassembly.

16. Install a new pump shaft seal. A piece of thin-wall tubing of suitable diameter can be used in place of tool J-22670.

17. Install the 2 dowel pins and a new pressure plate O-ring.

18. Slip shaft into the thrust plate with ported side toward the spline.

19. Install rotor, countersunk side toward the thrust plate, and secure with a *new* shaft retaining ring. This is a special ring, and no substitute should be made. Start ring with a brass drift, then seat, with a ⅜ in. socket as shown in **Figure 36**.

20. Install the shaft, thrust plate, and rotor assembly over the dowel pins.

21. Note the direction of rotation arrow on the pump ring. Pump rotates clockwise when viewed from the pulley end. Install pump ring with the arrow to the *rear* of the housing.

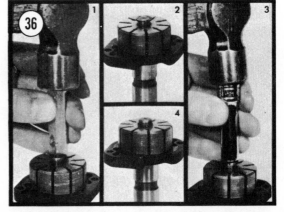

22. Insert vanes so that round edge is toward the pump ring.

23. Thoroughly lubricate pressure plate and exposed surface of pressure plate O-ring. Slide pressure plate over dowel pins with ported side facing the pump ring. Press pressure plate into place (approximately 1/16 in.) by hand, using a large socket. Install pressure plate spring.

24. Install new end plate O-ring in housing, and press end plate into place. Secure with the end plate retaining ring, locating the ends of the ring between the valve bore and the ⅛ in. diameter hole in the housing.

25. Insert the flow control spring and plunger (hex head screw first).

26. Lubricate new mounting stud and union square ring seals and a new reservoir O-ring seal, and install into housing.

27. Lubricate the sealing edges of the reservoir. Place it into the housing and press until it seats. Recheck position of stud and union seals.

28. Install union assembly and studs, using a new union O-ring seal.

29. Insert the Woodruff key into place on the drive shaft and slide the pulley onto the shaft. Torque a *new* pulley nut to 60 ft.-lb. (8.3 mkg).

Pitman Shaft Seal Replacement

Pitman shaft seals can be replaced with the steering gear in the car as follows.

1. Mark the pitman arm-to-shaft relationship. Using a suitable puller, remove the pitman arm, but do not hammer on the puller.

2. Clean the end of the pitman shaft and the surrounding parts of the gear housing.

3. Put a single layer of tape over the shaft splines to protect the new seal.

4. Remove the pitman shaft seal retaining ring.

5. Place a container under the steering gear, start the engine, and turn the steering wheel all the way to the left. Oil pressure should force the seals out of the housing; but if it does not, steering gear must be removed to install seal as described under *Steering Gear Overhaul.*

6. Lubricate the new seals. The single lip seal should be started into the housing only enough to insert the back-up washer and the outer seal. Install the outer seal back-up washer and, using a suitable socket, tap the seal into the bore only far enough to permit the retaining ring to seat. Install the retaining ring.

7. Check fluid level. Start engine, and let it idle for 3 minutes without turning the steering wheel.

8. Turn the wheel to the left against the stop, and check for leaks.

9. Remove tape, install pitman arm in proper location with respect to the shaft, and torque to 140 ft.-lb. (19.4 mkg).

Steering Gear Overhaul

Because it is often not necessary to conduct a complete steering gear overhaul, the following procedures highlight subassembly overhaul. The procedures can be followed in sequence for complete overhaul, however. Subassemblies include: adjuster plug, valve and stud shaft, pitman shaft and side cover, rack-piston, hose connector inverted flares, pitman shaft bearing, and seal (**Figure 37 and Figure 38**).

> NOTE: *Do not attempt steering gear overhaul without special tool J-8947, rack-piston seal compressor.*

1. Begin *steering gear disassembly* by removing the end cover retaining ring (retaining ring can be rotated until one end is near the ⅛ in. hole in the housing so that a punch can be inserted to assist in removal).

2. Rotate the stud shaft counterclockwise just far enough to force the rack-piston end cover from the housing. Discard O-ring.

3. Remove the end plug with a ⅜ in. extension. End plug may have to be tapped lightly with a brass drift to loosen.

4. Loosen the pitman shaft adjusting screw locknut, and remove the 4 cover-attaching bolts.

5. Unscrew the side cover enough to see the rack-piston and pitman shaft teeth, then center the pitman shaft teeth in the housing opening by rotating the stub shaft.

6. With a soft hammer, tap the pitman shaft and remove, with the side cover, from the housing. Discard the side cover O-ring.

7. Using ball retainer tool J-7539, or a suitable size shaft, retain balls in the rack-piston while turning the stub shaft counterclockwise to remove the rack-piston.

8. Loosen the adjuster plug locknut with a spanner wrench, and remove the plug. Discard the O-ring.

9. The valve and stub shaft assembly can now be removed. Discard the stub shaft cap O-ring.

10

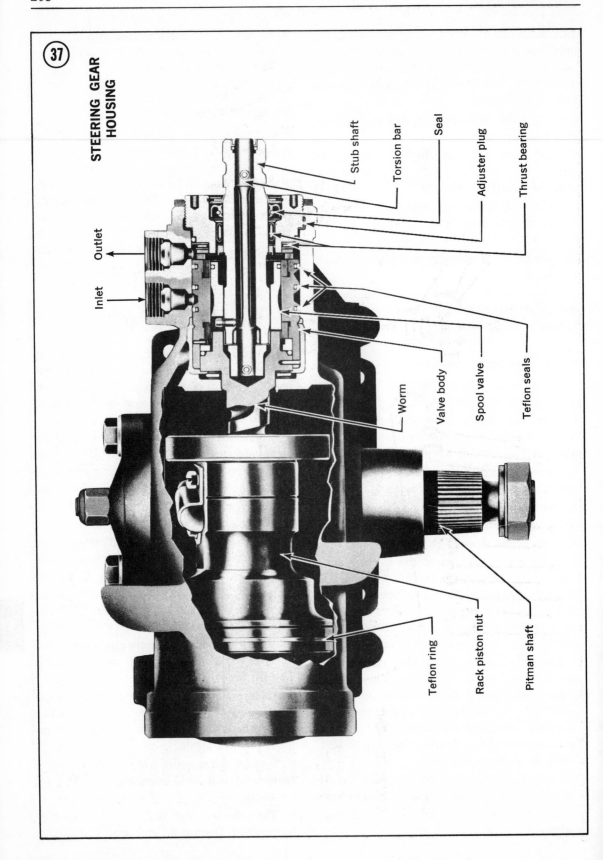

37

STEERING GEAR HOUSING

Stub shaft

Torsion bar

Seal

Adjuster plug

Thrust bearing

Outlet

Inlet

Worm

Valve body

Spool valve

Teflon seals

Teflon ring

Rack piston nut

Pitman shaft

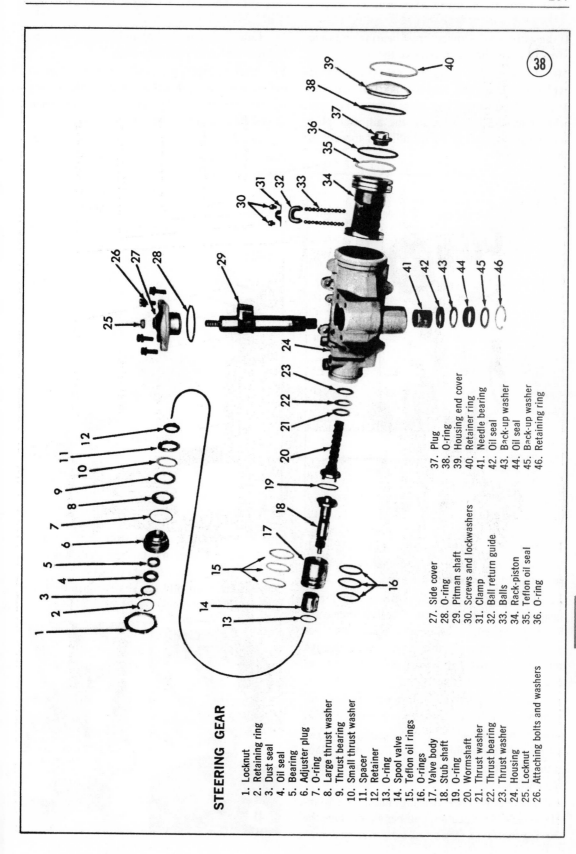

STEERING GEAR

1. Locknut
2. Retaining ring
3. Dust seal
4. Oil seal
5. Bearing
6. Adjuster plug
7. O-ring
8. Large thrust washer
9. Thrust bearing
10. Small thrust washer
11. Spacer
12. Retainer
13. O-ring
14. Spool valve
15. Teflon oil rings
16. O-rings
17. Valve body
18. Stub shaft
19. O-ring
20. Wormshaft
21. Thrust washer
22. Thrust bearing
23. Thrust washer
24. Housing
25. Locknut
26. Attaching bolts and washers
27. Side cover
28. O-ring
29. Pitman shaft
30. Screws and lockwashers
31. Clamp
32. Ball return guide
33. Balls
34. Rack-piston
35. Teflon oil seal
36. O-ring
37. Plug
38. O-ring
39. Housing end cover
40. Retainer ring
41. Needle bearing
42. Oil seal
43. Back-up washer
44. Oil seal
45. Back-up washer
46. Retaining ring

38

10

If the worm or the lower thrust bearing and race are still in the housing, remove them.

10. If the *adjuster plug oil seal only* is to be replaced (**Figure 39**), remove the retaining ring and pry the dust seal and oil seal from the bore with a screwdriver. (Secure the adjuster plug during this operation by installing it loosely in the housing.)

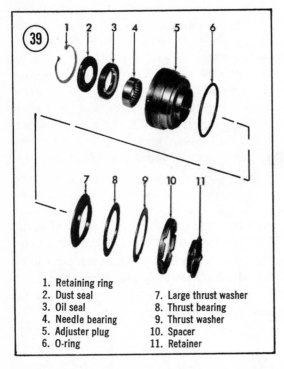

1. Retaining ring
2. Dust seal
3. Oil seal
4. Needle bearing
5. Adjuster plug
6. O-ring
7. Large thrust washer
8. Thrust bearing
9. Thrust washer
10. Spacer
11. Retainer

11. If the *thrust bearing* only is to be removed, pry the retainer with a small screwdriver at the 2 raised areas. Discard the retainer.

12. To replace the *needle bearing,* the thrust bearing must be removed. Carefully measure location of needle bearing in bore for correct re-assembly. With a suitable driving tool, remove the needle bearing, dust seal, and oil seal from the adjuster plug.

13. Wash all parts and blow dry. Inspect all bearings, spacers, and washers for wear, cracks, pitting, or scoring.

14. When reassembling the adjuster plug, place it on a block of wood to protect the thrust bearing surface.

15. Drive new needle bearings into place. Manufacturer's identification number should face the driving tool.

16. Lubricate new oil seal and install, followed by dust seal and retaining ring.

17. After lubricating, install large thrust bearing washer, upper thrust bearing, small bearing washer, and spacer. The grooves of the spacer should be away from the bearing washer.

18. Install a new bearing retainer, making sure that the raised areas do not project above the spacer and that the spacer is free to rotate.

19. Remove the *valve and stub shaft assembly* O-ring from the shaft cap end (**Figure 40**).

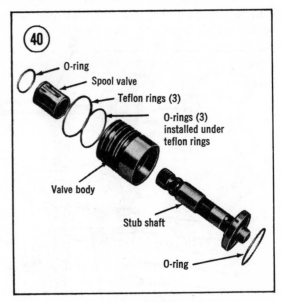

O-ring
Spool valve
Teflon rings (3)
O-rings (3) installed under teflon rings
Valve body
Stub shaft
O-ring

20. Holding the valve and stub shaft assembly as shown in **Figure 41**, tap the shaft against a wooden surface until the shaft cap is free of the valve body, then pull the shaft cap until it has cleared the valve body by ¼ in.

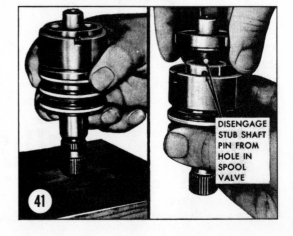

DISENGAGE STUB SHAFT PIN FROM HOLE IN SPOOL VALVE

21. Disengage the shaft pin as shown previously in Figure 39 and remove the shaft.

22. Referring to **Figure 42**, push the spool valve far enough out of the valve body to expose the dampener O-ring. Now, carefully rotating the valve body, remove the spool. Use extreme care in removing the spool valve. If it becomes cocked, realign it with the body and proceed with removal. Discard the dampener O-ring.

23. Replacement of the 3 Teflon oil rings requires that they be cut from the valve body. The O-rings beneath the Teflon oil ring should be replaced also.

24. Wash all parts and blow dry.

25. If the stub shaft or valve body drive pins are worn or broken, the complete valve and shaft assembly must be replaced.

26. Look for evidence of leakage between the torsion bar and the stub shaft. If any scores, nicks, or burrs on the ground surface of the stub shaft cannot be cleaned up with crocus cloth, replace the valve and shaft assembly.

27. Examine the valve body inner diameter and spool valve outer diameter for wear. If any nicks or burrs cannot be cleaned up with crocus cloth, replace the valve and shaft assembly.

28. Replace the complete valve and shaft assembly if the notch in the skirt of the valve body is worn.

29. With the spool valve dampener O-ring removed, lubricate the spool valve and valve body, and check to see that the valve rotates freely in the valve body. If any binding occurs, replace the complete valve and shaft assembly.

30. Lubricate and assemble O-rings and Teflon oil rings on valve body. Teflon rings may distort when installing, but oil heat during steering gear operation will straighten them.

31. After lubricating, slip the valve dampener O-ring over the spool valve. Lubricate the spool valve and valve body, and insert the spool valve into the body while rotating the spool. Continue pushing the spool valve through the valve body until shaft pin hole appears at the opposite end.

32. Slip the shaft assembly into the spool valve until the pin can be placed into the spool valve hole. Continue pressing the spool valve and shaft assembly into the valve body, aligning the notch in the shaft cap with the pin on the valve body.

33. Install a new O-ring in the shaft cap end of the valve body assembly after lubricating it.

34. Separate *pitman shaft and side cover* by unscrewing the adjusting screw.

35. Wash shaft and cover, and blow dry. Inspect for roughness, nicks, and wear on bearing surfaces. Examine teeth, and check for play in adjusting screw. If the adjusting screw is loose, or if it binds when turned in the pitman shaft, the shaft and screw assembly must be replaced as a unit.

36. Reassemble the shaft and cover by screwing adjusting screw all the way into the cover, then backing off ½ turn.

37. Wash all parts and blow dry. Examine the worm and rack-piston grooves, the balls, the rack-piston teeth, and external ground surfaces for wear. The worm and rack-piston is a matched assembly and must be replaced as such. Inspect the ends of the ball return guide halves for damage. Examine the lower thrust bearing and washers for wear.

38. Lubricate a new Teflon oil seal and O-ring, and install as shown in **Figure 43**.

39. Refer to **Figure 44**. Insert the worm into the

10

BACK-UP O-RING MUST BE INSTALLED UNDER PISTON RING

RACK-PISTON NUT

43

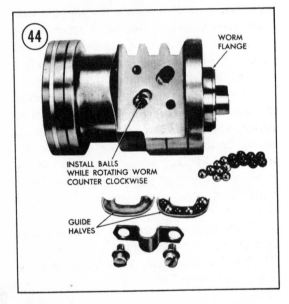

44

WORM FLANGE

INSTALL BALLS WHILE ROTATING WORM COUNTER CLOCKWISE

GUIDE HALVES

42. Start ball retainer tool into the rack-piston, and rotate worm out while replacing it with tool.

43. The *hose connector inverted flares* can be placed by tapping the connector hole with a 5/16-18 tap (2 or 3 threads deep only) and turning a 5/16-18 bolt, with a nut and a flat washer installed, into the tapped hole. Holding the bolt head with a wrench, tighten the nut to pull the connector from the housing.

44. Clean any tapping chips from the housing, and drive a new connector into place, using care not to damage the connector or housing threads.

45. The *pitman shaft needle bearing and seals* are shown in **Figure 45**. Remove the seals first, and carefully measure the location of the bearing for correct reinstallation. (Remove the retaining ring and outer seal washer, and pry out the first seal. Follow by removal of the second washer and prying out the inner seal. After measuring the location of the needle bearing, drive it out from pitman shaft side of housing.)

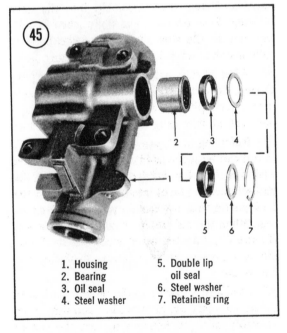

45

1. Housing	5. Double lip oil seal
2. Bearing	6. Steel washer
3. Oil seal	7. Retaining ring
4. Steel washer	

rack-piston, turning the worm until its groove is aligned with the lower ball return guide hole.

40. Lubricate the balls, and install 17 of them into rack-piston by slowly turning worm counter-clockwise. Alternate silver and black balls.

41. Install the 7 remaining balls into the return guide, making certain the balls at the guide end are of different color than those they will meet when the guide is installed, and install the guide assembly into the rack-piston. (Petroleum jelly will help hold the balls in place while installing the guide.) Install the clamp, and torque the 2 screws to 10 ft.-lb. (1.38 mkg).

46. Install a new needle bearing, with manufacturer's identification number against the driving tool, being careful that it does not bottom in the housing and become damaged.

47. Lubricate the oil seals and install. Drive the seals only to sufficient depth to allow the retaining ring to seat in its groove.

48. Begin *steering gear assembly* by installing the lower thrust bearing and washers onto the worm. Lubricate the assembly (**Figure 46**).

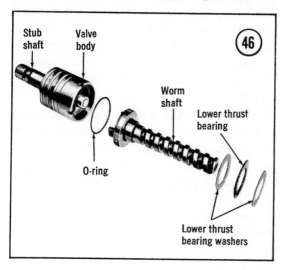

Figure 46

Stub shaft
Valve body
Worm shaft
Lower thrust bearing
O-ring
Lower thrust bearing washers

Figure 47

J-8947
Rack-piston
J-7539

49. With the *narrow notch* in the valve body aligned with the pin in the worm, install the valve and stub shaft assembly into the gear housing. Push on the valve body when installing, not on the stub shaft. The valve body is fully installed when it clears the oil return hole.

50. After lubricating, install a new adjuster plug O-ring. Cover the stub shaft spline with a single layer of cellophane tape to prevent seal damage, and seat adjuster plug assembly in the housing.

51. Referring to **Figure 47**, install tool J-8947 (a rod can be substituted), lubricate rack-piston Teflon seal, and insert the rack-piston (with the ball retainer in place) into the housing with the rack-piston teeth toward the pitman shaft opening. When the ball retainer contacts the worm (Figure 47), turn the worm clockwise to thread the rack-piston onto the worm, displacing the ball retainer.

52. Install a new O-ring in the pitman shaft side cover, and place the pitman shaft and side cover assembly into the housing so that the center tooth of the shaft engages the center groove of the rack-piston. Torque cover bolts to 30 ft.-lb. (4.14 mkg).

53. Install the rack-piston end plug, and torque to 75 ft.-lb. (10.37 mkg).

54. Install the housing cover ring, housing cover, and retaining ring.

55. Prepare to adjust bearing preload by cinching adjuster plug and backing off ⅛ turn.

56. With an in.-lb. torque wrench on the stub shaft, measure the seal and ball drag; it should not exceed 3 in.-lb. Now tighten the adjuster plug locknut, and recheck combined drag and bearing preload.

57. With pitman arm adjusting screw backed all the way out and then turned in ½ turn, rotate the stub shaft through its center of travel, noting the highest torque reading. Turn the pitman shaft adjusting screw until a reading of 3-6 in.-lb. higher than the combined drag and bearing preload reading is reached. The reading should not exceed 14 in.-lb.

58. Tighten the adjusting screw locknut, and recheck the adjustment.

59. When reinstalling the steering gear, position hoses as shown in **Figure 48**.

Steering Gear Adjustment

Only the pitman shaft adjustment can be made when the power steering gear is installed in the car. The combined seal, ball drag, and bearing preload torque must be determined before making the adjustment.

1. Disconnect the pitman arm at the relay rod. Loosen pitman shaft adjusting screw locknut, and turn screw counterclockwise to its limit.

2. Disconnect the battery ground cable, and remove the horn button or shroud. Turn the steering wheel gently to both stops and return it to mid-position.

10

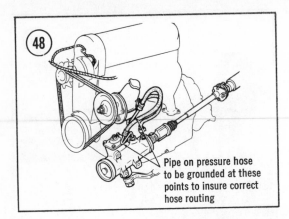

Pipe on pressure hose
to be grounded at these
points to insure correct
hose routing

3. Measure the combined seal, ball drag, and bearing preload with an in.-lb. torque wrench by turning the shaft through the center of its travel approximately ¼ turn in each direction. Note the highest reading.

4. Tighten the pitman shaft adjusting screw until a reading of 3-6 in.-lb. over the combined seal, ball drag, and bearing preload reading is reached.

5. Tighten pitman shaft adjusting screw locknut, and recheck torque. Total torque reading should not exceed 14 in.-lb.

Table 1   STEERING AND FRONT SUSPENSION SPECIFICATIONS

Standard Steering		
Gear ratio	20.9 : 1 (gear)	22.5 : 1 (overall)
Thrust bearing preload (over seal and ball drag)	5-8 in.-lb. (vehicle)	7 in.-lb. (bench)
Highpoint preload, or pitman shaft adjustment (over thrust bearing preload)	4-10 in.-lb. (vehicle)	14 in.-lb. (bench)
Total preload (maximum)	16 in.-lb. (vehicle)	21 in.-lb. (bench)
Power Steering		
Gear ratio	16.0 : 1 (gear)	16.6 : 1 (overall)
Pump pressure	900-1,000 psi ①	
Seal and ball drag	3 in.-lb. (maximum)	
Thrust bearing preload (over seal and ball drag)	½-2 in.-lb.	
High point preload, or pitman shaft adjustment (over seal and ball drag and bearing preload)	3-6 in.-lb.	
Total preload	14 in.-lb. (maximum)	
Wheel Alignment		
Camber	+ ¼° ± ½°	(Camber and caster
Caster	− ¾° ± ½°	setting for each wheel should agree to within ½°)
Toe	¼ in. to 1/16 in. toe-in (1971-1974) 0 in. to ⅛ in. toe-in (1975) 0 in. to ⅛ in. toe-out (1976-1977)	
Wheel Bearing		
Preload	0	
End-play	0.0001″ - 0.0008″	

① 750-850 psi for 1973-1977 models.

Table 2   TORQUE SPECIFICATIONS (1971-1974)

Steering column		Pitman shaft nut	93 ft.-lb.
Directional signal housing		**Power steering gear**	
Shroud	35 in.-lb.	Adjuster plug locknut	80 ft.-lb.
Switch	35 in.-lb.	Cover bolts	30 ft.-lb.
Dash panel bracket screws	15 ft.-lb.	Mounting bolts	70 ft.-lb.
Studs	19 ft.-lb.	Pitman shaft adjusting screw locknut	32 ft.-lb.
Flexible coupling nuts	18 ft.-lb.	Pitman shaft nut	140 ft.-lb.
Pinch bolt	30 in.-lb.	**Power steering pump**	
Ignition switch screws	35 in.-lb.	Brace rod-to-engine	18 ft.-lb.
Pot joint clamp	55 ft.-lb.	Bracket and brace rod-to-pump	25 ft.-lb.
Steering wheel nut	30 ft.-lb.	Bracket-to-engine	25 ft.-lb.
Toe plate	40 in.-lb.	Pulley	60 ft.-lb.
Steering linkage		Pump mount	33 ft.-lb.
Idler arm to: relay rod	35 ft.-lb.	Pump outlet union	33 ft.-lb.
Frame	30 ft.-lb.	Ball-joint nut, upper	30 ft.-lb.
Pitman arm to relay rod	35 ft.-lb.	Lower	60 ft.-lb.
Tie rod ball stud	35 ft.-lb.	Control arm, upper	60 ft.-lb.
Clamp	132 in.-lb.	Lower	125 ft.-lb.
Manual steering gear		Shock absorber, bolt	22 ft.-lb.
Adjuster plug locknut	75 ft.-lb.	Stud	116 in.-lb.
Cover bolts	18 ft.-lb.	Stabilizer bar, bracket	27 ft.-lb.
Mounting bolts	70 ft.-lb.	to control arm	90 in.-lb.
Pitman shaft adjusting screw locknut	15 ft.-lb.	Wheel spindle nut	12 ft.-lb.

Table 3   TORQUE SPECIFICATIONS (1975-1977)

	Torque		Torque
Steering linkage		Manual steering gear	
Pitman arm to relay rod stud nut	35 ft.-lb.①	Gear mounting bolts	70 ft.-lb.
Tie rod end stud nuts	35 ft.-lb.①	Adjuster plug locknut	75 ft.-lb.
Tie rod clamp bolt nuts	132 in.-lb.①	Side cover bolts	18 ft.-lb.
Idler arm to relay rod stud nut	35 ft.-lb.	Lash adjuster screw locknut	15 ft.-lb.
Idler arm to frame bolt nuts	30 ft.-lb.	Pitman shaft nut (1975)	93 ft.-lb.
Steering column		Pitman shaft nut (1976-1977)	140 ft.-lb.
Steering wheel nut	30 ft.-lb.	Power steering gear	
Steering wheel shroud	18 in.-lb.	Gear mounting bolts	70 ft.-lb.
Toe plate screws	70 in.-lb.	Adjuster locknut	80 ft.-lb.
Dash panel bracket to column screws	22 ft.-lb.	Side cover bolts	30 ft.-lb.
Dash panel bracket to dash studs	20 ft.-lb.	Lash adjuster screw locknut	32 ft.-lb.
Pot joint coupling clamp bolt nut		Pitman shaft nut (1975)	140 ft.-lb.
Manual	50 ft.-lb.	Pitman shaft nut (1976-1977)	185 ft.-lb.
Power	30 ft.-lb.	Power steering pump	
Flexible coupling to steering shaft		Pump mounting studs	25 ft.-lb.
pinch bolt	30 ft.-lb.	Pump outlet union	25 ft.-lb.
Flexible coupling to intermediate shaft		Bracket to engine bolts	25 ft.-lb.
flange bolt nuts	18 ft.-lb.	Brace rod to engine stud nut	18 ft.-lb.
Ignition switch to column screws	35 in.-lb.	Bracket and brace rod to pump	
Steering column lock plate cover screws	20 in.-lb.	bolts and nuts	25 ft.-lb.
Directional signal switch screws	35 in.-lb.	Power steering hoses	
Directional signal housing screws	60 in.-lb.	Pressure hose fitting (pump and gear)	25 ft. lb.
Directional signal housing shroud screws	18 in.-lb.	① Plus additional torque required to align castellation	
Tilt lever screw	35 in.-lb.	with cotter pin hole in stud (not to exceed 50 ft.-lb.).	

10

CHAPTER ELEVEN

REAR AXLE AND SUSPENSION

The rear axle assembly is connected to the transmission through the Hotchkiss-design drive shaft. It incorporates an overhung hypoid pinion and ring gear in a cast carrier and semi-floating axle shafts in welded tube housings. Depending on the engine and transmission used, axle ratio is 2.53:1, 2.92:1, or 3.36:1. See the table at the end of the chapter for specifications.

Both a regular differential and a limited-slip Positraction is available. Procedures specified in this chapter are applicable to both differentials. The Positraction requires a special lubricant specified in Chapter Two. Do not use regular gear lubricant. Torque and other specifications are given in **Table 1** at the end of this chapter.

> NOTE: *When equipped with Positraction rear end, the rear tires should be the same size and tread pattern to minimize wear on the Positraction cones. For the same reason do not continue to rapidly spin one wheel when the other is so deeply stuck the vehicle refuses to move (a condition which can occur even with limited-slip if one wheel is on extremely slippery surface. This does not necessarily mean the limited-slip rear end is malfunctioning).*

DRIVE SHAFT AND UNIVERSAL JOINTS

NOTE: *Whenever removing the driveshaft, it is wise to mark the relationship of the rear universal joint yoke to the companion flange yoke. If the front joint is to be disassembled, mark it also.*

1. Disconnect the drive shaft by removing the rear universal joint trunnion bearing U-bolts and pulling shaft from end of transmission.

2. If universal joints are not to be disassembled, tape bearing cups to trunnion.

3. Disassemble universal joints by removing snap rings and pressing out the bearing with the aid of suitable sized sockets and a vise.

4. Clean and inspect bearings, dust seals, trunnion and caps (**Figure 1**) for wear. Pack bearings with chassis lubricant (not required if replacement kit is used), making certain that the lubricant reservoir at the end of each trunnion is full.

5. Assemble with yokes located according to the marks previously made. Make certain snap rings are seated and that rear U-bolt trunnion bearing caps are correctly seated in the companion yoke.

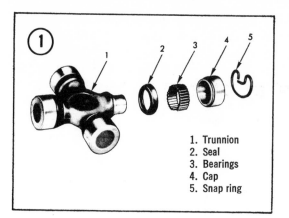

1. Trunnion
2. Seal
3. Bearings
4. Cap
5. Snap ring

REAR AXLE

Most rear axle maintenance and repair involves axle shafts, axle shaft bearings, seals, or the pinion shaft seal. If the correct ring and pinion gear adjustment and bearing preloads were made in production, and if there is adequate lubricant, there should be no need for differential adjustment or repair. Except for replacement of the housing or complete assembly, all rear axle repairs and adjustments can be accomplished without removal from the vehicle.

Axle Shaft, Seal, or Bearing Replacement

1. Raise the vehicle by the frame, until wheels clear the ground.

CAUTION
Use safety stands when working under the car. Do not rely solely on hydraulic or mechanical jacks.

2. Remove the wheels and the brake drums (Chapter Nine).

3. Place a container under the differential to catch lubricant, and remove cover.

4. Unscrew the pinion shaft lock screw, and remove the pinion shaft.

5. Without turning differential or axles, tap each axle toward the differential, and remove C-locks. Replace the pinion shaft and lock screw. Axle shafts can now be removed.

6. With a suitable puller, remove oil seal and bearing (**Figure 2**). If replacing seal only, it can be removed by inserting the lock end of the axle shaft behind the seal and prying it out of

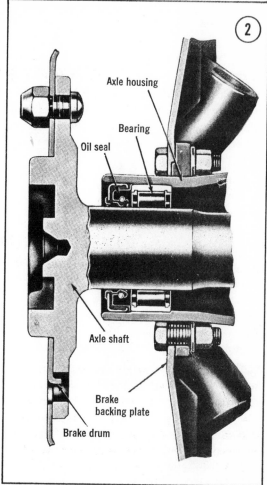

its bore. Use caution not to damage the bore with the shaft.

7. Lubricate the new bearing and seal lip cavity with wheel bearing grease. Install, referring to Figure 2.

8. Now is a good time to replace any damaged lug bolts in the axle flange; this can be done with the axle installed, however. Studs can be driven out (or pressed out with tool J-6627 or J-5504). A new stud can be drawn into place by starting it with finger pressure, then threading the lug nut on backwards and tightening until bolt head is seated.

9. When reinstalling the axle shafts, use care not to damage the seals.

10. Remove the pinion shaft, insert the C-locks, and pull the shafts outward to seat the C-locks in the recessed end of the side gears before rein-

11

stalling the pinion shaft. Torque all bolts to specifications.

Pinion Seal Replacement

1. With rear universal disconnected and rear brake drums removed, measure pinion bearing preload with an in.-lb. torque wrench on the pinion flange nut. Record the torque required to keep the pinion turning (for reference during reassembly).

2. Mark the pinion shaft-to-flange relationship for correct reassembly.

3. Holding the pinion flange, remove the self-locking nut.

4. With a suitable puller, remove pinion flange. Inspect oil seal surface, drive splines, and bearing cup surfaces. If deflector is damaged, replace it by tapping it from the flange, cleaning up the stake points and staking a new deflector into place at 3 new equally spaced locations. Be careful not to damage the sealing surface when staking.

5. Measure the old seal location with respect to the rim of the seal bore, and pry out seal. Install the new seal to that same location after applying grease to the cavity between the seal lips. **Figure 3** shows the position of the pinion oil seal. Note that the seal will be seated at the inner shoulder before its outside flange reaches the rim of the differential carrier housing.

6. Start flange onto pinion shaft, located accord to marks previously made, and tap lightly until 2 or 3 threads of pinion shaft are showing.

7. Using the old nut, draw flange onto pinion shaft *only until end play is removed*. Remove the old nut, apply a non-hardening sealer between the washer and the flange, and start the new nut onto the shaft. Tighten in small increments until previously recorded (Step 1) bearing preload is reached.

Differential Removal

1. With axle shafts removed, remove the differential pinion gear shaft. Identify the differential pinions and thrust washers, also the side gears and thrust washers. Then remove, keeping gears and thrust washers together.

2. Loosen the bearing cap bolts, after marking the caps and housing, and tap each cap lightly to unseat it; do not pry caps. A pry bar may be used to help release the caps by inserting one end into the differential case web—where the spider gears are located—then prying against the axle housing.

3. Identify cups, caps, and shims, and keep them together for each side.

Cleaning and Inspection

Wash all parts and inspect for scored, chipped, nicked, or worn bearing surfaces. Examine differential case for cracks. Inspect thrust washers for wear. Check fit of all splines.

Differential Bearing Replacement

1. Remove bearing using a suitable puller.

2. When replacing the second bearing, support the differential case so that pressure is not applied to the bearing cage.

Ring Gear Replacement

1. Remove the 10 bolts securing the ring gear to the differential case, and carefully tap it from the case with a soft hammer.

2. Before reassembling, make 5 guide pins as shown in **Figure 4**. Make the guide pins from $3/8$ in.-24 x $1\frac{1}{2}$ in. long cap screws.

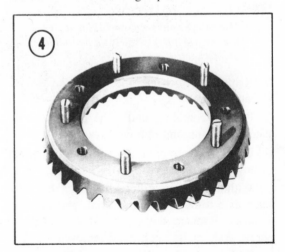

3. Put ring gear in place, with guide pins started through their holes in the case. Install ring gear bolts and lockwashers in the remaining holes,

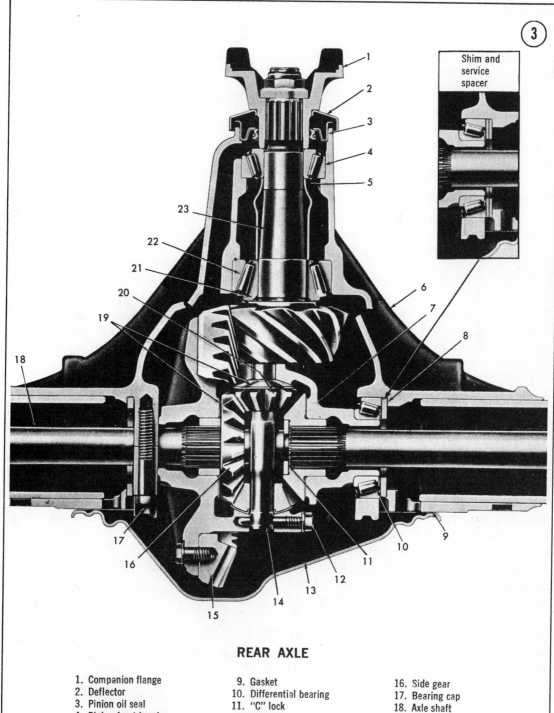

Shim and service spacer

REAR AXLE

1. Companion flange	9. Gasket	16. Side gear
2. Deflector	10. Differential bearing	17. Bearing cap
3. Pinion oil seal	11. "C" lock	18. Axle shaft
4. Pinion front bearing	12. Pinion shaft	19. Thrust washer
5. Pinion bearing spacer	lock bolt	20. Differential pinion
6. Differential carrier	13. Cover	21. Shim
7. Differential case	14. Pinion shaft	22. Pinion rear bearing
8. Shim	15. Ring gear	23. Drive pinion

11

tightening evenly until the gear is seated. Remove guide pins, and install remaining bolts. Torque bolts to 50 ft.-lb. (8.9 mkg).

Drive Pinion Bearing Replacement

1. Remove differential as previously described.

2. Measure pinion bearing preload with an in.-lb. torque wrench. Record the torque required to keep the pinion turning (for reference during reassembly).

3. Reinstall nut flush with end of pinion shaft, and tap out pinion with soft hammer.

CAUTION
Be careful not to damage bearings
while removing pinion from carrier.

4. Remove front bearing cone, and discard pinion bearing spacer.

5. Wash all parts and inspect for excessive wear. (Large end of rollers will be the first to show wear. The bearing races and rollers may show a "frosted" wear pattern with occasional light scratches; such a condition is acceptable.)

6. Tap out old cups with a brass drift. Inspect seats and bores for nicks or burrs, and clean up as necessary.

7. Tap new cups into place.

8. Remove rear bearing with a press or suitable puller. Record the shim thickness behind the bearing. This same shim may be used if the original ring gear, pinion, and rear bearings are to be reinstalled.

9. When installing new bearings or ring and pinion gear, shim thickness must be determined as shown in **Figure 5**. Lubricate bearings and install with gauge plates J-23597-3 and -5 together with plunger as shown in Figure 5. Tighten nut until 20 in.-lb. torque is required to turn the bearings.

10. With plates J-23597-4 assembled to J-23597-6, install the assembly into the differential side bearing bores. Install side bearing caps, and cinch bolts.

11. Install the dial indicator or the gauge post of J-23597-6 so that the gauge button rests on tool plunger.

12. Swing end of tool plunger across gauge plate. Stop at highest indicator reading, and set

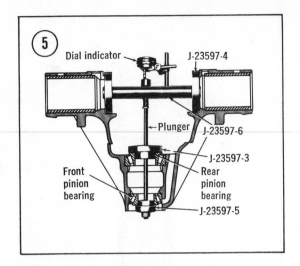

dial indicator to zero. Now recheck to see that the point of highest reading falls on zero.

13. Turn tool plunger off gauge button, and take reading directly from dial indicator. Service pinion gears are stamped with a code on the rear end of the pinion. **Table 2** shows the amount to be added or subtracted from the gauge reading according to the code stamped on the pinion. Use a shim with thickness equal to the dial indicator reading adjusted according to codes below.

Table 2   PINION GEAR CODE

Code	Inch
40	−0.005
41	−0.004
42	−0.003
43	−0.002
44	−0.001
45	−0.000
46	+0.001
47	+0.002
48	+0.003
49	+0.004
50	+0.005

14. Remove tool J-23597 and pinion bearings from carrier. Install shim and rear pinion bearing as shown in **Figure 6**.

15. Install front bearing and oil seal. (Note that oil seal will seat before its flange reaches the housing bore rim as shown in Figure 3.)

16. Carefully insert drive pinion into case and guide it through the front bearing and seal.

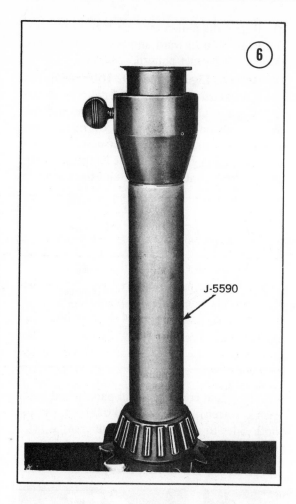

J-5590

17. Insert pinion flange and draw onto shaft with old nut *only until shaft endplay is removed.* Start new nut, tightening in small increments until original pinion shaft preload is reached.

Differential Installation and Adjustment

1. Lubricate bearings, position cups, and put differential assembly in the carrier. Support the assembly and slide a service spacer (0.160 in.) between each race and the carrier housing. The chamfered side of the spacer should go against the bearing race. Install left bearing cap to the support case.

> NOTE: *Cast iron preload spacers are used in production. If reused, they may break when tapped into place. Measure the thickness of the original spacers to help determine the thickness and number of service spacers required.*

2. From the total thickness measurement of the original spacer, subtract the total of the 2 service spacers plus 0.025 in. for gauging space.

3. Select 2 service shims whose combined thickness totals the difference found in Step 2, and install them between the right bearing cup and service spacer.

4. Determine the clearance between the right cup and spacer using a feeler gauge. Make sure the left bearing cup and spacer are properly seated, but do not apply pressure on bearings to preload them.

> NOTE: *Use a progressive check technique for this measurement. Begin with a feeler gauge of considerably less thickness than the distance to be measured, and insert several times with a slicing motion while turning the differential case to get the feel of the gauge. Increase gauge thickness in 0.002 in. increments until a noticeable drag increase is felt. The gauge used just before the noticeable drag increase is the correct measurement.*

5. With the service spacers remaining in the carrier, remove the previously installed shims.

6. Install 2 equal shims whose total thickness equals the feeler gauge measurement plus the thickness of the 2 shims removed in Step 5.

7. Install the 2 new shims between each side bearing race and service spacer (**Figure 7**).

8. Install both caps and mount a dial indicator to check ring and pinion gear backlash. With

indicator button perpendicular to tooth angle and in line with gear rotation, measure backlash at 4 equally spaced points around gear. The readings at these 4 points should vary no more than 0.001 in. and should fall between 0.003 in. to 0.010 in. (A backlash within the range 0.005 in. to 0.008 in. is preferred.)

9. If readings vary more than 0.001 in., measure ring gear runout. If runout exceeds 0.002 in., check for nicks, burrs, or dirt which may have been overlooked previously between gear and case.

10. If backlash does not fall within required range, change shim thickness by 0.002 in. for every 0.001 in. change in backlash. Always maintain the total shim thickness when adjusting backlash by adding to one side what has been removed from the other.

11. Prepare to check ring and pinion gear contact pattern by installing axle shafts and brake drums. Expand brake shoes until a torque of 60 ft.-lb. (8.3 mkg) is required to turn pinion shaft.

12. Clean the ring and pinion gear teeth. Paint the ring gear teeth with a mixture of powdered red lead and oil so that the contact pattern can be determined.

13. Rotate the pinion through 4 or more revolutions in both forward and reverse directions. Inspect the contact pattern.

14. Refer to **Figures 8 and 9**. Too little or too much backlash is indicated by patterns shown in "B" and "C" respectively. A face or flank contact can only be corrected by moving the pinion in or out, respectively. Excessively worn ring and pinion gears cannot be adjusted to produce correct contact pattern and backlash.

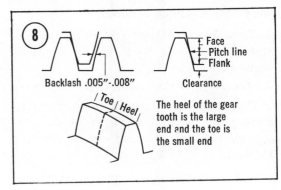

15. Now that correct contact pattern and backlash has been established, add 0.004 in. shim to both sides to produce correct differential bearing preload. (Shim replacement may be neces-

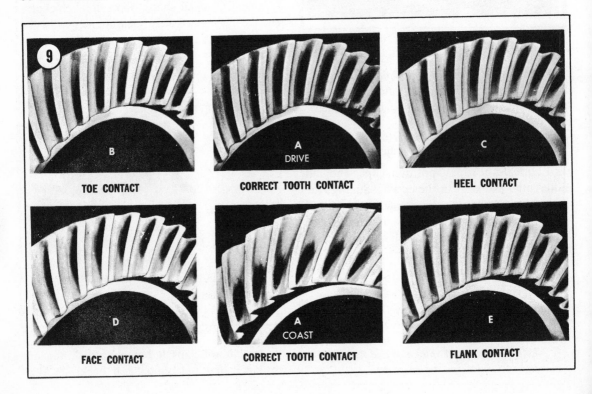

B TOE CONTACT	**A** DRIVE — CORRECT TOOTH CONTACT
	C HEEL CONTACT
D FACE CONTACT	**A** COAST — CORRECT TOOTH CONTACT
	E FLANK CONTACT

sary if 0.004 in. shims are not available. This is acceptable providing that the net increase for each side is 0.004 in.)

> NOTE: *Final shim installation is easier if case is partially removed, then rotated into position with shims being tapped into place at the same time.*

REAR SUSPENSION

Rear Axle Assembly Removal

1. Raise vehicle by frame to allow clearance for rear axle assembly removal. Provide a portable support for the rear axle.

2. Remove drive shaft as previously described.

3. On 1976-1977 models, disconnect and remove tie rod as shown in **Figure 10**. Also disconnect and remove torque arm as shown in **Figure 11**.

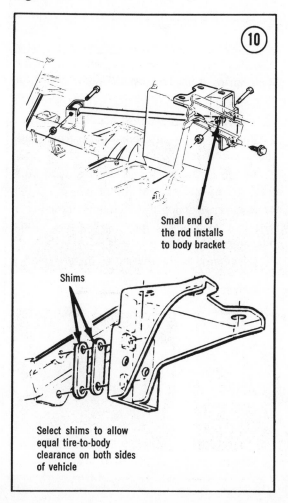

Small end of the rod installs to body bracket

Shims

Select shims to allow equal tire-to-body clearance on both sides of vehicle

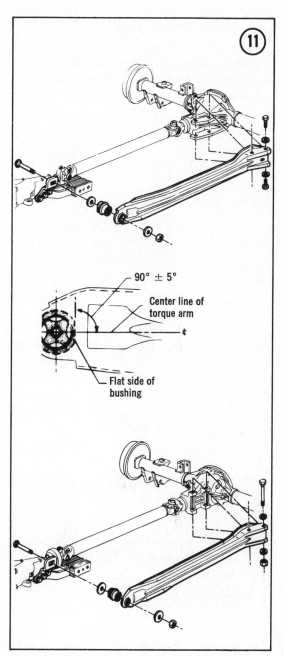

90° ± 5°

Center line of torque arm

Flat side of bushing

4. Disconnect the shock absorbers and upper control arms.

5. Disconnect rear brake line rubber hose at body-mounted brake line connection.

6. Disconnect emergency brake cable and release from clips.

7. Disconnect lower control arms at axle. Lower axle assembly until spring tension is released. Remove axle assembly.

Control Arm Bushing Replacement

CAUTION
Remove only one control arm at a time to prevent rear axle from slipping sideways.

Control arm bushings are press-fit. Note that control arm bushing holes have different diameters. When tightening control arm pivot bolts, car must be at curb height.

Stabilizer Bar

When reinstalling stabilizer bar, add shims to fill gap between stabilizer and control arm. Divide shims equally, and torque attaching bolts to 47 ft.-lb. (6.50 mkg).

Curb Height

Curb height must be measured at curb weight (full gas tank, spare, jack, and no passengers). Car must be level and supported by all 4 wheels. The height from the lower to upper spring seat should measure as specified in Table 2.

Rear Shock Absorber Replacement

1. Raise vehicle and support rear axle assembly.

WARNING
Use sturdy jackstands for supporting both chassis and rear axle. Do not depend on jack.

2. Remove 2 upper and one lower attaching bolts as indicated in **Figure 12**. Remove shock absorber.

3. Replacement is reverse of removal.

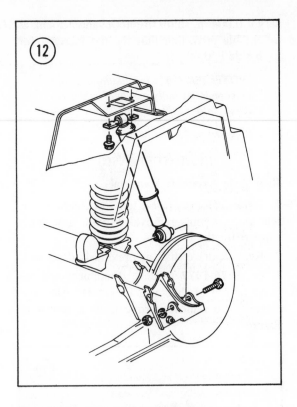

Rear Spring Removal/Installation

1. Raise car and support rear axle. See WARNING under *Rear Shock Absorber Removal*.

2. Remove lower attaching bolts from both shock absorbers.

3. Attach a safety wire or chain around both rear springs and around rear axle.

4. Being careful not to stretch brake hose lower rear axle assembly, remove spring and spring insulator from either or both sides.

5. Installation is the reverse of these steps.

Table 1   DIFFERENTIAL AND REAR SUSPENSION SPECIFICATIONS AND TORQUES

	1971-1975	1976-1977
Lubricant capacity	2.8 pints	2.8 pints
Filler plug	20 ft.-lb.	20 ft.-lb.
Differential carrier cover	20 ft.-lb.	20 ft.-lb.
Ring and pinion backlash	0.005 in.-0.008 in.	0.005 in.-0.008 in.
Pinion bearing preload, new	10-25 ft.-lb.	10-25 ft.-lb.
used	8-12 ft.-lb.	8-12 ft.-lb.
Ring gear	50 ft.-lb.	50 ft.-lb.
Differential bearing caps	55 ft.-lb.	55 ft.-lb.
Upper control arms	60 ft.-lb.	
Lower control arms	80 ft.-lb.	80 ft.-lb.
Rear shock absorber, upper	18 ft.-lb.	18 ft.-lb.
lower	42 ft.-lb.	42 ft.-lb.
Universal joint to axle	14 ft.-lb.	14 ft.-lb.
Rear stabilizer bolts	47 ft.-lb.	47 ft.-lb.
Riding height at curb weight	$9\frac{5}{16}$ in.-$10\frac{1}{16}$ in.	$9\frac{5}{8}$ in.-$10\frac{3}{8}$ in.
Torque control arm		
Front bracket to transmission		30 ft.-lb.
Front bracket to torque arm		50 ft.-lb.
Torque arm to rear axle housing		115 ft.-lb.
Tie rod bolts		85 ft.-lb.
Jounce bumper		25 ft.-lb.

11

INDEX

12

12

MAINTENANCE LOG

DATE	TYPE OF SERVICE	COST	REMARKS

NOTES

1971 ENGINE COMPARTMENT WIRING

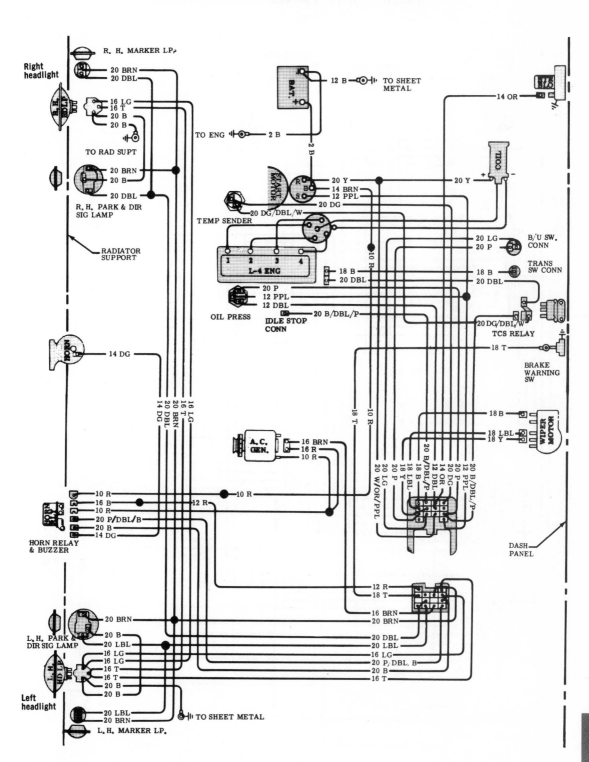

Right headlight

R. H. MARKER LP.

20 BRN
20 DBL

16 LG
16 T
20 B
20 B

TO RAD SUPT

R. H. PARK & DIR SIG LAMP

20 BRN
20 B

20 DBL

RADIATOR SUPPORT

HORN

14 DG

16 LG
16 T
20 DBL
20 BRN
14 DG

HORN RELAY & BUZZER

10 R
16 B
10 R
20 P/DBL/B
20 B
14 DG

L. H. PARK & DIR SIG LAMP

20 BRN
20 B
20 LBL
16 LG
16 LG
16 T
20 B
20 B

Left headlight

20 LBL
20 BRN

L. H. MARKER LP.

TO SHEET METAL

TO ENG   2 B

BAT.

12 B   TO SHEET METAL

TEMP SENDER

20 DG/DBL/W

L-4 ENG
1 2 3 4

OIL PRESS

20 P
12 PPL
12 DBL

IDLE STOP CONN

20 B/DBL/P

20 Y
14 BRN
12 PPL
20 DG

18 B
20 DBL

A.C. GEN.

16 BRN
16 R
10 R

10 R

12 R

18 T
10 R

12 R
18 T

16 BRN
20 BRN

20 DBL
20 LBL
16 LG
20 P/DBL, B
20 B
16 T

TO SHEET METAL

14 OR

COIL

20 Y

20 LG
20 P

18 B
20 DBL

20 DG/DBL/W
TCS RELAY

18 T

18 B

18 LBL
18 Y

WIPER MOTOR

B/U SW. CONN

TRANS SW CONN

BRAKE WARNING SW

20 B/DBL/P
12 PPL
20 DG
20 OR
14 OR
18 B
18 LBL
20 B/DBL/P
20 P
20 Y
20 LG
20 W/OR/PPL

DASH PANEL

1

1971 INSTRUMENT PANEL WIRING (PART I)

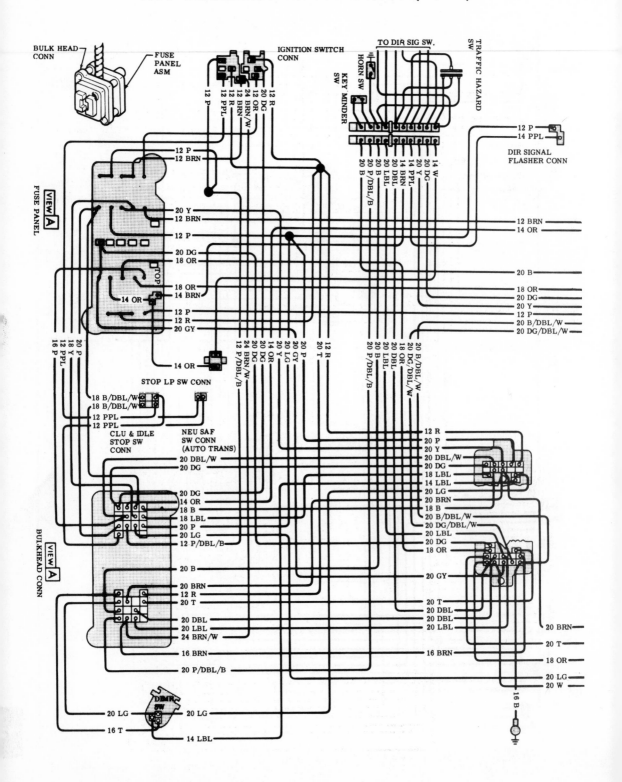

1971 INSTRUMENT PANEL WIRING (PART II)

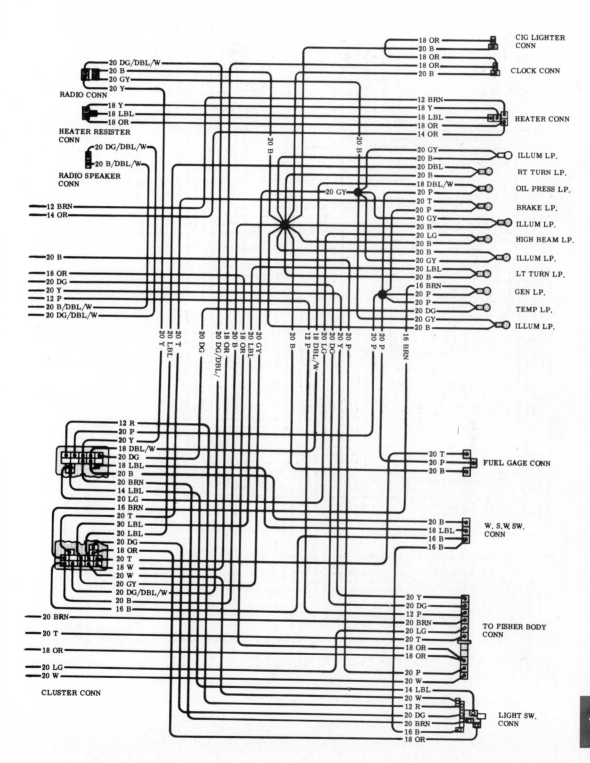

1971 BODY WIRING

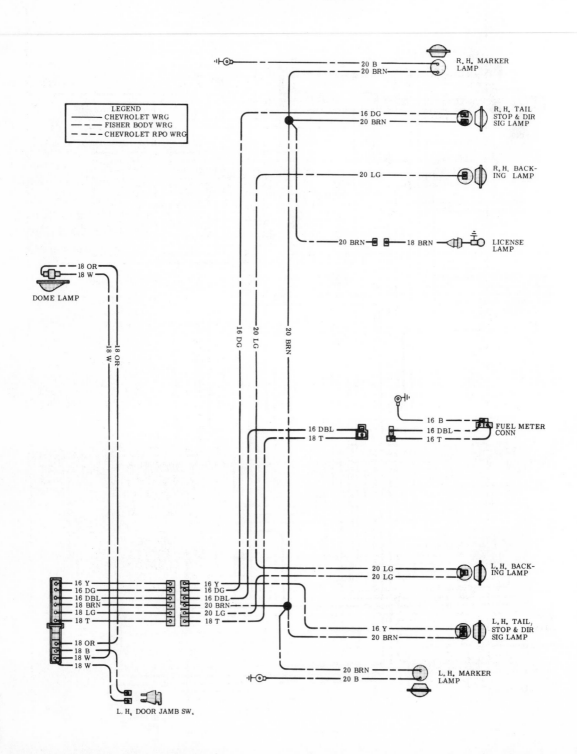

1972 ENGINE COMPARTMENT WIRING

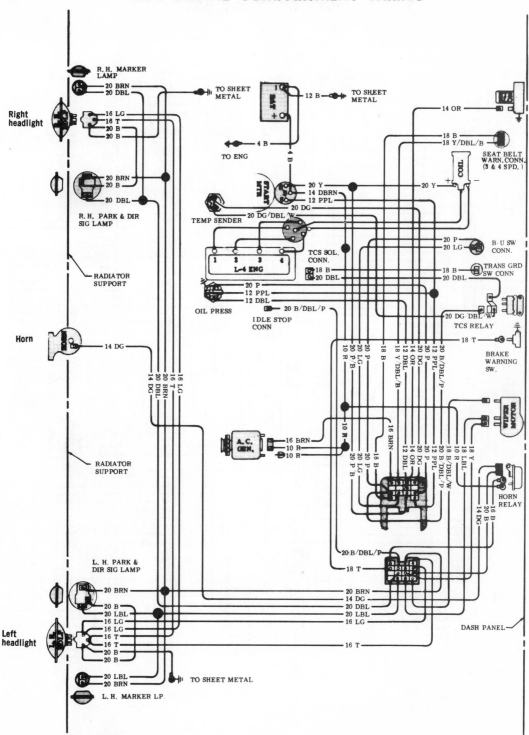

1972 INSTRUMENT PANEL

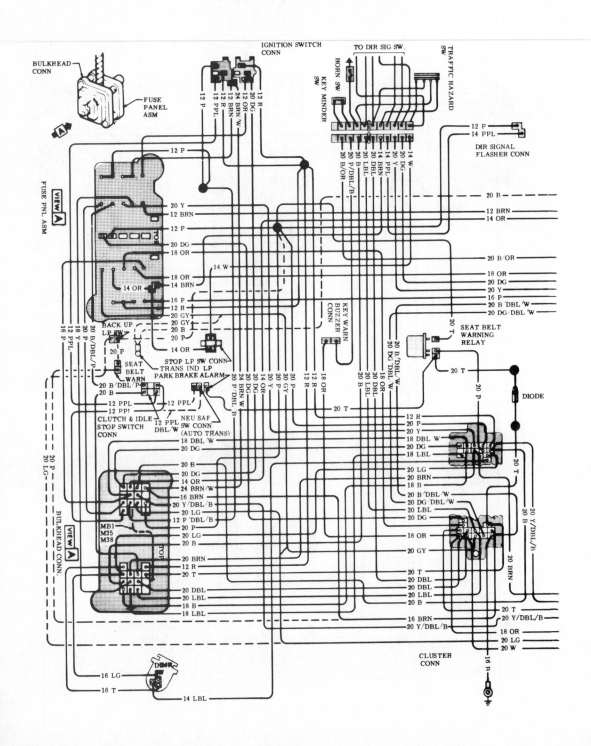

1972 INSTRUMENT CLUSTER

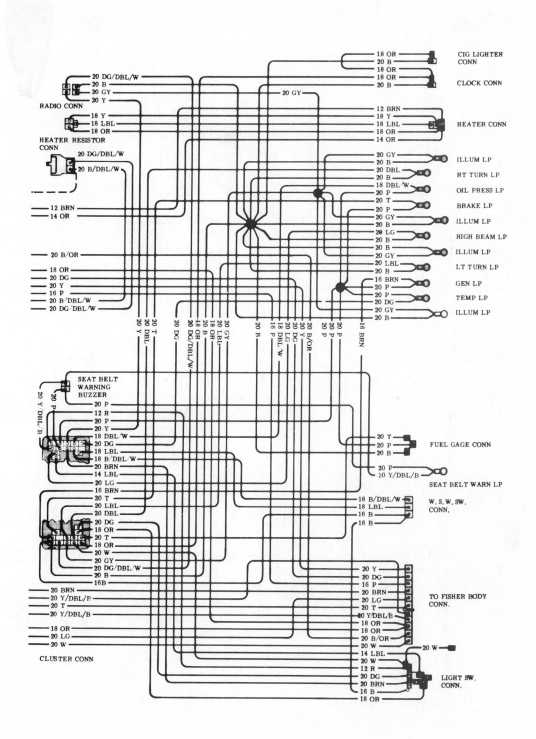

1972 BODY AND REAR LIGHTING

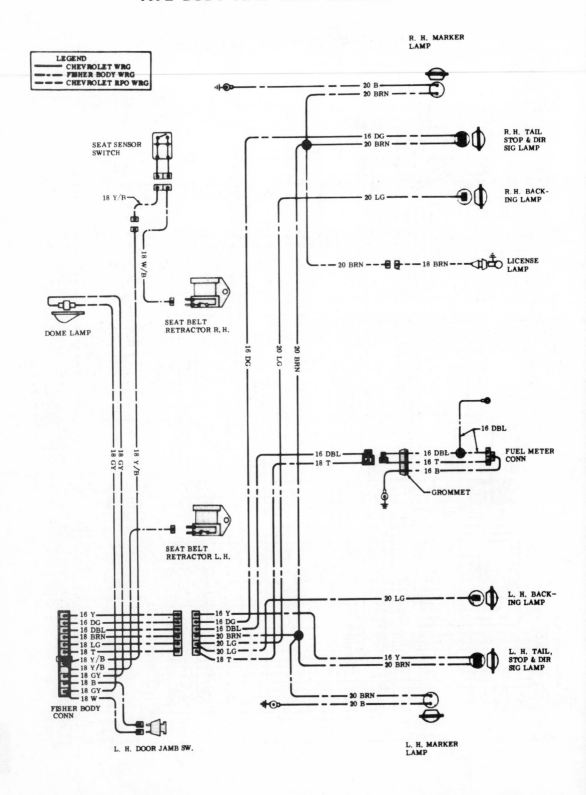

1972 GAUGES — RPO Z29 (PART I)

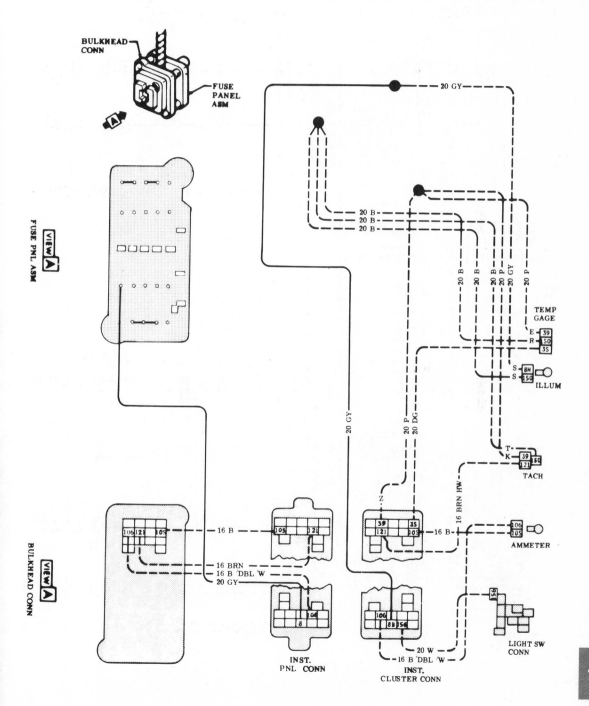

BULKHEAD CONN

FUSE PANEL ASM

FUSE PNL ASM VIEW A

BULKHEAD CONN VIEW A

20 GY

20 B
20 B
20 B

20 B
20 B
20 B
20 P
20 GY
20 P

TEMP GAGE

E 39
R 150
35

S 8N
S 150
ILLUM

20 GY

20 P
20 DG

T· 39 150
K 121
TACH

16 BRN HW

Z·

16 B

106
105
AMMETER

106 121 105

16 B

105 121

39 35
121 105

16 B

16 BRN
16 B DBL W
20 GY

8
04

INST. PNL CONN

106
8B 56

20 W
16 B DBL W
INST. CLUSTER CONN

56

LIGHT SW CONN

13

1972 GAUGES — RPO Z29 (PART II)

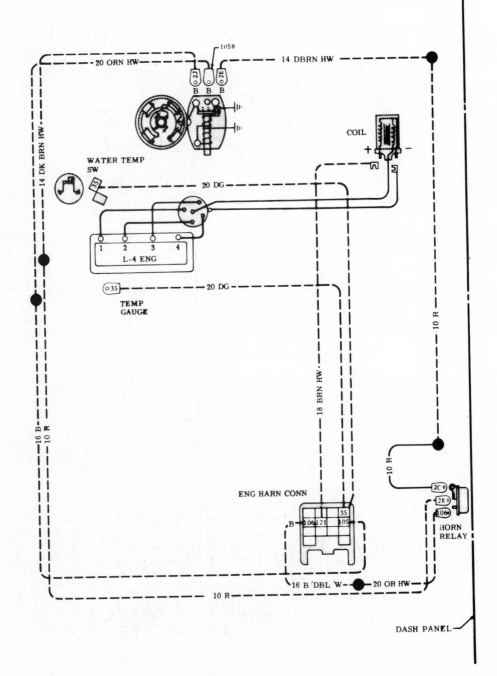

1973 ENGINE COMPARTMENT

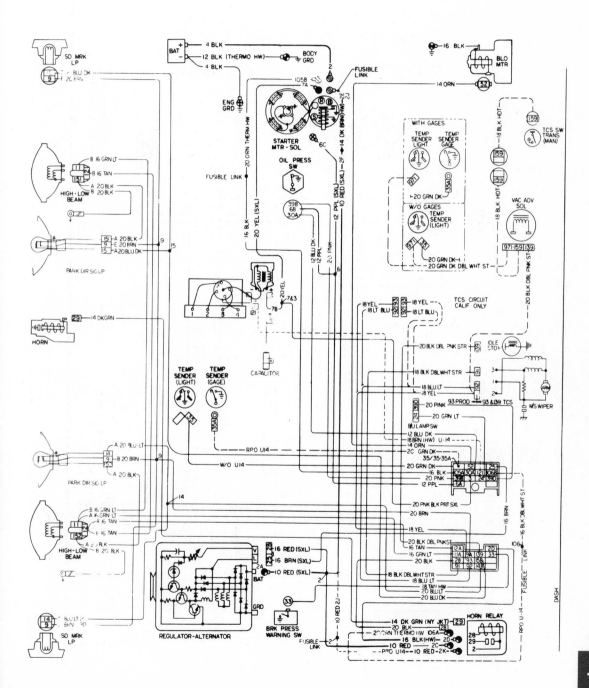

1973 INSTRUMENT PANEL

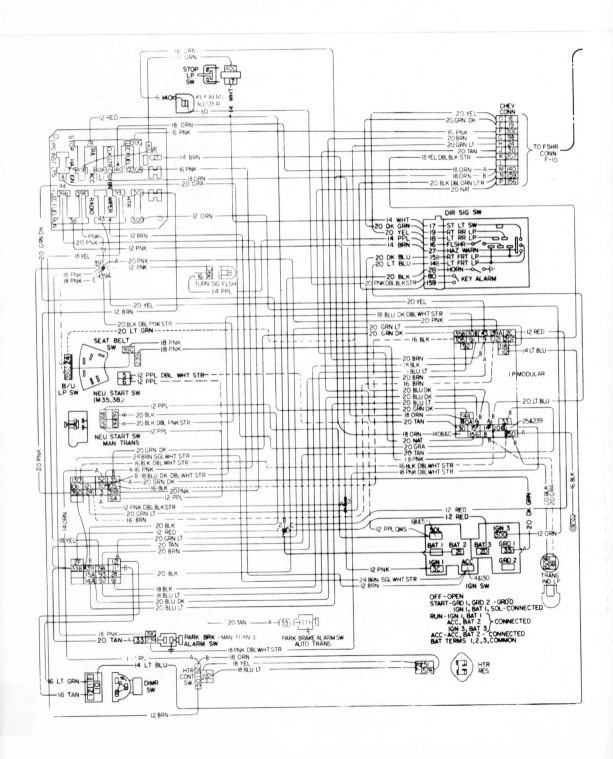

1973 INSTRUMENT CLUSTER

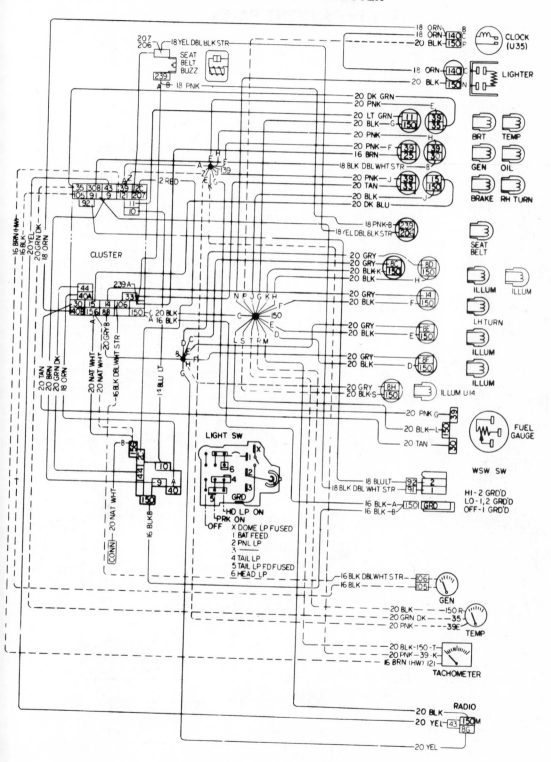

1973 BODY AND REAR LIGHTING

DOME LP

TO CHEV
CONN
F-18

FSHR
CONN

18 D
19 E
31 F
9 G
24 H
30 J
207 K
L
40 M
159 N
156 P

18 WHT HW
18 WHT HW

ST SNSR SW

207 205

LEFT ST
BELT RETR

207 18 YEL BLK HW

18 YEL BLK HW

207
207 18 YEL BLK HW

18 YEL BLK HW

205

RIGHT ST
BELT RETR

18 WHT HW
18 BLK
18 TAN
18 LT GRN
18 BRN
16 DK BLU
16 DK GRN
16 YEL

SD MRK
LP

150 20 BLK 9
150

20 BRN

20 BRN 9
16 DK GRN 19

20 BRN

20 BRN

20 LT GRN 24
(HW)

TAIL, STOP,
+ DIR LP

B/U LP

A 18
B 19
C 31
D 9
E 24
F 30

18
19
31
9
24
30

16 YEL
16 DK GRN

20 BRN
20 LT GRN

9 9 18 BRN

LIC LP

18 TAN
16 DK BLU

150 16 BLK HW

30 30 16 TAN
31 31 16 DK BLU

FUEL PUMP
&
SENDER UNIT

20 BRN

20 LT GRN 24
(HW)

B/U LP

59
91

LEFT DR
JAMB SW

150 20 BLK 150
9

20 BRN

SD MRK
LP

16 YEL 18
20 BRN 9

TAIL, STOP,
+ DIR LP

1973 GAUGES — RPO Z29 (PART I)

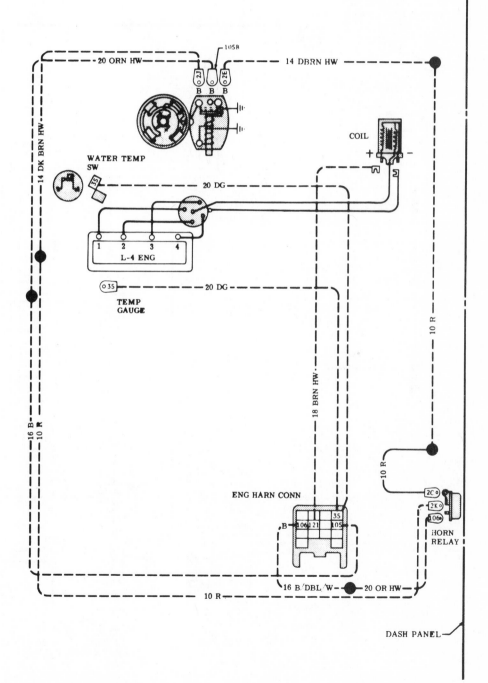

20 ORN HW

105B

14 DBRN HW

B B B

COIL

WATER TEMP
SW

20 DG

35

1 2 3 4

L-4 ENG

14 DK BRN HW

35

20 DG

TEMP
GAUGE

18 BRN HW

10 R

16 B
10 R

ENG HARN CONN

B 106 21 35 105

2C

2K

106

HORN
RELAY

10 R

16 B DBL W

20 OR HW

10 R

DASH PANEL

1973 GAUGES — RPO Z29 (PART II)

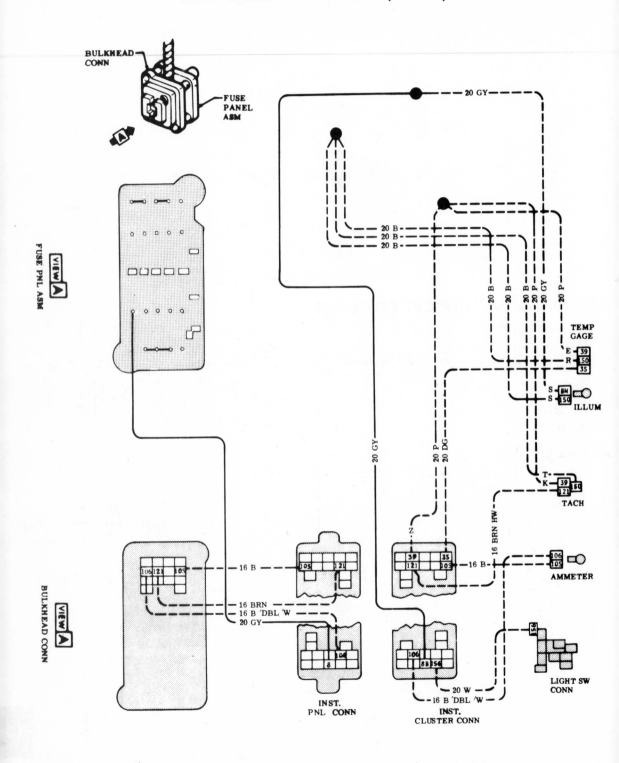

1973 RADIO

975 --- 18 BLK --- 975
977 --- 18 GRN LT --- 977

WIRE ASM – RADIO SPKR

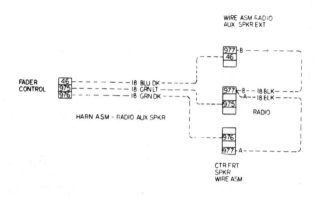

WIRE ASM RADIO
AUX SPKR EXT

977 B
46

FADER
CONTROL
46 --- 18 BLU DK
975 --- 18 GRN LT
976 --- 18 GRN DK

977 B --- 18 BLK
A --- 18 ELK
975

RADIO

HARN ASM - RADIO AUX SPKR

976
977 A

CTR FRT
SPKR
WIRE ASM

1973 REAR WINDOW DEFOGGER

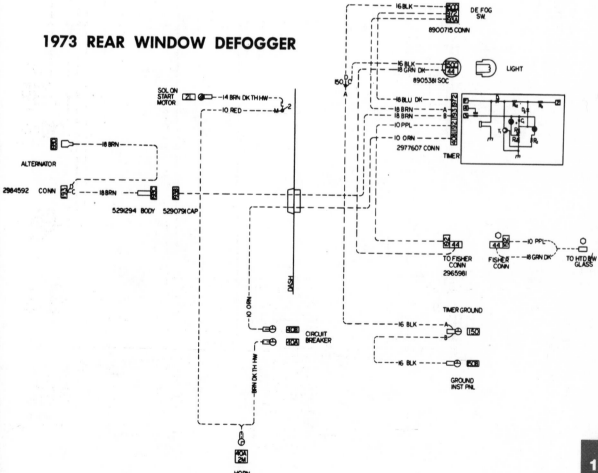

1974 ENGINE COMPARTMENT

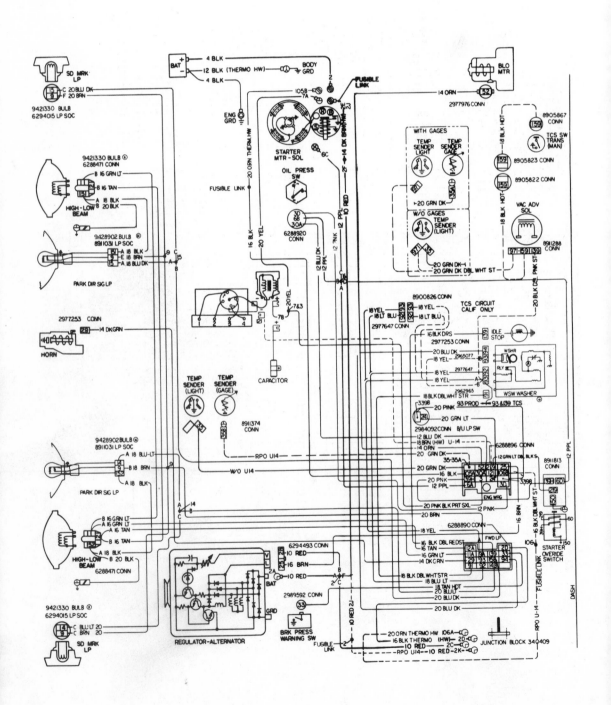

1974 INSTRUMENT PANEL

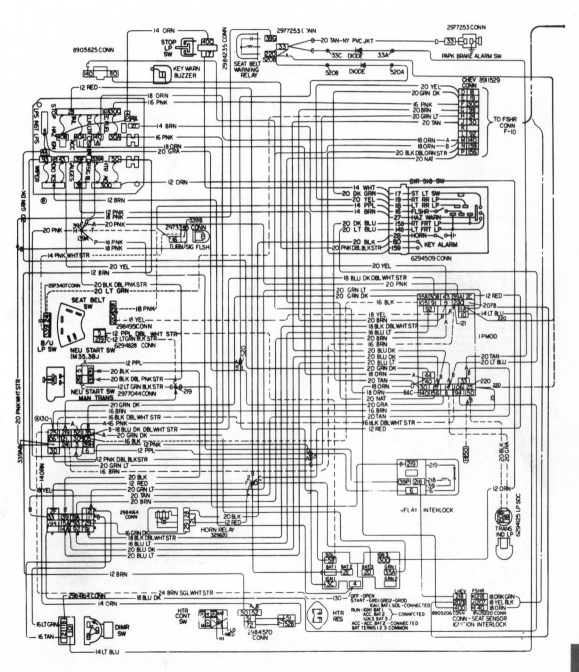

1974 INSTRUMENT CLUSTER

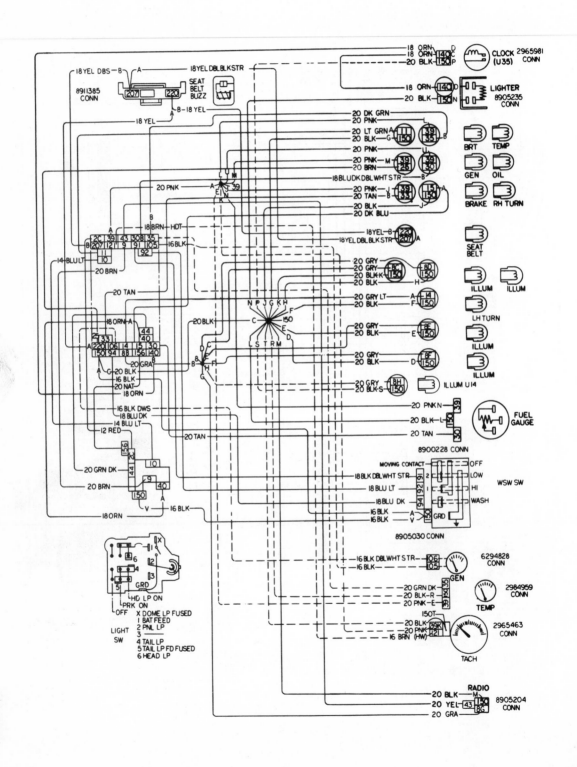

1974 BODY AND REAR LIGHTING (COUPE)

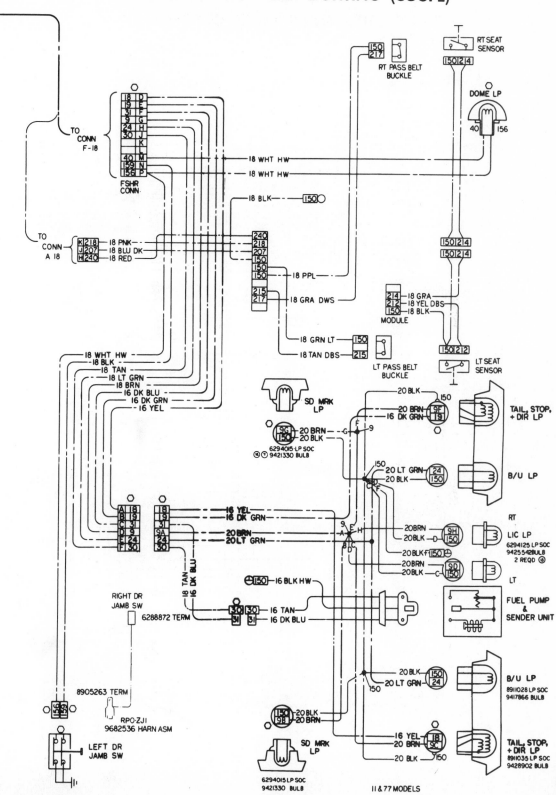

1974 AIR CONDITIONING

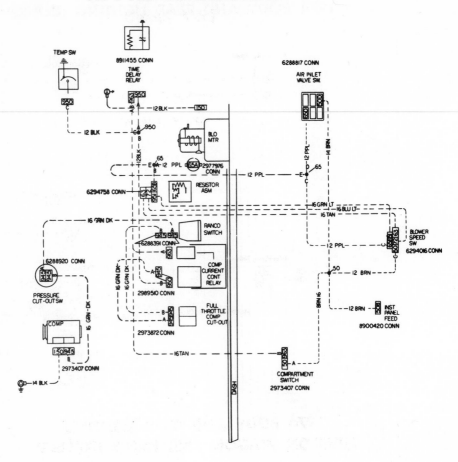

1974 REAR WINDOW DEFOGGER

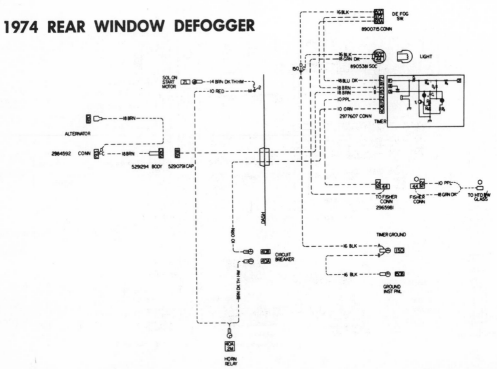

1974 RADIO

8905206 CONN

| 975 |
| 977 |

—— 18 BLK ——
—— 18 GRN LT ——

8900444 CONN

| 975 |
| 977 |

WIRE ASM – RADIO SPKR

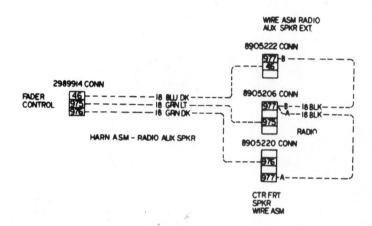

WIRE ASM RADIO
AUX SPKR EXT.

8905222 CONN

| 977 | B |
| 46 |

2989914 CONN

FADER
CONTROL

| 46 |
| 975 |
| 976 |

—— 18 BLU DK ——
—— 18 GRN LT ——
—— 18 GRN DK ——

8905206 CONN

| 977 | B | — 18 BLK —
| 975 | A | — 18 BLK —

RADIO

HARN ASM – RADIO AUX SPKR

8905220 CONN

| 976 |
| 977 | A

CTR FRT
SPKR
WIRE ASM

1974 BODY AND REAR LIGHTING
(STATION WAGON AND PANEL EXPRESS)

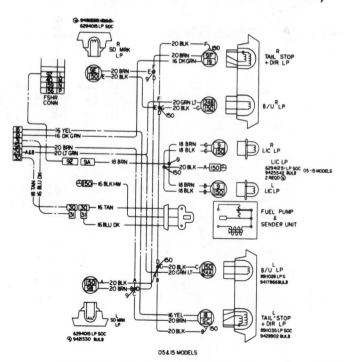

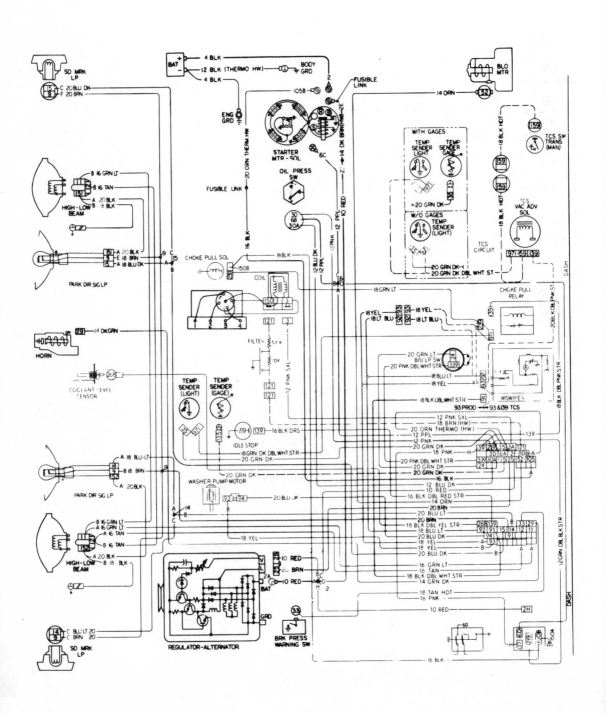

1975 INSTRUMENT PANEL

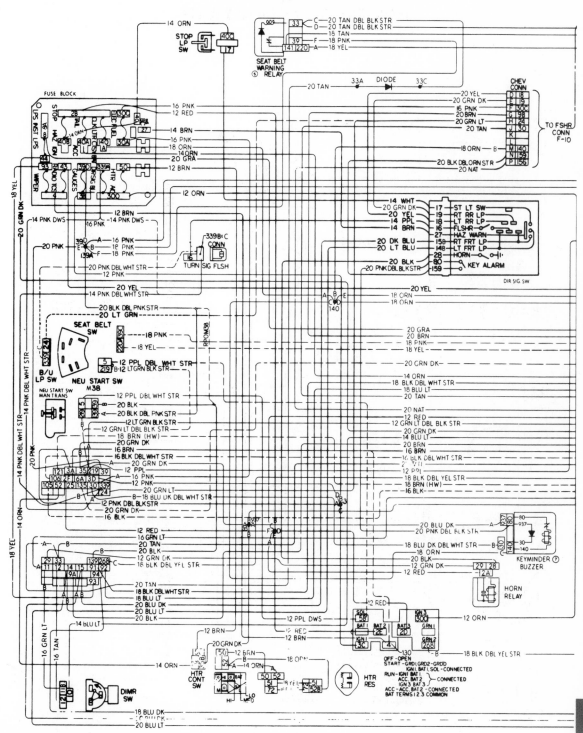

1975 INSTRUMENT CLUSTER

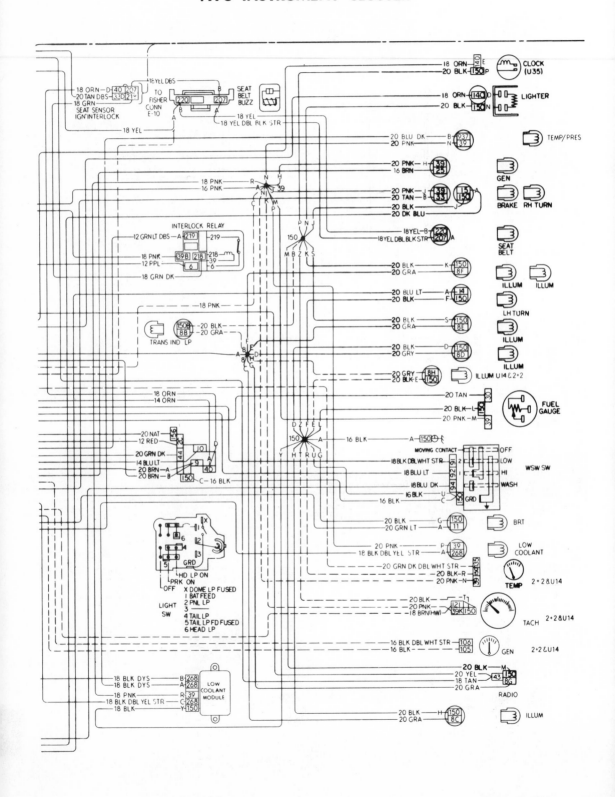

1975 BODY AND REAR LIGHTING (COUPE)

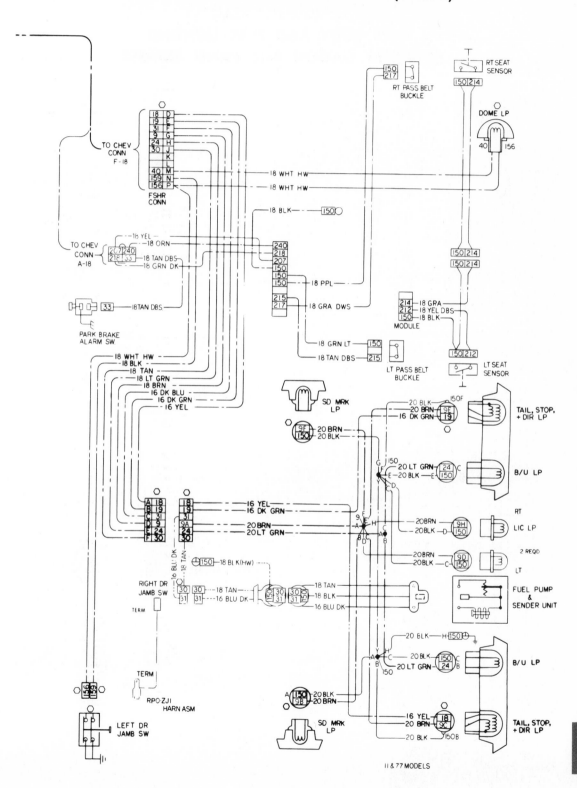

11 & 77 MODELS

13

1975 BODY AND REAR LIGHTING
(STATION WAGON AND PANEL EXPRESS)

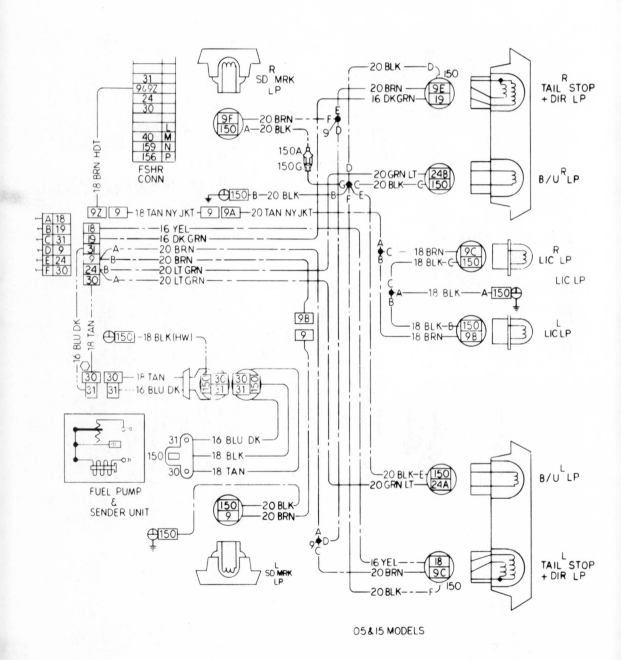

05 & 15 MODELS

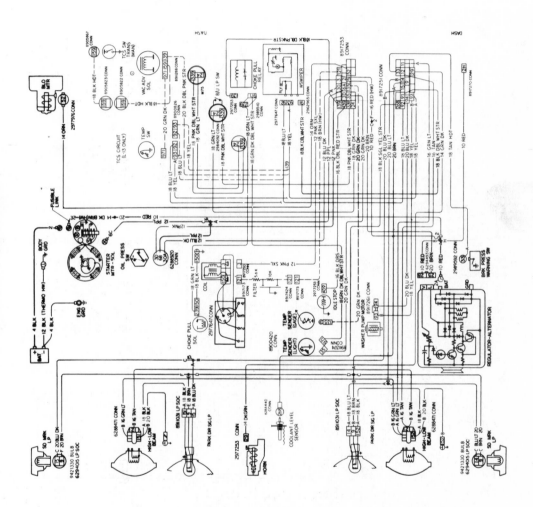

1976 FRONT LIGHTING

13

1976 INSTRUMENT CLUSTER

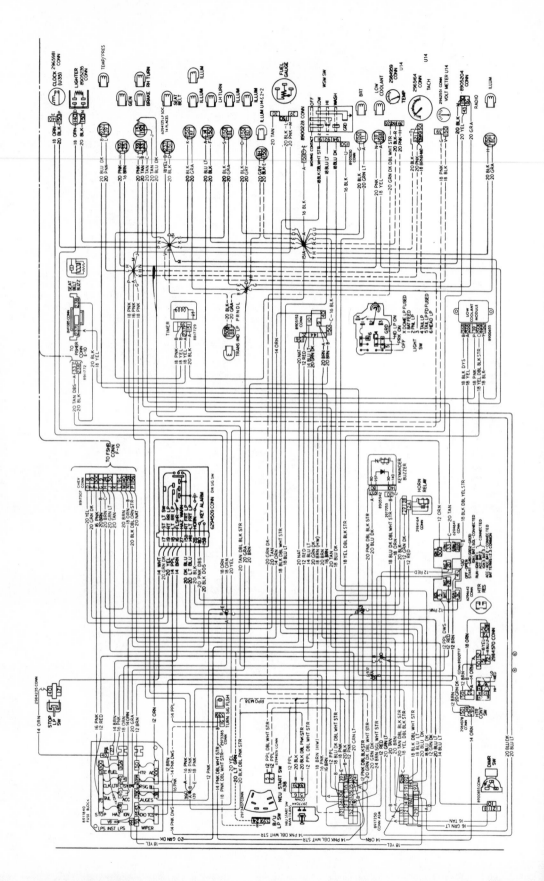

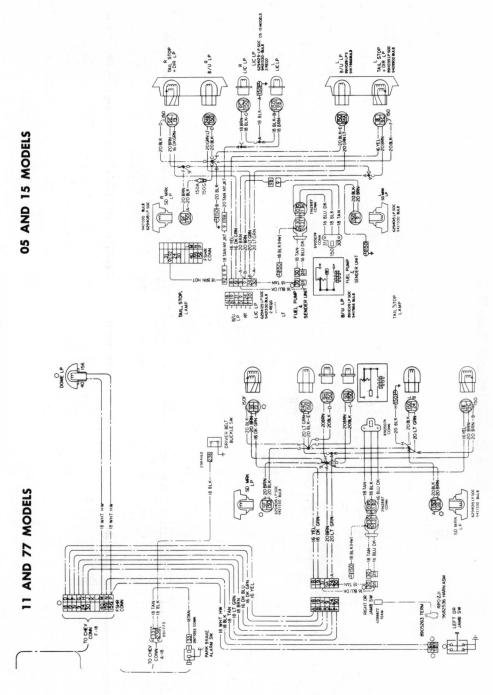

1976 REAR SECTION

05 AND 15 MODELS

11 AND 77 MODELS

1976 ACCESSORIES

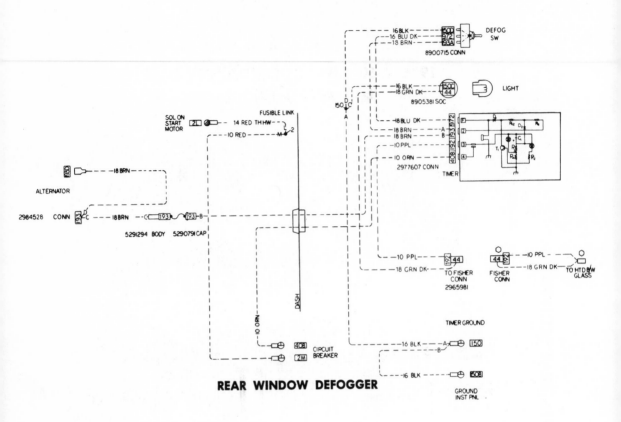

REAR WINDOW DEFOGGER

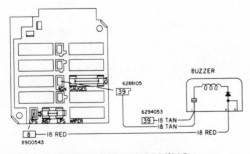

UNDERHOOD LAMP RPO

WIRE ASSEMBLY
(RADIO SPEAKER)

HEADLAMP WARNING

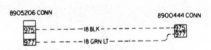

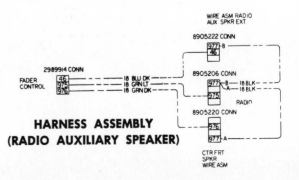

HARNESS ASSEMBLY
(RADIO AUXILIARY SPEAKER)

1976 C-60 AIR CONDITIONING
(L-11 AND L-13)

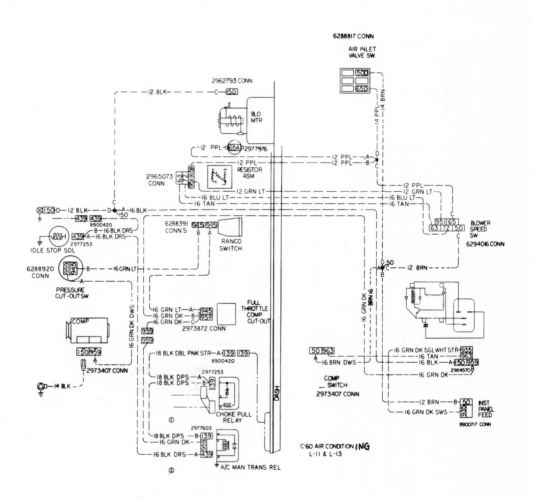

1977 Front Lighting

1977 INSTRUMENT CLUSTER (PART I)

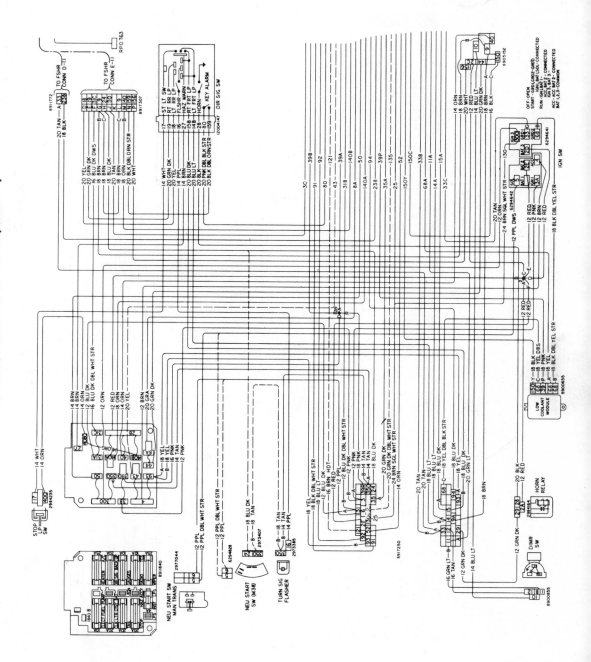

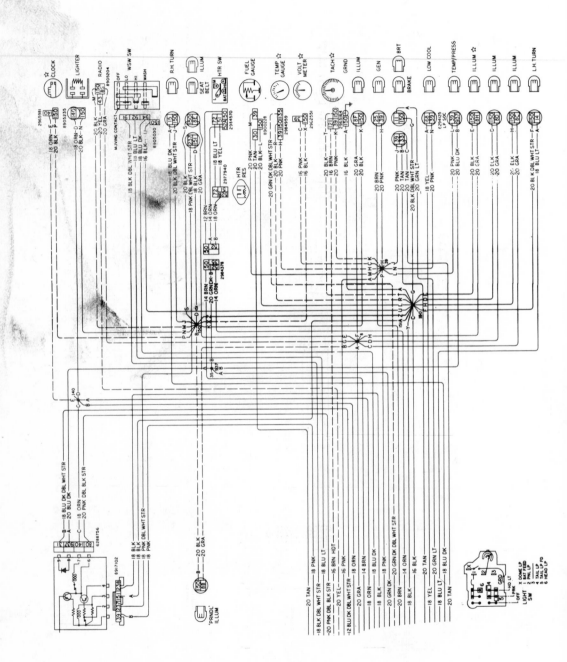

1977 INSTRUMENT CLUSTER (PART II)

1977 REAR SECTION

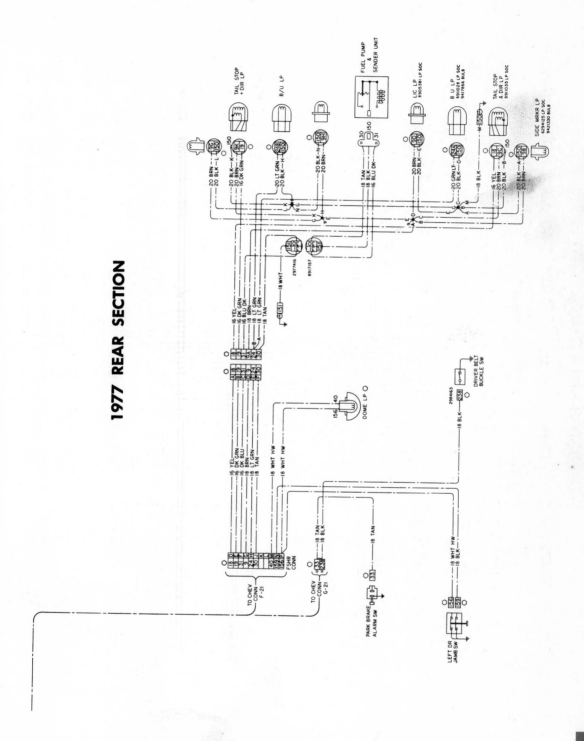

13

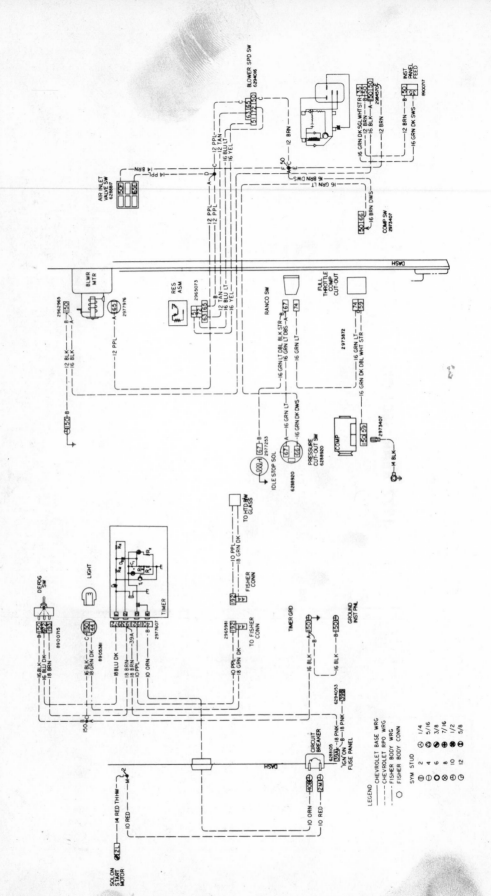

APR -- 1983

1977 C-60 AIR CONDITIONING (L-11 AND L-13)

1977 REAR WINDOW DEFOGGER